DEE

DEEPER LIFE

The extraordinary growth of the
Deeper Life Bible Church

Alan Isaacson

With a foreword by W.F. Kumuyi

HODDER AND STOUGHTON
LONDON   SYDNEY   AUCKLAND   TORONTO

All scriptural quotations are from the New International Version of the Bible © 1973, 1978, 1984 by New York International Bible Society. Used with permission. Quotations are also taken from the Koran (translated by N.J. Dawood, Penguin Books, fourth revised edition 1974) and from the *World Christian Encyclopedia* by David Barrett, Oxford University Press, 1982.

British Library Cataloguing in Publication Data
Isaacson, Alan
deeper life.
1. Nigeria. Deeper Life Bible Church
I. Title
289.9

ISBN 0-340- 52342-5

For Hilda

Contents

Foreword
by W. F. Kumuyi
General Superintendent, Deeper Christian Life Ministry

This book is the substance of Alan's sense of responsibility to the body of Christ and an unalloyed commitment to truth. He sought the truth first-hand, found it, documented it and minded less whose ox is gored.

Alan visited Nigeria between mid-September and early November 1988. He was with us in our worship sessions at the Central Headquarters Church, Gbagada, Lagos. We all studied the Bible together in our weekly Bible study. He joined our leaders in their Zonal meetings. Alan saw all our overseers and had interviews with a few of them in their states.

On the selection of materials, Alan has been reasonably fastidious. Vital and representative information based on interviews, interactions, and discussions from within the official orbit of Deeper Christian Life Ministry form the bulk of his account. For an objective and broad-based presentation, Alan went outside Deeper Life. He spoke with distinguished men of worth and credit in the Nigerian Christian world.

For a full-orbed account, he travelled outside Lagos. He went to the frontier States of Nigeria, primarily Borno and Kano States. Along the southern coast, he witnessed our work in Imo and Bendel States. He traversed thousands of kilometres by air and land. He went hinterland and interacted with the rural folks right at the native setting, just to get facts first-hand! The mixed grill has been mashed together for a balanced meal, the book – *Deeper Life: The extraordinary growth of the Deeper Life Bible Church.*

In doing this, Alan was deliberately let into the heart of Deeper Life Bible Church and her inter-church relations arm, the Deeper Christian Life Ministry. In seven short weeks, he saw as much as he would see if he spent seven months. He saw the church unrehearsed, unconditioned, and of course unretouched. He saw some things he would approve of and others he would disapprove of. He heard the word as preached by our ministers. He saw our ways of life. In summary, he saw the ministry through and through. He saw the men God used to develop the ministry. He heard the message of the men. He looked intently into the methods of administration. He saw the miracles God is doing among us. And finally, he saw the relevance of the ministry to the church life of Nigeria in particular and Africa at large.

I need to say a word of caution on the miracles experienced through the ministry. The stories of miracles documented here may unseat some sincere minds. I blame them not. Some may feel miracles are not for today. Others may think all the church should care for is the salvation of souls. But in Africa and amongst the black people of the globe, hard-core Gospel preaching may not give the desired result. The Gospel must be preached with "signs following". The proof and evidence of the love and concern of God pave the path of the Gospel in Africa. It prepares the heart of the people for the word of God.

God, in the growth of Deeper Life Bible Church, has strategically and prudently used miracles to make all come to him (John 3.26) in Deeper Life. Needless to mention, the miracle of conversion is, by all parameters, incomparably greater than every other miracle, even the raising of the dead. Conversion, the new birth or the regeneration of heart which follows a decisive act of repentance is and will always be a cardinal issue in Deeper Life. Thus, the generality of the people in Deeper Life are "persuaded by simple proclamation of the Gospel" (p.74). We take Christian living and holiness seriously.

It appears to me as much as possible, Alan has been dispassionate, detached and disciplined. His honesty and candid thoughts are peculiarly striking. His disciplined mind gave him an advantage in his position as an observer. Like an impartial judge, he has weighed the evidence before him and with Christian maturity and liberty noted his observations. Not all comments and criticisms are favourable to the church. At times he is downright sharp and unsparing.

He wrote as he saw through his lens. Though objective, he could not but be subjective, at least, within the frame of his Christian perception, religious philosophy and denominational background. With a sense of duty, he has tried to correct some things he appeared not to approve of in the ministry.

While I may not always share his conclusions, his zeal for the truth is nevertheless impressive. He stands as a much needed example in the present-day church world. Lest anyone jump into an hasty, unguided and unconsidered verdict on the life and practice in Deeper Life Bible Church, it is worth noting that there are some incidental occurrences alluded to. Such occurrences, either from members or local pastors of the Deeper Life, are not to be taken as the official practice or view of the ministry.

Lagos
January 1989

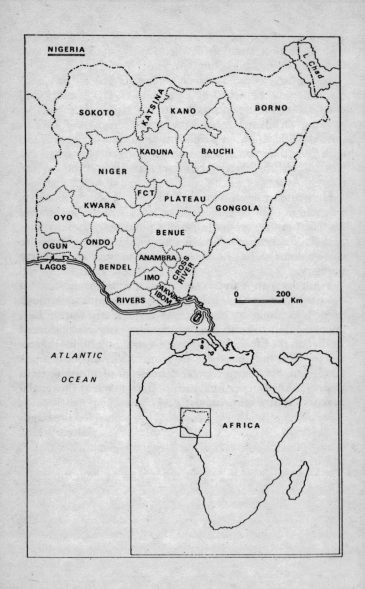

Introductory Note

In 1986 the Deeper Life Bible Church of Nigeria sent a missionary to Britain, and so we in the West first began to hear something of the remarkable story of Deeper Life. It seemed a story worth telling. I had worked in Nigeria myself (before I was married), as an English teacher in a rural secondary school for a couple of years in the late 1970s, so I knew a bit about the country. Since then I have been involved in different ways in writing, education, mission and church growth in Britain. When the phone call came asking if I'd be prepared to visit a new independent church in Nigeria, Hilda agreed to release me – by the time I made the trip we had two small sons, and a third on the way! The visit would inevitably involve a lot of travelling which would not be feasible with a young family, so I deserted my family – which wasn't easy for any of us – but I felt peaceful about leaving them in the care of our loving and supportive church family in Sheffield.

The advance on royalties for this book paid for the return flight, while Deeper Life were responsible for my welfare while I was in Nigeria. My job was mainly journalistic – to report on Deeper Life for you, the reader – but it was also to begin to interpret and understand Deeper Life so that we may begin to know how to react to their message and learn from them. Deeper Life themselves were anxious to have an "outsider" come to visit them, so that they could interact

with a "partner in the Gospel", while ultimately benefiting
from the credibility which an outsider's report can give,
rather than simply presenting a self-written review. How
many churches in Britain would welcome – even initiate – a
public "inspection" by a not-totally-sympathetic outsider?

Deeper Life

So it was that for seven weeks at the end of 1988 I visited
W. F. Kumuyi, his inter-denominational Deeper Christian
Life Ministry, and the Deeper Life Bible Church which has
grown out of the work of the Ministry. For short, both these
organisations are referred to as "Deeper Life".

Briefly, Kumuyi was working as a maths lecturer at
the University of Lagos in 1973, and started an inter-
denominational Bible study group on Monday evenings.
The group began with fifteen adults. Kumuyi started the
group because he was under pressure with so many people
coming to him for counselling that he needed to ask them to
come to his flat just once a week, and all together! Kumuyi
himself was a member of a North American based church
which is in the Pentecostal/Holiness tradition.

The Bible study grew and by 1975 loudspeakers were set
up outside for the 500 people who gathered each Monday at
Kumuyi's flat. The first Deeper Life "Retreat" was held in
December 1975, and 1,500 people attended. The movement
continued to grow, with regular meetings on Thursdays
added for Evangelism Training.

Growth

In 1976, Deeper Life members who travelled from Lagos to
other parts of the country started their own Deeper Life
fellowships – as in later years did those members who
travelled to other countries – initially Ghana. Numbers
continued to increase. Forty-five thousand attended the

retreat in 1981, but by then members were coming under pressure from the churches to choose where their primary affiliation lay – with their church, or Deeper Life. At the end of 1982, Kumuyi gave way to pressure and started the Deeper Life Bible Church, for the first time offering Sunday worship.

Many members of the older established churches in Nigeria seem to regard Deeper Life as sheep-stealers, but I met some who were more positive about the challenge that independent churches bring to, for example, the Anglicans. At the end of the last century the SIM (then Sudan Interior Mission) started church planting, out of which have grown the independent, indigenous ECWA (Evangelical Churches of West Africa). My time in Nigeria in the 1970s had been in an ECWA school, so I met up with some of my old ECWA friends – and they were now only slightly hesitant about Deeper Life. Due to the pressure on my time – my main purpose was to visit Deeper Life – I regretfully had little contact with the older established independent churches such as the Cherubim and Seraphim. In the early days of Pastor Kumuyi's ministry, relationships with the churches were strained because his followers often felt their loyalties were divided. His original vision was to support the churches through a Bible study ministry, but by the time he started Sunday worship, he was effectively leading a new, independent, indigenous church. "But," he said to me at one time, "I've been telling my pastors that it is not our business to be seeking converts from other churches. Our first targets must be the unreached and the unchurched."

Deeper Life now strategically seek to plant churches throughout Nigeria and Africa. The Lagos church is divided into districts, while the Federation of Nigeria is divided into states. Each state has a Deeper Life "State Overseer" (the Lagos districts have "District Co-ordinators") and it is these gifted men (together with a "Women's Co-ordinator") who form Deeper Life's leadership team with Pastor Kumuyi as the "General Superintendent". In each place there is then a pastoral structure of Pastors, male and female

Zonal Leaders, Area Leaders, and male and female House
Caring Fellowship Leaders. Within Deeper Life, each state
or Lagos district has missionary responsibility for a different
country. I met two young men from the Lagos district whose
responsibility was Tanzania. They were using their annual
leave, and travelling at their own expense, to make an
exploratory visit to Tanzania. On their return, if they felt
called, and were affirmed in that by their district, they were
prepared to be sent as missionaries.

Meeting needs

In 1983, in response to the needs of the – mostly poor – people
attending Deeper Life, the Thursday Evangelism Training
was changed to a "Miracle Revival Hour". Miracles –
particularly healings – had been seen before, but now
the expectation was deliberately increased. I met many
people with testimonies of miracles: healing, deliverance,
provision, and conversion. To make a gross generalisation,
many Nigerians may tend to blame a demon for anything –
if you haven't been promoted in the past three years, you
must have a demon. The other side of that is an over-
simple dependence on God – some students who would
rather spend an evening praying for success than revising.
That said, I met many genuine (I felt) and remarkable
testimonies of deliverance. In terms of miracles of provision,
the expectation was not of the "prosperity gospel" kind,
which is attracting a large number of people in Nigeria
today.

Doctrine

Deeper Life's stance as a genuinely independent, indigenous
church seems to be based on a reaction against clearly
unchristian practice in local churches (e.g. animal sacrifice).
Such practices seem to be widespread, despite normally

being contrary to the teachings of the leaderships of the churches. But when I was first asked if I would be prepared to visit one of the new independent churches in Nigeria, I really did not know what I would find, and whether I would be able to worship with them at all! For all I knew, they might have been engaging in practices which would seem strange or even evil to me. However, I had also heard that they had grown significantly – attendance at the Lagos church now being over 50,000 each Sunday, with English as the medium of communication and simultaneous translation into a dozen or more other languages. Moreover, they had planted congregations in many other countries, including Britain. So I also half expected a major stadium, with soft seating, air conditioning, and headphones – something like the United Nations General Assembly building, perhaps. Deeper Life had promised they would look after me while I was in the country – but one person's notion of hospitality can differ from another's, so I was unsure how comfortable I would be.

As it turned out, their style of worship was probably more Westernised than the average independent church, out of a kind of counter-reaction to some of the independents, while still dealing openly and effectively with the spirit world. Their buildings were very simple – a minimum standard – if they had a building at all in a particular place. And Deeper Life exceeded any hopes I might have had, and made me ashamed of my fears, with their open-ended generosity, humility, and love.

Doctrinally, some might even call them fundamentalist, but Kumuyi is most influenced by Western Evangelical/ Pentecostal/Holiness tradition, and perhaps too wary of being too African in worship or practice. Pastor Kumuyi is anxious to see uniformity of teaching throughout Deeper Life.

The first work of grace is conversion – a definite experience of being born again. The second is sanctification – again a definite experience which you know you have had, and after which you do not sin (although you still need to grow in grace). The third is the baptism in the Holy Spirit, evidenced either "always" or only "normally" (depending on whom I spoke to) by speaking in tongues.

Membership

When I visited in 1988, the main building in Gbagada, Lagos, seated 12,000 people, and they were holding five services on a Sunday – a regular attendance of about 50,000. In the rest of Nigeria, about a thousand other Deeper Life Bible Churches have been planted. Numbers attending these churches range from double figures up into the thousands for the major cities. The total membership in Nigeria is in the region of 200,000. The growth has come probably mainly from the traditional denominations: Anglican, Baptist, Methodist, Roman Catholic; but also from the older African independent churches, such as the Cherubim and Seraphim and the Celestial Church of Christ. I also met a significant number of converts from Islam, and from traditional African religions.

The main emphasis of Deeper Life is on individual and corporate Bible study and personal evangelism. Caring is encouraged through their House Caring Fellowship system, and I came across many examples of sympathetic (and what we in the West would probably regard as sacrificial) giving and caring. In this way there is a personal response to injustice in society. At the corporate level, "development" is getting on their agenda – though of course there is a struggle between vision, priorities, and money. Kumuyi himself only gave up his job at the university in 1983, and he is the only full-time pastoral worker at Gbagada. In other locations, a Deeper Life pastor can only go full-time if his membership has passed 100, and if the congregation are prepared to support him. Despite these restraints, Deeper Life has always been, and remains, a totally indigenous movement and completely self-supporting. Long may it remain so.

Schiphol – outward

Pastor Pre Ovia of the Deeper Life Bible Church in London wanted to come to Heathrow to see me off – but I was flying from Manchester. He still tried to come and see me off, even though it didn't work out. But he did try; the time involved didn't matter. It was an example of the warmth and hospitality I found in so many Nigerians who turned to me as a brother. And it was similarly Nigerian that failure or success didn't matter; what was important was that he tried.

I had some hours to spend at Schiphol Airport, Amsterdam, waiting for my connection to Lagos, and I saw a "Place of Worship" signposted. It proved to be a small room, with just sixteen seats. On the wall was a simple picture of a fishing boat with a mast that looked like a cross, and woven into the brown carpet at one corner was the representation of a compass: the four corners of the world. It was a quiet room, set in the heart of the airport. The whole world was buzzing outside the doors.

A small bookcase contained Bibles in different languages. A large book of plain paper was available for people to write in. One recent message was from a man, thanking God for the peace he had received "after a violent and sad trip". I sat and prayed for a while. Then a young man came in, obviously out of curiosity. He looked to see what was in the bookcase, walked around the room restlessly, then found the visitors' book. He took some moments to read the comments, then wrote something and walked quickly out of the room. Other people came and went as I rested there, each seeming to find some peace or pleasure in the silence, such a stark contrast to the shopping mall, the money changers, and the constant flight announcements beneath.

Before I left I went to take another look in the book. The young man had taken a whole page to draw an angry face, with the phrase, "Just do it," written beside. This message – typical of modern Western culture – seemed to have no idea of how small a human being can feel, nor how great God is, and how he can bring us into his greatness. If you think you can do without God, you will never find him. Most Nigerians know they need God and are searching for the best way to serve him, to be in contact with him, and to receive from him. I knew I would be entering a very different culture when I arrived in Lagos.

I came out of the silence to the stress and hubbub. My flight was called, and I was on my way again. Soon after take-off I was handed a box of aeroplane food. The fact that the packaging had a picture of a pig crossed out on it told me that this was food acceptable to Muslims and others whose religion forbids them to eat pig. This was a reminder that from now on I had to be aware that the expectations and assumptions of people around me might be very different from my own. Although I had plenty of time for reflection during the flight, nothing can quite prepare you for the differences between Western and Nigerian cultures. Here are just some of the assumptions and ideas that are rooted in Western culture, but which are challenged by what I found. If you agree with more than four of these statements, then you may find this book very difficult:

1 I don't believe in miracles.

2 Dreams aren't real.

3 There are no such things as demons.

4 Herbalists (local "native doctors" who are healers and diviners, but who may also curse) are never really harmful (if they really exist).

5 Most illnesses are psychosomatic.

6 There's always a rational explanation.

7 You can't take everything in the Bible at face value.

8 All religions are basically the same.

1

One in a hundred million

To get from Lagos to Benin City, the capital of Bendel State, you travel eastwards along the thickly wooded coast. Rivers snake through to the sea, and no doubt snakes twist through the undergrowth and round the trees. There is mile after mile of deciduous trees and palms. Benin City itself is spacious, and mostly flat. The city centre swirls with cars, but there are hardly any traffic jams on its wide streets. Its modern, impressive buildings with corrugated iron roofs on concrete or mud walls are usually free-standing, but occasionally grouped into compounds. There are lots of green spaces and clumps of trees in the city – some of the trees very big indeed. It is a city carved out of the forest, and it comes as no surprise to learn that wood carving is a major feature of the local culture of the Edo people. At that time of year – October – when it was so dry in the semi-desert of the north of the country, Benin City was wet! The atmosphere was heavy with humidity, and some roads impassable, having been virtually washed away.

Late one afternoon we set off to leave Benin City for the village of Ugbine on the Gili-Gili road. Cool gusts of wind were blowing, and within a minute we were in the middle of a violent downpour of rain. Huge muddy puddles formed immediately, as the storm drains filled. People ran for the nearest shelter, their heads covered with a bag, or a magazine. Some had umbrellas. Street traders rushed for cover, some carrying their stock with them. Others left their stall in the open, but took refuge on a verandah or under a tree within sight of it. Some of the more permanent roadside traders have shelters of wood with iron roofs.

The wide streets of Benin City and the smart two-, three-, and four-storey offices and shops, painted pale yellow, light blue or white, were washed clean by the storm. Very quickly all the men and women had found shelter – but some children were still running around. Driving became hazardous – because of the puddles you couldn't see the potholes, and visibility was reduced anyway because of the rain. Two petrol stations we passed were closed because the attendants refused to come out in the wet (I didn't blame them!). The third was open; it had a more effective shelter over the pumps. An attendant wearing a black plastic bag upside down over her head served us, pushing through the congestion caused by people looking for any kind of protection from the downpour.

As we drove out of the city the rain became lighter and we sped along a smooth tarred road; but after fifteen minutes the road ended in a mud track which we followed through a string of small villages. The land was mostly cultivated, but still thick with vegetation. The track had a switchback effect, as each vehicle passing made the puddles deeper. We would slide over a mud hump, only to drop into fifty centimetres of water, then up to the next hump, and down again. My travelling companions were worried that we might get stuck – or even that we might get to Ugbine but then be unable to make the return trip.

"Don't worry," said our driver. "This is a miracle vehicle."

Forty-five minutes later, evening was drawing in as we drove into Ugbine, and the rain was finally stopping. This is an area where idolatry is predominant, with most men worshipping Ovia, most of the women Omero. A local product is rubber from the trees which form a part of the forest surrounding the village. Outside most of the houses were long horizontal poles, on which small oblong sheets of rubber were hanging to dry.

We made our way to a house belonging to an old woman, Osahenkhoe Emwenruwa. I was accompanied by an interpreter because the old lady does not speak English, and I can't speak Edo. She is a widow, and shares four rooms in the mud house with her daughter, also widowed, and nine grandchildren. Two tenants occupy two other rooms. We could hear sounds of cooking and smell woodsmoke behind the house. When I asked Osahenkhoe how old she was, she just laughed. She did not know – except that she had been one year old at the coronation of the King of Benin, Oba Eweka. There were two oil lamps to light our conversation – and conversation was all that was happening in every other house in the village, now that it was dark. Snatches of laughter or singing carried from house to house. I asked how they made a living for themselves, and she explained that her daughter concentrates on growing cassava, and trades in it successfully. Her daughter and the children also work to grow their own food, but four of the children are in primary school.

Osahenkhoe Emwenruwa sat on a wooden stool opposite me across the clean-swept concrete floor. She wore a wrapper and head-tie, and a simple cowrie shell necklace. When I asked if I could take her photograph, she was delighted, but went to change into something a little more special! I asked her to tell me her story, and as she spoke to our interpreter I noticed there was still a breeze from the rain. Occasional flashes of lightning lit the room for a split second while thunder rumbled in the distance. Two toddlers sat on the floor between us, mesmerised by the oil lamp, while two other children stood one at each arm of their grandmother, occasionally interrupting her story to put in extra details. She talked quietly and carefully.

When she had finished, our interpreter began to relate the details to me:

"She is very grateful for the question you asked her. Her problem was from her waist to her neck – because of being bent over, her neck was paining her. For more than ten years she wasn't able to stand upright at all – she had to get around the house and the village permanently bending at the waist, usually on all fours. During those ten years she tried many different places for help. She went to lots of herbalists and local healers, anyone she heard of. Sometimes they gave her something to drink, at other times something to rub on the waist – but there was no solution. It cost a lot of her children's money – she doesn't have any money of her own. Last year a relative told her about a Deeper Christian Life Ministry retreat in Lagos, where they would prove God's promise that the lame will walk, the blind will see. She told him, 'That's a lie. I don't want to go there.' But the in-law managed to persuade her to go. He gave her a date, and she got ready, but when he arrived it was to apologise that he had got the date wrong. The retreat had been the day before. Now they were too late. 'Don't worry,' she told him. 'Who is that God anyway? Leave me alone and let me die!'

"Then a year later he came again, and told her the same man was coming to Benin City. She said, 'What have you come here for? You always come to deceive me.' But he persuaded her again, and this time gave her the correct date!

"'You make sure it really is that day!' she told him. The in-law said he would go with her.

"When the day came she got ready early in the morning, but by midday he still had not arrived, so she went back to get changed into her everyday clothes, and started fetching water for the family. Then she heard a vehicle coming and sent a child to find out who it was for. It was for her – so she came in and changed again."

The story was obviously well known to the interpreter, and he was enjoying telling it despite occasional inter-ruptions from others, or when, for instance, two children brought a couple of goats through the house from the front to the back. He continued:

"Some of the Deeper Life members supported her to the vehicle and helped her to get in. When they arrived, they carried her to the 'miracle ground'. The people were clapping and singing already, and the programme was not due to start for another hour and a half! She asked her relative, 'Why are all these people shouting and dancing?'

"'Their big man – Pastor Kumuyi – has come from Lagos,' he told her.

"'Is he God, then?'

"'Something is going to take place tonight.'

"'OK-oh,' she replied, not really believing anything was going to happen at all.

"When the ministration started, a young woman member of Deeper Life came and asked her what she wanted. Osahenkhoe described her condition, and the young woman told her, 'OK, you are going to walk soon.' Osahenkhoe was angry. 'Don't you joke with me. I'll never walk again.' The young woman prayed for her and then asked her to get up. She did try, but she couldn't lift her back straight. So her relatives carried her to the Deeper Life Bible Church building in Benin where they slept that night in order to go to the second miracle service the next morning.

"She was carried to the miracle ground again for Pastor Kumuyi's second service on July 23rd, 1988. The Deeper Life pastor for Ugbine, John Osayomwanbo, told her, 'Mummy, you are going to walk.' She just retorted, 'This thing isn't a joke. Don't play with me.' He tried to make her walk on the strength of the previous night's prayer, but she couldn't. Then before the end of the ministration that Saturday morning, she felt something fly out of her neck, although she didn't see anything – but then she found she could move her head without any pain.

"John Osayomwanbo said, 'God has done it. You may not be able to walk here, but you will be able to walk when you get home.' After the service he tried to get an appointment for her to see Pastor Kumuyi, but there were so many people, it wasn't possible to meet him. They carried Osahenkhoe Emwenruwa back to their vehicle, and as they were driving home she told them, 'You see now – everybody in the village has heard that I've gone to Benin, and now they will laugh at me. They will say I'm a real sinner because nothing has happened to me.'

"The drivers who worked between Ugbine and Benin had been telling stories of the crusade in the villages. They told Osahenkhoe's daughter some of the stories, 'But,' they added, 'we didn't see your mother.' When the vehicle finally reached home, Osahenkhoe found her daughter weeping and crying for her with disappointment. The old woman was looking for someone to carry her down from the vehicle, but she found herself strong, just stood up, jumped down, and walked!

"There was jubilation throughout the whole village. The dancing started, and everybody in Ugbine began celebrating and bringing her gifts. They danced all night through to the next morning, all through that day and the following night, right through to the morning after that. Then the people decided they must go back to their farms! It had been a long time since Ugbine had seen such a celebration. Ever since then she has been able to walk upright, while before she was only properly able to get around on all fours. She decided to join the Deeper Life Bible Church in Ugbine. She hadn't attended church before, she had been an idol-worshipper. She used to keep her idol, Ehi, in a corner. It was an oval shape moulded out of chalk, representing an angel or intermediary. But she has now accepted Christ as her saviour. Since then her daughter and the children have also joined Deeper Life."

I asked Osahenkhoe if she had any prayer requests, now that she was walking upright again. She had two requests. Firstly, that now God has raised her up, she wants it to be permanent. Secondly, that God will keep all the children safe. As we said goodbye, she added, "If you meet anyone who has a similar problem, tell them, this is the way I have passed. If they can pass the same way, it will be well with them."

The little Deeper Life Bible Church started in this small village in 1984. Over four years the number at Sunday worship had reached only around twenty adults. After

the Miracle Crusade of July 1988 in Benin led by Pastor
Kumuyi, over sixty have been worshipping in the church
there.

Osahenkhoe is just one of the many people I have met
whose lives have been dramatically changed by an encounter
with Christ through the Deeper Christian Life Ministry
in Nigeria. A hundred million people live in this vibrant
country, a country with a vigorous and diverse history.

Early history of Nigeria

Civilisation and culture have existed in Nigeria for centuries.
Archaeological finds of the "Nok" culture on the Jos Plateau
(now in Plateau State) suggest a settled people flourishing
in that area between 900 BC and AD 200. They probably
cultivated grain for food, and quite early on developed
iron-smelting techniques. Some of the terracotta sculptures
which have been found suggest a developed culture with
wealth and leisure available to a few at least.

In the ninth and tenth centuries, the "Igbo-Ukwu" culture
arose in the south-east of what is now Nigeria. Intricate and
beautiful ceremonial objects made from copper and bronze
have been discovered. As copper is hardly found in this
area at all, trade must have developed with other peoples
hundreds of miles away – probably in North Africa.

Between the twelfth and fifteenth centuries, dignified and
realistic bronze heads were cast in Ife (now Oyo State). Ife
was the centre for the Yoruba people – now mainly living
across the south-west of modern Nigeria – and these heads
were probably depictions of the "Oni" (King) of Ife. The
Benin kingdom further to the east (now Bendel State) was
at its most powerful from the fifteenth to the nineteenth
centuries, a period of nearly five hundred years. It seems
that the Benin bronze-casters may have learnt their craft
from an Ife artist in the fourteenth century. Benin bronzes
are some of the finest works of art that may be seen anywhere
in the world. The kingdom was ruled by the "Oba" and his

court, until a British punitive expedition sacked Benin City
and exiled the Oba in 1897.

Modern history of Nigeria

Nigeria's modern history has been most deeply scarred
by the Atlantic slave trade which began in 1520, and
continued through to the nineteenth century. That horrific
trade in people's lives was supplemented by the export
of raw materials for European industries, on which the
European industrial revolution and wealth and power have
been built to this day. In order to be able to control
trade more effectively, the British annexed Lagos as a
colony in 1861. British Protectorates were established over
much larger tracts of land, until in 1900 the whole of
present-day Nigeria (nearly four times the size of Britain)
came under direct British colonial administration. Initially
government continued to be through local rulers, but the
1922 constitution provided for Nigerians to be elected to
a Legislative Council. Political parties began to develop
but it was not until 1953–4 that the British agreed to a
federal constitution, and the possibility of self-government.
On October 1st, 1960, Nigeria finally gained independence
from Britain – a Nigeria composed of over 500 language
groups. The four largest of these are the Hausa, Yoruba,
Ibo, and Fulani.

Dr Nnamdi Azikiwe was Governor-General until 1963,
and then President of the first Republic until January 1966
when a coup toppled the civilian government. General Ironsi
then became head of the Federal Military Government,
followed by General Yakubu Gowon in July 1966. In
May 1967 Lieutenant-Colonel Ojukwu made a unilateral
declaration of independence for the "Republic of Biafra"
in the east of the country. A full-scale civil war
developed, of tragic proportions, which ended only in
January 1970 with the collapse of Biafra. Twenty years
later, the wounds are still there.

Soon after I arrived in Lagos I met Bunmi Odetola, one of the editors responsible for Deeper Christian Life Ministry publications. We were talking together in the simple office where I was based. This tall, articulate young man dressed and spoke as impeccably as he studied the Scriptures and wrote Bible study materials. He leant over the desk and told me of his memories of that war:

"The civil war and the years immediately following were the Dark Ages for Nigeria. The problems affecting so many people, and the scarcity of everything, gave rise to some 'survival churches' which were really only on the look-out for what they could get. There was a dearth of the word of God. Doctrinally and practically there was a decline in Nigeria's spiritual climate. The 'occultic churches' became stronger. In the early seventies, therefore, there was a hunger and thirst for a real spiritual experience. New movements like the Deeper Christian Life Ministry helped to feed those who were spiritually hungry while the churches were not meeting the needs of the people. There were churches that held the Gospel truth, but they were 'closed' in the sense that they felt they were only just surviving, and even under siege. It was difficult to join one of these churches as a newcomer and be assimilated. Movements like Deeper Life were 'open' – it was easy to belong and identify yourself with them, whether you were a mechanic, a student, or a professional. As we became part of Deeper Life after those war years, we had tremendous zeal. We had felt like some scorched land, and now there were at last some showers. The ground wanted to cry out, 'I'm wet – I'm getting something!' So we would preach the Gospel everywhere we went: on the streets and in the buses. If we were on a bus together, we would even compete to see who could start preaching first."

For those in other parts of Nigeria, the civil war may not have seemed so significant, but when I travelled to the east I heard the same story.

To the east of the River Niger lie the states of Anambra, Rivers, Imo, Akwa Ibom, and Cross River. Much of the early missionary spread of the Lagos-based Deeper Christian Life

Ministry came about through a combination of personal vision and individual commitment, rather than central funding and directive strategy. Most of the senior leaders in Deeper Life across the country gained their initial experience in Lagos, and went out from there. Their "State Overseer" for Anambra, Emmanuel Ogbodo, explained how he had become a Christian in 1970 when he was working for a surveying firm in Lagos. He joined Deeper Life soon after the Ministry started in 1973. As he participated in the Bible study and evangelistic outreach he began to "feel a burden" for his people in Anambra. Emmanuel is a slender and intelligent young man who spoke out of pride for his people and devotion to them. Whenever I met him, he was dressed in the same workmanlike light blue shirt and trousers. His eyes always shone with excitement at the work in Anambra.

"I wanted to go back home to share the Gospel," he told me, "so I asked the Lord to provide a job for me there. Not long after, I got an interview, and in July 1977 I went to Enugu, the state capital. I started a small Bible study group there in the August. In 1980 I changed to another job which gave me more time to devote to Deeper Life. In 1981 I started working full time for Deeper Life. Now we have over a hundred Deeper Life Bible Churches in Anambra, and around 6,000 Deeper Life members."

Emmanuel Ogbodo described to me how at the end of the Biafran war the Gospel became meaningful to many of the easterners. A lot of people – especially the young – were asking what life was all about, after so much suffering. Obinna Nkemjika, a stouter man than Emmanuel, with a round face and a permanent smile, is Imo State Overseer. He added, "In 1970, revival started in the east. In my own village we had never heard a Gospel preacher until then. The war had a great impact, opening the way for the Gospel."

Working with Obinna Nkemjika is the Assistant Pastor of the Owerri Deeper Life Bible Church (Imo State), Charles Egonu. Both Obinna and Charles combine their pastoral and teaching duties with working full time as college lecturers in Owerri. Charles Egonu felt that before the civil war, people had been religious, but the Christians were by and large only nominal and their faith superficial; they could not relate Christian teaching to real life. Now there has been a spiritual awakening which has shown what God can do. During the war, life was hard. There was a lot of uncertainty, and people were living under all kinds of threats, but that brought a stronger consciousness of God's ability to help. As people were really struggling to survive, they began to gather into groups to pray and fast.

"Every morning," Charles remembered, "the women in my village would meet in the primary school to pray together. People were praying a lot, and they talked more about God. After the war that spiritual sense continued. They were receptive to an experience of the Holy Spirit because they were looking for something deeper. They had gone through nominal Christianity, but they were hungry for God to manifest himself and his power. The experience had always been available, of course, but at that time people were really looking for it. I grew up as a Roman Catholic, and was interested in the things of God, but when I was truly converted in 1975, I started seeing the Scriptures in a new way. Whatever is happening in Nigeria now is in agreement with Joel:

> I will pour out my Spirit on all people.
> Your sons and daughters will prophesy,
>   your old men will dream dreams,
>   your young men will see visions.
> Even on my servants, both men and women,
>   I will pour out my Spirit in those days . . .
> And everyone who calls
>   on the name of the LORD will be saved . . .
>   (Joel 2.28,29,32)

The word of God is being fulfilled in real, practical experience."

General Murtala Muhammed took over from Gowon in July 1975, but was assassinated in February 1976. His Chief of Staff, Lieutenant-General Olusegun Obasanjo, became the next Head of State, and he led the country to civilian rule in the second Republic when Alhaji Shehu Shagari became President in 1979. Instability in the nation's life prompted the military coup of December 1983 under the leadership of Major-General Muhammadu Buhari. Major-General Ibrahim Babangida took over the Presidency in August 1985, with a view to civilian rule being re-established in 1992.

Nigeria today

Nigeria's population is over 100 million – the largest population of any country in Africa. The Federal Republic of Nigeria has twenty-one states, with a developing Federal Capital Territory in the geographical centre of the country. Until the 1970s, it was principally an agricultural country, but since then its wealth has been created by the exploitation of oil resources. Significant material development has taken place since Independence, with the construction of roads, universities, airports, and industries.

The desire for national unity is strong. The Buhari regime introduced the "War against Indiscipline" which continues on five fronts: Queuing Up, Improved Work Ethics, Nationalism and Patriotism, Anti-Corruption, and Environmental Sanitation. The Babangida regime has declared a state of economic emergency, and launched the Structural Adjustment Programme (SAP). The value of the Naira has plummeted – many who once considered themselves wealthy now find it very hard to get by – but this has already resulted in lessening Nigeria's dependence on imports. When I was visiting the country, Nigerian unemployment was approximately seven per cent on average, while a shoe-mender was earning N30 a week, a welder N50 a week, a graduate teacher N100, and an officer manager N150. Legal and medical professionals were earning over N250. The exchange rate was N10 to £1, and prices were comparable with Britain.

There is a lively press: the newspapers are critical – but positively so – of government and institutions. Nigerians should be proud of their attitudes and their history, which has had its sad moments, but which is also one of fruitfulness and dynamic achievement. The pace of development in recent years has really been remarkable. The high moral tone and expectations of the newspapers and the Nigerians I met are certainly signs of hope for the future of their dynamic country.

2

People and religion

Driving from Ayobo, where I was staying, to Gbagada in Lagos where I was to be based for a while, our car slid through the mud to get to the main road where puddles obscured the potholes and so made for a bumpy ride. A minibus with a flat tyre couldn't get off the road because it was stuck in the mud, so it blocked the road while they changed the wheel.

There were people carrying water to their homes, and floods of youngsters in school uniform with bags and satchels of books – even the little ones – under their arms, on their shoulders, or on their heads. Young women were sitting in shady spots plaiting each other's hair. Other groups of two or three, some men, some groups of women, just sat in the shade, talking. A lot of the children were barefoot. All had been hard at work since before dawn.

The noise of the traffic, the traders, and the loudspeakers broadcasting music, Muslim calls to prayer and Christian evangelism blotted out the human voices singing while they worked, and the crickets, cicadas, and crowing cocks which came through if there was an unexpected moment of quiet.

Although there are plenty of cars – more than enough to cause a number of jams – most people who want or need to travel have to go on foot or by bus. At some places the pavements are crowded three and four deep for hundreds of metres with people waiting for a ride. At motor parks long, long queues wait patiently for occasional buses. I saw hardly any new buses – but a lot of very old ones. The buses that do run are filled to twice their capacity, and have their bumpers removed, or spikes added, to stop hopefuls clinging on for a free ride. Neither measure seems to be effective.

Most people walk if they need to get somewhere. Some stand by the roadside in the hope of a lift in a car, or a foothold of a few cubic centimetres on a bus. Usually they just walk (or "trek"), wearing sandals, trying to avoid the muddiest parts. Some carry bags. There are mothers or elder sisters with babies strapped to their backs – the baby's head nestles in the small of the carrier's back, its legs rest on the hips. Other people walk freely, but carry loads on their heads. Some of the loads are so heavy, it takes two or three others to lift them on to someone's head.

Most women wear traditional Nigerian dress, as do some men also – but most men in the south of Nigeria have adopted Western styles of dress.

There are regular police check-points (a policeman is usually armed with a pistol or a rifle) which are relaxed: not many vehicles are stopped.

Street traders are everywhere: men and women, boys and girls – some very young children and some very old adults. Some sit by the roadside with their produce on a table – bananas, yams or eggs. Others hawk what they can carry – a few loaves of bread, or the day's newspapers, a couple of torches, or packets of biscuits. If you show the slightest interest they surround you. People sell everything: onions, peppers, groundnuts, cassava, fish, spinach, tomatoes, oranges. A young boy sells black plastic bags. "Free-range" chickens scratch for food. Clean drinking water is for sale in little clear plastic bags. There are books, pens, plantains, maize, locks and keys, okra.

The centre of Lagos, like every other city, is a procession of modern, gleaming skyscrapers. Further out on the main roads are two-, three-, and four-storey blocks,

some offices, some flats. There is always construction work
going on. Most buildings are made of concrete, natural grey
or painted pastel colours; they have louvre windows; and
in the more prosperous houses fine netting screens to keep
out mosquitoes. A few have air-conditioning. Some have
flat roofs, but otherwise virtually all have sloping roofs of
corrugated iron.

Further out, crowded communities are separated by tracts
of open land. Here most buildings are single-storey, some
built of cement blocks, others of mud. They have louvre
windows, or wooden shutters, or nothing in the windows
at all except maybe a light piece of cloth for a curtain.
The roofs of the older houses are a patchwork of rusted
corrugated iron. Occasionally, amongst the older houses,
you catch sight of a shrine to an ancestor or a spirit.

At night in Lagos, traders' stalls with flickering oil lamps
line the roads. Rarely is there street lighting – more often
light escapes through open doors and windows, and most
buildings have outside lights. There are darker areas where
fewer buildings have electricity, and people move about by
moonlight, occasionally caught in the dazzling headlights
of a passing vehicle. Artificial light is a mixed blessing – at
least you can see clearly, but it also attracts all the bugs and
mosquitoes, which are at their most aggressive in the night
hours.

In all this diversity of people and activity twenty-four
hours a day, there is diversity of religion too.

To estimate religious affiliation is a controversial matter,
because of the current debate over whether, and to what
extent, Islamic Sharia law should be adopted in the country's 1992 constitution. Many Muslims want the full Sharia
law enshrined in the constitution, while many Christians
oppose any mention of Sharia at all. Suffice it to say that
Christians and Muslims each claim well over forty per cent
of the population. The Deeper Life Bible Church has now
reached nearly 200,000 members. A full quarter of that total
attend the central church in Gbagada, Lagos. A further
quarter are in the state capitals, while nearly 100,000 are

members in the towns and villages. The largest Christian grouping in Nigeria is the Roman Catholic Church, which alone accounts for maybe twelve per cent of the population. Next comes the Anglican Church of Nigeria with over eight million members – the largest national Anglican community outside England.

Traditional worship

Traditional worship continues throughout Nigeria, with many worshippers professing only a nominal allegiance to either Islam or Christianity, because these two world faiths have not in general effectively embraced the African need and desire to be in touch with the spirit world. There are very few Nigerians who would count themselves "agnostic" or "atheist". There is usually a loyalty to a supreme being, manifested through lesser deities – who may be represented by idols – and ancestral spirits. Magical practices and rituals are part of everyday life, and often practised by the local herbalist (or "native doctor", a healer/diviner who may also place curses for a fee) offering healing, divination, or meeting other needs in the community through contact with the spirit world. The traditional religion in an area will often be connected closely with the local ruler – as the Oba of Benin had been very much part of Osahenkoe Emwenruwa's life and traditional worship.

Samuel Kolawole Osinaike, whom I met in Gbagada, is a cheerful young man, full of confidence in the faith which he has been taught in Deeper Life, and has learnt by his own experience. We established an immediate rapport when we discovered that we had both taught at the same school, although at different times. He had spent 1975–6 at Playfair Memorial College, Oro-Ago, while I had been there from 1977 to 1979. He had subsequently pursued a career in banking, which had brought him to Lagos – and here I was, ten years later, interviewing him. He was born and brought up an Anglican, but also grew up to depend on magic charms, which he has now utterly abandoned. I asked him what he meant by "magic charms".

"There are different kinds of charms," he explained. "For example, the witch doctor may gather some leaves and make incantations over them. Now, when he curses you, it will happen to you. Or if you take one of those herbal concoctions, it can influence you in the spiritual realm. Or if you wash with soap which has been mixed with a herbal concoction, it will have a negative effect on you. There are evil forces around – you may see yourself flying at night. These forces are real. I have seen somebody carrying a heavy grindstone with a single cotton thread. It should have been impossible, but he was able to do it by magic. These people can mar your life – but Jesus can destroy their power.

"In your village there may be a special tree which you dare not cut down, unless you have a special spiritual power to cut it down. If you are covered in the blood of Jesus it will not affect you. In my own family we had a twin god idol. We worshipped it so that the twins in my family would not die."

Islam

David Barrett, in the *World Christian Encyclopedia*, notes: "Islamic influence was first felt in the eleventh and twelfth centuries, and by the fifteenth century Kano had become a flourishing centre for Muslim culture and commerce. A new thrust came in the nineteenth century when a Fulani crusade swept over the Hausa area leaving permanent marks on the culture and social system." The ancient city walls of Kano, and the majestic Emir's Palace, still stand as a testimony to that importance and power. The spiritual head of Islam in Nigeria remains to this day the "Sultan" of Sokoto, now Alhaji Ibrahim Dasuki.

Religious life in Nigeria can now be broadly determined as Muslim in the north, and Christian in the south. To many Christians, the idea of Nigeria as a secular state has been compromised by the decision in 1986 to seek full membership of the Islamic Conference Organisation (OIC). A hardening of positions on both sides of this issue, and of the proper role of Sharia law in the life of the nation as a whole, is making solutions to these problems difficult to find.

Islam in Nigeria seems to be a united faith, although a number of groupings within the religion have identified themselves. There are also individuals and groups who take a more flexible approach to being Muslims and accept various aspects of traditional worship into their spirituality.

In the dry climate of the north I visited Kano. The Harmattan was already beginning – the dry season when dust from the Sahara Desert drifts south in thick clouds, covering every surface in minutes and making you thirsty in a few moments as your throat gets parched. In a corner of the Kano Deeper Life Bible Church I met Abdul Maruf, who explained to me in broken English how he came to be there. He was thirty-five years old – and he had been a Muslim for all of those thirty-five years:

"I always said I would die a Muslim. I came to Kano in 1971 to work as a printer, and I liked to see the Muslim–Christian riots – I was happy to see the Christians being persecuted. I married an Ibo woman in 1981 – she had been a Christian but she changed to Islam and we were married in the mosque. But sometimes I was not happy with Islam – there seemed to be no life in me. I didn't drink alcohol, I prayed five times a day, I read the Koran – but I found it difficult to understand.

"I bought many books about Islam – I wanted to go to the College of Islamic Theology in Maiduguri to learn more. I read the Koran about John, and Jesus and the unbelievers – and was confused."

And as he [Zacharias] stood praying in the Shrine, the angels called out to him, saying: "Allah bids you rejoice in the birth of John, who shall confirm the Word of Allah. He shall be princely and chaste, a prophet and a righteous man." (Al-Imran 3.39)

Allah is the supreme Plotter. He said: "Jesus, I am about to cause you to die and lift you up to Me. I shall take you away from the unbelievers and exalt your followers above them till the Day of Resurrection. Then to Me you shall all return and I shall judge your disputes." (Al-Imran 3.54–55)

Abdul felt uneasy about these passages. He went to visit a Muslim friend who told him not to worry – but at the same time his wife was beginning to argue with him that she wanted to serve God more fully, and she soon converted back to Christianity.

"But I didn't want her to go to churches where members drank alcohol or joined secret societies," explained Abdul. "I had heard Deeper Life didn't do such things, so I allowed her to attend Deeper Life."

In 1987 Abdul started to make plans for a pilgrimage to Mecca, but he was still perplexed by passages in the Koran such as:

We sent . . . Jesus the son of Mary. We gave him the Gospel and put compassion and mercy in the hearts of his followers. (Al-Hadid 57.27)

It would only be proper to note that there is much in the Koran which condemns and criticises Christians – which is precisely why Abdul was getting so confused. At the same time, these discoveries of Abdul's were from his own searching of his Scriptures, and the conclusions he reached were his own.

"I was confused," he went on. "One night I was crying in my bed, and I prayed, 'Lord, I want you to show me the way.' I felt that God was telling me to look in the Bible and I found Psalm 30."

To you, O LORD I called;
    to the Lord I cried for mercy . . .
You turned my wailing into dancing;

you removed my sackcloth and clothed me with joy,
that my heart may sing to you and not be silent.
O LORD my God, I will give you thanks for ever.

(Psalm 30.8,11,12)

So Abdul was led to repentance and conversion to Christ.
At first he did not want to go near a church – he was afraid
they might use magic and the occult, which he had always
avoided as a Muslim. But his wife took him to the Deeper
Life pastor, who advised him to continue attending the
mosque, but also to come to the weekly Bible study so that
he could learn more about God.

"I read where Jesus calls himself the way, the truth, and
the life (John 14.6) and the good shepherd (John 10.11). I
meditated, and prayed. Now I am happier than if I had
won millions of naira! I will die for Christ. I'm wearing
this badge," (he showed me a badge with 'Jesus makes
a difference' written on it) "and I will never backslide.
Some of my family have rebuked me and tried to make
incantations over me, but they can't do anything against
me. I am strong in the Lord. I have told my father to
remove all the medicines and charms in his house. A lot
of the Imams [Muslim leaders] are using incantations over
me, but they can't touch me. They are still persecuting me.

"I was born again in December 1987. I didn't go to
Mecca. This Deeper Life Bible Church is my Mecca!"

Emmanuel Ene – formerly Tahir Hamza – is from Enugu,
Anambra State. He was a Muslim, and as there was a
shortage of Islamic teachers in his area he was sent to Kano
to study the Koran. He arrived in May 1988 and was given
a room at the Fagge Central Mosque. He studied hard, and
used to go out preaching Islam. In September 1988 he met
a young man reading a pamphlet, and because he wanted
to talk to him and help him to become a Muslim, he asked
if he could read the pamphlet.

"I saw the phrase, 'Decide for Jesus now'. We agreed
to talk about this: I went to collect my Hadith [not the
Koran, but a compilation of traditions of Islam], and then

he brought me to Deeper Life. He showed me this passage
from the Koran:

> *Alif lam mim.* Allah! There is no god but Him, the Living,
> the Ever-existent One. (Al-Imran 3.1)

and then showed how Christ was God:

> In the beginning was the Word, and the Word was with
> God, and the Word was God. (John 1.1)

Then he showed me where it seemed that Mohammed
wasn't sure of what would happen to him!

> 'I am no prodigy among the apostles; nor do I know
> what will be done with me or you. I follow only what is
> revealed to me, and my only duty is to give plain warning.'
> (Al-Ahqaf 46.9)

compared with:

> 'I am the way and the truth and the life. No-one comes to
> the Father except through me.' (John 14.6)

I accepted defeat casually, but I wasn't convinced. I
went back to the mosque and contemplated. I thought,
'Mohammed didn't promise us rest, but Jesus said he was
the way.' I checked my own Koran – and I couldn't sleep
that night. I wanted to pray, and I talked to God, not in
the traditional Muslim way. The next day – a Friday – I
came to the Miracle Revival Hour, then I went back to the
mosque and continued praying. By now I was convinced that
I had found the truth. I was convinced that Christ was the
Son of God, and I accepted him as my personal Lord and
Saviour."

That was in September 1988, and I was talking with
Emmanuel in the October! I asked him what he was going
to do now. He explained that he had abandoned the course

he had started, and joined the Deeper Life Bible Church. He was going to stay in Kano for a while to get "spiritually well-equipped" before returning to Enugu.

I asked Deeper Life pastor Ransom Bello about Islam. He told me that Kano was really an Islamic state – but that usually there were no problems between Muslims and Christians. They greet each other, relate to each other, and can live in the same houses without conflict. But sometimes there can be friction – sometimes Deeper Life members walking down the street have been abused just for carrying Bibles, and there can be distrust between the communities.

"But at the personal level relations are good," he affirmed. "The Lord is helping us. I know Muslims who are honest, trustworthy, and devoted, and who don't believe in fanaticism. They keep to high moral standards. At the normal human level, they are 'good' – but except by the cross of Christ, no one is good enough for heaven. We Christians have some things to learn from the Muslims, though. Some Christians complain about what we teach on modest dress – but I tell them to look at the Muslims and the decent clothes they wear. Their level of devotion is high: they pray five times a day. In Deeper Life we have prayer meetings, but in many churches you can't get people to pray often. Also, the Muslims are generous for the cause of Islam. If I pastored 4,500 Muslims rather than 4,500 Christians as I do here in Kano city, we would have no financial problems at all!"

Christianity

Catholicism first came to Nigeria with the Portuguese in the fifteenth century, but the faith only really began to take root with the second wave of Catholic mission which began in 1865. In 1842 the (Anglican) Church Missionary Society and the British Wesleyan Methodists had sent missionaries to start work on the southern coast. Jamaican Presbyterian missionaries followed in 1846, and Southern Baptists from the USA in 1850. Christians from all denominations whom

I met in Nigeria spoke with pride and affection of the early missionaries: their sacrificial faith which planted the Church, and their involvement in the ending of the slave trade.

Ernest Iyade – the Administrative Secretary for Deeper Life in Lagos – expressed genuine and deep affection, gratitude, and respect for the work of Western missionaries. He and others told me that they hoped that many of those who had worked in Nigeria would hear of the life and vitality of the churches in this country which they loved, and would be able to praise God for the fruit which has grown. At the same time he criticised African converts for failing to separate themselves sufficiently from their culture for the sake of the Gospel. This has enabled "backsliding" to occur, and occultism to penetrate the churches. Perhaps the early Western missionaries failed to penetrate and address those aspects of local culture, at the same time attaching to the Gospel as essential what were only products of Western culture.

One young woman I met in Lagos – Elisabeth Ifeagwu – was born and brought up a Roman Catholic. She told me her story:

"I was a Catholic. I came across the Scripture Union at school in Ibadan, and I started attending their meetings and using the daily Bible reading notes, *Daily Power*. The Lord started talking to me, and I just loved reading the Bible. I began to feel guilty in the Catholic Church – I felt it was as if we were worshipping the images, bowing down to them. I was converted through SU in 1972. I had always had the zeal to please God – I even wanted to become a Reverend Sister. But I would keep malice with people. I had a bad temper. I saw I was slighting the God I wanted to love. I gave my life totally to the Lord, and the moment I stood up, as I was still praying, I felt light, as if a burden had been lifted off me. I felt peace within me. I went to a senior girl I had been annoyed with, and apologised for not talking to her – even though nobody had taught me about restitution. I kept on going to the Catholic services because at the school, once you were registered with a particular church you had to stay with it. I told the Reverend Father I had some questions, but he was not able to convince me. I took the Bible as my standard. When I came to Lagos in 1973, I didn't go to any particular church, but I did go to one Christian gathering at the racecourse – and was invited to a fellowship in Surulere. It was there that I heard about the weekly Deeper Life Bible study at Flat 2 in the University of Lagos. I joined them in 1974 and I have been involved in all the programmes. I was a Bible study leader at the April 1976 retreat in Lagos. I went to the weekly Thursday Evangelism Training School and was a member of an evangelism team (later, I became the team leader). In the evangelism teams we would gather on a Sunday, brothers and sisters together, to pray and go out on house-to-house evangelism, brothers in pairs and sisters in pairs, to evangelise our own sex, inviting people to the Bible study."

Two thousand five hundred people attended that April 1976 Deeper Christian Life Ministry retreat. Others, like Elisabeth, were finding in Deeper Life the opportunity they wanted to study and apply the Bible in commitment and faith.

Independent churches

Catholic Christianity has remained fairly unified, while Protestants have seen a wide diversity develop through the twentieth century. Churches planted by European and North American missions seem to fall into three groupings: "Orthodox" (Anglican, Methodist, Baptist, for example), Evangelical and Pentecostal. In 1918 there was a virulent influenza epidemic which ravaged West Africa. The churches planted by European and North American missions appeared powerless against this epidemic, while there were those African Christians who believed God would wish to protect his people. Yoruba Christians formed

prayer and healing groups, which ultimately broke away to
become independent, indigenous churches: among them the
Cherubim and Seraphim, the Church of the Lord (Aladura),
and the Christ Apostolic Church. The Christ Apostolic
Church, for instance, began as a renewal movement within
the Anglican Church, but by 1920 it had separated. David
Barrett estimates that the total number of Christian denominations in Nigeria in 1970 had reached 860. By 1980
the number had risen to 960, and it is rising still.

Some of these independent churches are called "white
garment" churches – because their worshippers wear white
garments in an effort to worship God as he requires:

> After this I looked and there before me was a great
> multitude that no-one could count, from every nation,
> tribe, people and language, standing before the throne
> and in front of the Lamb. They were wearing white robes
> and were holding palm branches in their hands. And they
> cried out in a loud voice:
>> "Salvation belongs to our God,
>> who sits on the throne,
>> and to the Lamb." (Revelation 7.9,10)

As these churches were seeking a more effective, more
appropriate expression of Christianity, so there appeared
to be some aspects of local culture which the Western
missionaries had rejected, but which in fact were felt to
be acceptable to the Nigerians. To take as an example
just one issue where many have rejected what they see
as merely Western practice: the Christ Apostolic Church,
in line with the teaching of the early European and North
American missionaries, does not allow polygamy, while the
Cherubim and Seraphim may allow polygamous marriages,
except for bishops and deacons. The Celestial Church of
Christ advocates polygamy as normal marital practice. By
contrast, most Nigerian Christians would describe divorce
as being unacceptable to God, while many Western churches
are giving an increasing number of divorces their blessing.

In terms of worship, there are many traditional practices which are widespread among these independent churches – for example, burning candles, singing and dancing, praying aloud individually at the same time as everybody else, use of "medicine", and animal sacrifice. These and other practices may be used in local expressions of Christian worship, with or without the consent of the national leadership of the church concerned. It is often in negative response to the local expression that a breakaway group has formed, while that local expression may not be what the leadership want or intend. Dissatisfaction with the local expression of Christianity has therefore prompted a search for a "better" expression of the faith, and one which meets the people's needs – particularly needs for healing, material security, protection from demonic attack, divination, and a tangible relationship with ancestors. (I think all the Nigerian Christians I have met would witness to experiencing each of these quite often, as spiritual needs.) It is a testimony to the power of the Gospel in Nigeria, and to the inherent faith of the people, that most of those who break away do so to form a "more" (or "better") Christian grouping. Our experience in Britain, when there has been a dissatisfaction with the local expression of Christianity, is usually for only a minority to seek a deeper Christian faith. The majority turn to agnosticism or even atheism, with a significant number exploring other world faiths such as Islam, Hinduism, Buddhism, and, more recently, Ba'hai.

Towards the end of October 1988 I drove along the smooth roads towards Ilorin, the state capital of Kwara, where the majority of the people are Yoruba. It was significantly greener than the far north which I had left behind me, with clumps of thick vegetation by the roadside, and plantations of maize and cassava, though nothing like the thick jungle of the southern coast. We found the Ilorin Deeper Life Bible Church in Osere on the outskirts of the city. This is a new development area, and although the original Deeper Life building is not very old, it has already built extensions in a lean-to manner along one side and at the back, to more than double its capacity. The atmosphere was much more humid than in the north. There was the smell of fruit and vegetables in the air, and the sounds of people talking, children playing, and cocks crowing. It felt like a village rather than a city. Also in this area are new buildings for the Jehovah's Witnesses, the Alafia Oluwa Baptist Church, and His Grace Evangelical Church. These, along with a number of new mosques, demonstrate the spiritual intensity which I found all over Nigeria.

I sat on a bench under a tree outside the Deeper Life Bible Church waiting for a service to begin. A distinguished-looking man in a green and brown traditional suit and hat came and sat next to me. As we talked slowly in the evening sun, he explained that he had been a member of the Cherubim and Seraphim for many years, but had recently joined Deeper Life. He told me his story. An elder in society, with a wife, eight children and (so far) two grandchildren, I.O. Sodeko was born in Abeokuta, in Ogun State, in 1911.

"I served in the Cherubim and Seraphim Church for over fifty years, and had risen to the post of senior apostle. I was the chief usher for the Cherubim and Seraphim in Ilorin. Then in 1980, Deeper Life held a meeting adjacent to my house so I could hear them preaching. One day I decided to go and listen.

"After a Cherubim and Seraphim committee meeting one Tuesday I went to Deeper Life because I had problems with high blood pressure and diabetes. I asked for their leader to pray for me, but he was busy counselling so the assistant was called. I told him my problems, and he asked me to bow my head to pray. I wanted to remove my shoes, but he told me it wasn't necessary. He prayed for maybe four or five minutes, and I was expecting a vision or a prophecy from him, but suddenly he just stopped! I asked him, 'Have you finished the prayer already?' 'Yes,' he replied. Well, I was surprised! When I got home I told my wife, 'Ah-ah! These people don't know how to pray – they're wasting their time!'

"I refused to go back for three weeks, but then attended once again. The teaching on that day pained me, and I promised myself I would be at the next meeting. They were telling me to trust God, repent of my sins, and put my cares on God. When I was in Cherubim and Seraphim I used to tell lies, and was afraid of wizards and witches. But in 1981 I went on a Deeper Life retreat at Akure, and I decided there to put all my cares on the Lord. When I got back, I packed up all the 'medicines' and charms in my house and threw them into the river. So I left the Cherubim and Seraphim after fifty years. It wasn't easy – they tried to stop me going.

"After that 1981 retreat my diabetes and high blood pressure seemed to get worse – but I decided that rather than go to Satan for help, it would be better to die and go to my Lord. Since then I've not taken any drugs, and if I feel any of the symptoms coming on I just tell them they're wasting their time, and they go away.

"With all my past behaviour, my last place would have been hell. Now I've started to learn under Deeper Life. I used to get into debt, but I've learnt to tithe, and now I'm always in credit. I have enough money to care for my family – I have no problems! My wife and children are all staunch members of Deeper Life now."

At the same time as groups have been splitting off from the European and North American planted churches in Nigeria, the presence of Christianity has itself been an influence upon the traditional beliefs and worship in different places.

Churches – and cults

In Lagos I met a man who worked in a bank. He had been born and brought up a Muslim, but had come to faith in Christ through contact with a cult. He explained:

"At primary and secondary schools we had Bible knowledge classes, but I thought the Bible was just a story book. I did not know the Lord Jesus. I used to lead Muslim worship at school when I was in Class Four. I left school, started work, and got married. Although I was a Muslim, I hardly ever went to the mosque, but I always prayed and fasted, and was preparing to go to Mecca. If I had not become a Christian, by now I would be an *Alhaji* [the prestigious title given to a Muslim who has made a pilgrimage to Mecca]. I was married, but my wife and I could not have any children. We went from one doctor to another, but could find no solution. There was no success coming to us that medical way. We were living in Port Harcourt in Rivers State at the time (1975), and somebody said that if I went to an occult temple he knew, there was a prophet who could help me. When I got there, I saw some occultic, magical items. There was a book wrapped in brown paper which the prophet would beat with a wooden cross. There were candles that we had to look into, and leaf juice that we had to drink. At the same time the people were singing Christian choruses!

"Somebody said the name of the prophet was Danger. He said, 'Somebody has stolen my wristwatch, I want it back!' From nowhere, I saw a red handkerchief appear on the table. The prophet's watch was inside. Although I was a Muslim, I remembered what Jesus had said about false prophets, and I understood that Danger was a false prophet.

"The prophet knew what I was thinking. He cast a spell over me with a charm and kidnapped me, taking me to another town a long way away in the next state. He wanted to do evil and kill me. But I saw the hand of the Lord Jesus. The Lord came down and defended me. The prophet said, 'If I can't kill you, I will turn you mad!' He cast a spell with a charm and I lost my senses. The prophet Danger then told me all my sins from when I was about ten years old. Everything came out one by one, like a cassette tape playing back everything you have recorded. The prophet was saying it all in the presence of about thirty people. I didn't open my mouth. I just looked at him and thought, 'This must be Jesus. Like in the Bible, he knows everything I ever did. You are Jesus. I want you to forgive me.' All of a sudden, I was given a bottle, and saw "rescued" written inside the bottle. But the prophet said, 'No one can rescue you.'

"But the Lord Jesus came down and broke the power of evil in that place. Jesus told me, 'I allowed everything to come before you, and you prayed sincerely.' I was talking to Danger, but the Lord knew my prayer was sincere and he answered. He has the power to forgive sins. Then the Lord spoke specifically to me from the Bible:

> So do not fear, for I am with you;
> do not be dismayed, for I am your God.
> I will strengthen you and help you;
> I will uphold you with my righteous right hand.
> All who rage against you
> will surely be ashamed and disgraced;
> those who oppose you
> will be as nothing and perish.
>
> (Isaiah 41.10,11)

And the Lord brought me safely back to Port Harcourt. I had been away for twenty-four hours.

"After two weeks the Lord told me to go and preach to the prophet. I went, and rather than threatening me, he started to hide! I took out and threw away all his *ju-ju* (evil charms) and magic items. I bought a megaphone and started preaching to him at five o'clock every morning!

"I wasn't receiving any Christian teaching or fellowship at this time – the Lord himself was telling me what to do and which Scriptures to read – for three or four months. I didn't go to any church – I still considered myself a Muslim – but I read the Bible voraciously. It was as if the Lord was sitting in front of me and talking to me. But eventually I joined a Baptist church."

The dividing lines between groups such as the one which "kidnapped" this man and some other groupings which might call themselves "independent churches" are not always clear, and in the end, people of faith will differ as to whether and how much one particular grouping is Christian, or whether it is possible to be a Christian and remain in that group.

Doing what God wants you to do, being where he wants you to be

One of the smallest Deeper Life fellowships I visited was in Oro-Ago, the village where I had worked as a teacher for a couple of years in the late seventies, at a school run under the auspices of ECWA (Evangelical Churches of West Africa). On the tarred road from Ilorin to Omu-Aran, it takes just one hour to drive the eighty kilometres, but from there to Oro-Ago it takes another hour to travel just twenty-eight kilometres! The mud roads here were bumpier and slower than farther north where the drier atmosphere after a shorter rainy season means the roads can be levelled; though not as bad as in the far south where I had travelled to visit Osahenkhoe Emwenruwa's village. This track is hilly, the road bending round farms and peaks, alternately sandy, rocky, and muddy, a few streams crossing the track or even joining it for a short distance. The road goes over two rivers. The first bridge was just a car's width, the second was broken. You had to go up a ramp to the edge of the bridge, then a sharp drop down to where it had broken in the middle, and up the other side before bumping back down to the road again. This poor road contributes to a sense of isolation in Oro-Ago, but also a peacefulness and an independence, which are not bad characteristics.

Esther Adelike's bungalow, which she shares with another young woman who is also a member of Deeper Life, has just two small rooms – a sitting room and a bedroom. The atmosphere was clean and bright, and she was delighted to welcome us – if you live in Oro-Ago you don't get many visitors! She is a graceful young woman, showing a committed and resilient attitude to work and a dedication to serve God and discover his will for her life. She is responsible for the small Deeper Life Bible study group that meets in Oro-Ago, and I found it encouraging to meet a woman entrusted with leadership. I got the feeling, though, that women are only asked to lead when there are no men around. But at least Deeper Life are open to women leading at all. Perhaps the time is coming when women's potential contribution to leadership will be more fully recognised.

Esther moved to Oro-Ago in January 1986, and the following September a Deeper Life brother from Ilorin started a Deeper Life Bible study group there. He would travel out each week to lead them. Then in 1987 he handed over to another brother, who would travel in from Osi. But by the end of that year sister Esther had been asked to take care of the group.

It is somehow strange to return to a place after ten years and find that it hasn't changed! I had left Oro-Ago in 1979 (without having heard of Deeper Life at all) thinking that I would never see the place again – and indeed at the school where I had taught, of all the teaching staff I worked with, only one remained. Mr Bamgboye greeted me with his infectious laugh, observing with pleasure that whereas before I had used a motorbike, this time I had arrived in a car. His only anxiety was over whether I was married yet. I was able to satisfy him on this point.

The two maintenance men welcomed me: "Ah, Mr Isaacson," as if I had only been away a few days. It was a reassuring visit – which lasted only an hour or so – but it was a joy to me to discover that just as Oro-Ago became and remained part of me, so I have remained part of Oro-Ago. There is fruitfulness and permanence if you can place yourself where God wants you to be, whether near or far from your birthplace.

Esther is where she feels God wants her to be, doing the work she feels he wants her to do. That is enough. We will not always understand the purpose, or see the result.

"Although we aren't many in the Deeper Life fellowship here," Esther told me, "the few are committed, and want to fellowship together, and that encourages me. The group helps me personally – it's a challenge to me to study the word of God, and what I am teaching helps me as well. I expect an increase – but there isn't any growth yet."

Esther (who came originally from Oke-Opin) became a Christian in 1978 when she was teaching at Omupo. She was invited to the 1978 Deeper Life retreat in Ilorin where Pastor Kumuyi was ministering. She gave her life to Christ and joined Deeper Life. It does seem to be true that most of those who are most committed to Deeper Life and in the leadership have had some kind of personal encounter with W.F. Kumuyi, who is one of the most significant church leaders in Africa today.

3

Kumuyi

Sunday worship at Gbagada

In Gbagada Deeper Life Bible Church, Lagos, there are five
services each Sunday: at 7 a.m., 9.30 a.m., 12 noon, 2.30
p.m., and 5 p.m.. The church is divided pastorally into
various geographic "Districts" and "Zones", and you attend
a service according to which Zone you live in. I arrived one
Sunday morning as the first service was coming to an end
at around nine fifteen. The church building was filled to
capacity: about 12,000 seated. Most of those present seemed
to be in the age range of twenty to forty-five, although some
older people were also members of the church. I was the only
white person there. Around 3,000 people were also packed
into the surrounding grounds, on the streets, and on the
steps of houses and shops overlooking the rather ramshackle
(to Western eyes) but dignified building.

The building has concrete walls and pillars supporting a
corrugated iron roof. As the congregation has grown, so the
building has been expanded in the easiest way – the added
extensions being more like adjacent buildings with no walls
between rather than a continuation of the main building, so
that there are gaps in the roof where the rain comes in, and
storm drains which dissect the floor to take the water away.

The people sitting outside had their Bibles open and were taking notes as loudspeakers broadcast what was going on inside. The atmosphere outside was less conducive to joining in the singing and praying, while within the church an efficient army of young men and women acting as ushers guided people to their seats, and distributed the song sheet for the day, which also contained that week's and next week's memory verses.

Everything is conducted in English – the nation's official language and the language of education – but there are also "language classes" where you can sit and hear everything simultaneously translated into one of fifteen other languages. The Sunday worship begins with half an hour in Zonal groups in a "Search the Scriptures" study. All the members have a book to prepare the study for themselves, and their daily Bible readings have been leading up to the Sunday study. Certain people in the church are appointed "Search the Scriptures" leaders, and spend Saturday evening preparing together. Two people work full time for Deeper Christian Life Ministry preparing the "Search the Scriptures" books. This week the topic was "Self Denial", with the text:

> [Jesus said] "Anyone who loves his father or mother more than me is not worthy of me; anyone who loves his son or daughter more than me is not worthy of me; and anyone who does not take his cross and follow me is not worthy of me. Whoever finds his life will lose it, and whoever loses his life for my sake will find it." (Matthew 10.37–9)

Our young leader drew out the main points: "Our consecration must be renewed day after day. We need to reject luxury and forgo the benefits of compromise. Our cross will be made by the world, and we must be prepared to carry it for our Master. The measure of our love for Christ is the amount of self we can deny."

The poverty of the people and the immediate impact of this teaching made it clear that although this church is one which preaches the power of prayer, they could not be accused of preaching a "success" or "prosperity gospel" like so many groups which take Scripture to mean that God will give material prosperity to his most faithful followers.

After that session, time is spent in prayer – maybe emotional, but controlled. The cue is given to pray, and everybody starts praying aloud at once, each person individually talking to God, simultaneously. Some have seen this as the mode of prayer described in Acts 4.24 ("they raised their voices together in prayer to God"). Your relationship with God is your responsibility and you have to speak to him. At the sound of a bell, or an announcement over the loudspeakers, people will end their prayers.

We spent some time in prayer in the Zones, then Pastor W.F. Kumuyi – the founder and overall leader of the Deeper Life movement – came to the pulpit. We were all called together to hear any questions. A hush descended as the thousands present who owed their spiritual standing to Pastor Kumuyi listened carefully to what he had to say.

The early history of Deeper Life is very much the personal story of W.F. Kumuyi. He is a gifted man, clear-thinking and humble. He is a dedicated Christian, and deserves the title, "the man of God", which his followers have given him. Since he was a young man, Kumuyi has devoted his time to reading and studying the Bible. He knows the Scriptures inside out, and has struggled to understand and apply them. As he shares that struggle and his love for the word of God, so people have been drawn to him for advice, or simply to listen. When he preaches, his message is clear, simple, and profound. Poor street traders who can barely read sit next to university professors, all equally captivated by the way Scripture becomes suddenly relevant to them. Kumuyi's own Christian life developed because he took the Bible so seriously, and so the Deeper Christian Life Ministry has developed in the same way. Kumuyi has preached Deeper Life into existence. People like Esther in Oro-Ago (p. 55) and Elisabeth in Lagos (p. 46) have had their whole lives just turned around by Christ directly through Kumuyi's preaching.

As he has preached, so some of his followers have learnt the same skill, and been gifted by God in a similar way, so that people like Sodeko in Ilorin (p. 50) and Abdul in Kano (p. 41), while searching for God, have come to a deeper, fuller faith through a local Deeper Life pastor.

Kumuyi is not tall, and does not have a larger-than-life character. He does not dominate, nor has he accrued power to himself. He walks slowly, is relaxed, and has a gentle sense of humour with a warm smile and a twinkle in his eyes. He dresses simply, eats simply, lives in a small flat, and does not draw a salary from the ministry which has flourished under his leadership. He could have assumed titles to himself as the Deeper Life Ministry developed – most people enjoy the trappings and regalia of status which followers gladly give. But he calls his followers "brothers and sisters", and treats them as colleagues. The ministry has developed with a minimum of structure: a Deeper Life Bible Church may have a pastor, and Kumuyi is the "General Superintendent" of the movement.

Status is so important to a Nigerian that one is usually referred to by one's position rather than one's own name. To British ears it sounds oddly formal to talk about "the GS", or "the Pastor"; while to Nigerian ears it sounds strange simply to use a personal name. Members of Deeper Life refer to each other as "brother" and "sister".

Kumuyi was born in 1941 into an Anglican home. "It was a very strict Christian home," he told me. "We would get up in the morning, read the Bible, sing hymns, and go to church regularly. When I went to secondary school I lost interest in the church because our principal taught us atheism. But after a while I thought again and started going to various churches in the town. Eventually, in 1963, a group of singers and preachers from a Gospel church got permission to come to the school. I understood the Gospel message, and was born again on April 5th, 1964. I read John Wesley, Charles Finney, Spurgeon, and a lot of other books. I got involved with the Scripture Union, and I grew."

Kumuyi gained a first-class degree in Mathematics at the

University of Ibadan; and then went back to Mayflower School to teach. After five years he went to the University of Lagos to do a Postgraduate Certificate in Education and became a lecturer there in August 1973; and that was when he started a small "Deeper Life" Bible study group. The opportunity to study and question the Bible in that small group is carried on in Deeper Life practice today, and the quarter of an hour after "Search the Scriptures" in Sunday worship is always an opportunity for questions arising out of the study to be put to the pastor. Many members spoke to me with pride of this aspect of the life of the church: the accessibility of the pastor in matters of understanding and applying Scripture. Questions are invited, you raise your hand, an usher brings you a microphone and you speak out your question. People were open and uninhibited in their doubt and confusion! Young and old, men and women, educated and uneducated, all had a chance. Kumuyi always dealt with the questions sympathetically and firmly.

This Sunday a young woman came to the microphone to ask how we can apply Matthew 10.37 when we may have children, brothers, sisters, or a husband who does not come to the Deeper Life fellowship. I was impressed by the fact that it was a woman who asked the question, and that it was something which was of real concern to her. It also revealed that, although there was a consensus on needing uniformity of teaching, it is possible to challenge and question the leadership. It may sound fine from the pulpit, but can it work in practice? Kumuyi teaches with authority, but he is not an authoritarian.

Kumuyi answered the woman by saying that it was important to look at other Bible texts to get a balanced interpretation. Everybody opened their Bibles, ready to follow word for word Kumuyi's answer – the woman had obviously asked the key question which was on everybody's mind: self-denial and commitment to Christ are accepted and agreed, but it is not easy if you are anybody in a family except its head. Kumuyi quoted:

Jesus said, "And why do you break the command of God for the sake of your tradition? For God said, 'Honour your father and mother' and 'Anyone who curses his father or mother must be put to death.' But you say that if a man says to his father or mother, 'Whatever help you might otherwise have received from me is a gift devoted to God,' he is not to 'honour his father' with it. Thus you nullify the word of God for the sake of your tradition." (Matthew 15.3–6).

"Jesus supported and emphasised the Old Testament," explained Pastor Kumuyi. "God expects children to honour and support their parents. Consecrating so much money to God that they could not support their parents was emphasising commitment to the point where it contradicted other teachings of the Bible. We should honour, respect, love, and provide for our parents, whether they are 'born-again' Christians or not. And it is the same for our children: we must love, educate, train, and care for them."

It is a traditional African virtue – and one to be proud of – that parents are given respect and obedience by their children. In traditional terms, this virtue should be unquestioning and total. To stand up to parents at all can be seen as total rebellion and rejection, causing hurt through the whole extended family. To suggest that there may be a cut-off point where obedience to parents should end is a painful teaching for an African to accept and apply, but one which goes right to the heart of the confrontation between the Gospel and culture. Time and again I saw Kumuyi and other Deeper Life leaders effectively applying Scripture to the main concerns and needs of the people, and dealing openly with their questions. The pastor continued:

"But don't forget Matthew 10.37! When the demands of relatives contradict the demands of God, *stay on the side of God*. Love and fear your parents, but love and fear God more. If your parents want you to worship, consult, or make a sacrifice to an idol, you must refuse and explain why. You must stand up to them. They may disown you, but you must not disown them. Likewise, for example, if your daughter wants to marry a non-believer, you must not support her: but you must explain to her why."

Kumuyi was not shying away from the issue, nor was he being unrealistic about the nature of the problem. By providing the topic and the text for study in the first place, and then by allowing and receiving the question, he was making a courageous stand against the harmful effects of total obedience to parents or misguided support for children, while also affirming, after God, the primary demands that the whole family makes upon an individual.

The pastor then encouraged us to pray aloud, individually – to talk to the Lord about how we could serve him first, and love him more than parents, children, and relations; but still love our families. And so the teaching was indeed applied and rooted in the spiritual lives of the Deeper Life members.

This was followed by a hymn: congregational songs such as R. Kelso Carter's "Standing on the promises of Christ my King", Johnston and Towner's "Grace greater than all our sin," and Walton and Gordon's "In tenderness he sought me". The music was thus usually fairly Western in style – nineteenth- and early twentieth-century Baptist or Pentecostal hymns from the USA or the UK – accompanied by an orchestra of violins and cellos, trumpets and trombones. The music was good – but not very African.

Continuing up to the end of the first hour of the service, there would be some testimonies of what God had done for people in the past week, together with some prayer requests from members. It is something to have your personal request prayed for by 12,000 people! The prayers, led from the front, went on to cover intercessions for the nation, for the churches, and for all the needs of people everywhere.

Gifts were invited. If you wanted to make an offering, you raised your hand to have the gift prayed over, then the money was collected by the ushers in a time of prayer. There was no sense in which anybody was forced to give, or in which anybody knew how much anybody else was giving. Average giving was about N1 per person per week.

The second hour began with a welcome to newcomers – at every service I went to in every place (except the smallest villages) there were always newcomers. They were invited to stand and move to a special section of the seating which was reserved for them near the front. This meant that they could see and hear better what was going on, and also that they could be properly welcomed and followed up at the end of the service. Then there would usually be one or two notices, followed by the sermon.

The sermon would normally last an hour, and Kumuyi's own sermons were captivating. I would class him as one of the greatest living preachers, giving a straightforward Bible-based message. Although they would count themselves as Pentecostal, I only rarely heard any specifically "Pentecostal" (as opposed to "Evangelical") teaching from the pulpit. If Kumuyi was preaching, the hour would go quickly and the congregation would all be using their King James Bibles and taking notes. Many of the people are poor and uneducated, and as I watched, they found their KJVs difficult to handle because the language is very unlike the common English spoken as the national language in Nigeria. I felt they would much more easily be able to use a translation like the Good News Bible, without losing any depth of meaning or precision in teaching. Indeed, more time could be spent developing the text and applying the meaning, rather than using the sermon time simply to explain in more modern English what the rather more difficult English means! Deeper Life, of course, cannot afford to provide "pew Bibles", so everybody brings their own heavily-marked copy. The King James is the only Bible widely and cheaply available in Nigeria, and Pastor Kumuyi later explained to me why Deeper Life have not sought to change to another version.

"I think we have become used to it," he said, "because from the early years most of the Pentecostal and Evangelical churches have used the King James version. We have come to appreciate it. Then, maybe because of lack of information, or through misinformation, we feel that the new versions are not as faithful to the original. This is what we have gathered over the years: that the King James version is more faithful to the originals and that the translators were more God-fearing, whereas the translators of the new versions, some of them, are probably modernistic in their views.

"Then, to change for thousands of people means a real cost, because if I am preaching from a new version, and they have to change to that version in a space of one year, you are really talking about a large amount of money.

"But it's an area where sometimes you do what you do because that is the level of your understanding. I think it's just that this is what we have become used to. Human nature is hard to change. Not that we are so negative and feel that all the churches that are not using King James version are not following the Lord – far from that!"

For the sermon that day Kumuyi gave us an exposition of Psalm 15, calling it "The qualifications for heavenly citizenship". This sermon was just one of many that I heard preached by Pastor Kumuyi and others while I was with Deeper Life. As such, it is typical in that it was a serious attempt to understand and faithfully apply Scripture. While one sermon, such as this, taken at random, cannot be held as presenting either the main, or the distinctive, features of a church's faith and practice, I think this one vindicates Kumuyi as being in the mainstream of (Evangelical/Pentecostal) Christian thinking in the world today, and also shows one or two more characteristic beliefs current in Deeper Life. The sermon is therefore reproduced in detail in the Appendix.

Kumuyi's sermons were thorough and straightforward expositions of Scripture, and always personally challenging. He always gave a wide range of cross-references which were read in their context, supporting, clarifying and expanding his main points. He spoke clearly and authoritatively to the Nigerian situation. He dealt sensitively with African culture, but also made a firm stand in highlighting the points where local culture was incompatible with the will of God. While stressing the high moral tone which is one of the virtues of most African cultures at their best, he was at pains to specify those aspects of local culture which were unchristian and even evil. In this way he was not only concerned with some kind of personal holiness, but also genuinely seeking the wholeness and harmony of the community at large, where truth, honesty, and justice should be the predominant characteristics.

The Sunday worship would end with a time of prayer, and finish two and a quarter hours after it started. It had to finish then: in fifteen minutes' time the next service would start! In that time 12,000 people had to get out, and another 12,000 get in. On Sundays there is a permanent traffic jam in Gbagada.

Every Sunday, members also meet in one of the 5,000 House Caring Fellowships, using notes provided on the same theme as "Search the Scriptures". These notes would normally have been written by one of the District Co-ordinators. The House Caring Fellowship leaders meet on Saturday evening to prepare the Bible study.

Monday Bible study

On Mondays in Lagos there are three sessions of Bible study: total attendance when I was there was between 23,000 and 26,000. The meeting consisted of opening worship, including welcoming newcomers, and an hour-long exposition of Scripture, either following a thematic series or working through a particular book of the Bible. For the most committed, the Bible study is the highlight of the week, where they learn and grow. It is through the Bible study that Deeper Life has itself grown and gained its reputation. Like the Sunday worship, it is conducted in English with simultaneous translation. Kumuyi is usually responsible for writing the Bible study notes, which are distributed free each week to all those who attend. Sometimes the English of these notes demands a higher than average level of education to understand it clearly, but the members are thoroughly committed to understanding and applying Scripture, so even the least educated work at it. In a roundabout way, Deeper Life is making a significant contribution to increasing the literacy of its people in a country where primary education is far from universal, and only a minority attend secondary school. Reading and understanding your Bible every day is necessary if you want to grow in the Spirit.

When I asked Kumuyi what he felt was distinctive about Deeper Life he told me, "I would say that we interpret the Bible literally wherever possible. We take the commandments and warnings as seriously as we take the promises. I would think that is the major characteristic that the country and other churches know us for, and what we also feel distinguishes us. We are not just taking a part of the Bible, and doing away with the commandments and warnings. The corollary to that is that we take Christian living, or 'holiness', seriously."

Thursday Miracle Revival Hour

Bible study has always been the foundation of Kumuyi's own Christian life, and the Bible is the only authority in Deeper Life. But in response to need, particularly in relation to interference in the Christian life from the spirit world, Deeper Life have begun to develop ways to effectively counteract spiritual attack and spiritual disease. The average Nigerian has no problem in understanding that every aspect of life has a significant spiritual dimension. So Osahenkhoe Emwenruwa in Ugbine (whose story began Chapter 1) and many hundreds, if not thousands, of others like her have come to a "crusade", and received the touch of the Holy Spirit on their lives through the preaching and prayer of Kumuyi and Deeper Life members.

Every Thursday in Gbagada there are three sessions of "Miracle Revival Hour" (each lasting approximately two and a quarter hours!) with a total attendance of around 50,000 – though one Thursday when I was there attendance reached 69,000.

It was raining lightly that evening when I went to the church. People were baling and brushing out some of the water which was collecting in puddles and pools on the floor. Half an hour before the service was due to begin there were already probably 4,000 people in the building. Men and women were sitting together. Some children were with their parents, others were in small groups on their own – most of the children go to their own Children's Miracle Revival Hour. The Deeper Life brothers and sisters who act as ushers were already at their positions, guiding people to seats. After fifteen minutes another 2,000 had arrived. By the time the service began there were maybe 8,000 seated, and after a further quarter of an hour the building was filled to its 12,000 capacity. All those who came later (about another 2,000) stood outside in the rain.

The first fifteen minutes were spent in clapping and singing choruses, some of them more African in style using a repeated refrain in answer to a solo leader. Then there was a time of prayer for various requests that had been received. An offering was taken, and newcomers welcomed. Then another quarter of an hour was spent listening to three or four detailed testimonies from people declaring they had received a miracle from God: maybe conversion or healing, deliverance or provision.

The testimonies were followed by an opportunity to pray as individuals; then came the sermon, an hour long, on a theme connected with faith in God's loving provision, and our need for perseverance and expectancy.

Kumuyi came forward to lead us in a simple prayer:

"Whatever you want, call upon the Lord – ask him to do something great, something spectacular in your life. It may be healing, you may have problems, you may need deliverance from the powers of darkness."

The topic of Kumuyi's talk this evening was "Sevenfold persistence". He explained that we need a spiritual hunger and thirst before God will pour out his blessings. Basing his talk on Joshua 6 – the capture of Jericho – he told us', "You are now on the very border of the Promised Land. The Lord is ready to solve your problem – but it will take spiritual hunger and thirst. You need to see it in your heart and mind before you will see it with your eyes.

"The Israelites kept marching round Jericho, but nothing seemed to happen. If you will be persistent, you will get your miracle. All those people who have given their testimonies here did not come only once. They came often – and after persistence they saw their miracle. It will take persistence to see your miracle. People come here – they say, 'I must be there – whether there is rain, or opposition, or persecution, or no transport.' If you take that attitude, you will never miss your miracle. If you say, 'I can't be there,' I'm not sure you'll ever be able to have your miracle. It is like the people who carried the man on the bed to Jesus. He must have said, 'I don't care what you do, I must be there.' It was shocking: Jesus publicly called that man a sinner. You might say, 'He called me a sinner – I can't be there. He told me I had to repent, but I've always been a Christian.' But if you say, 'I want to be born again' – you will see your miracle."

In this way Kumuyi clearly communicated his theme of persistence, using two familiar Bible stories, applying them in terms of what might be called practical spirituality. I found myself reflecting, though, that God had given the Israelites a specific promise, which he fulfilled as they obeyed him. I am not sure that that is the same thing as saying, "Obey, and you will get your miracle." Likewise, Jesus' primary concern for the man on the stretcher (Luke 5.17–25) was, it seems, to forgive his sins. The physical healing was a special demonstration of the presence and power of God. We don't know what miracle the man himself was hoping for. Would he have been content to have been lifted out of the house on the stretcher, still paralysed, but with his sins forgiven? The message of these Scriptures to me is more our need to be in God's presence, to obey him, and have faith in him – to receive from him what he chooses to give us. He may choose to give us a miracle. He may not.

"Keep coming," Kumuyi continued; "if you're in a wheelchair and you 'must be there' – one day you'll be pushing your wheelchair home. Look at Joshua 6.16:

> The seventh time around, when the priests sounded the trumpet blast, Joshua commanded the people, 'Shout! for the LORD has given you the city!'

It came to pass at the seventh time. Be persistent. Call upon the name of the Lord."

We went on to 1 Kings 18, where there is famine in Israel under King Ahab. The Lord gives Elijah a definite promise, then we see Elijah wrestling with God in prayer (v. 42); looking, but seeing nothing – until the seventh time (v. 43); the reward for persistence (v. 44); and a great miracle on the way (v. 45).

Kumuyi concluded his message by moving on to 2 Kings 5 – the account of the healing of Naaman the leper:

"It will take paying the price to get your miracle," he warned us. "Look at the sevenfold persistence that God requires, and our own problem, in verses 10 and 11:

> Elisha sent a messenger to say to him, 'Go, wash yourself seven times in the Jordan, and your flesh will be restored and you will be cleansed.' But Naaman went away angry and said, 'I thought that he would surely come out to me and stand and call on the name of the LORD his God, wave his hand over the spot and cure me of my leprosy.'

But the miracle came, after persistence, in verse 14:

> So he went down and dipped himself in the Jordan seven times, as the man of God had told him, and his flesh was restored and became clean like that of a young boy.

'Seven' means complete, total, and without any holding back. Repent and give yourself fully to the Lord."

So now it was our turn: we all stood to pray, and around the vast building (and outside in the rain) people started talking to God. For more than five minutes the believers just talked and talked, in the expectation that they were getting through to God. Everybody was asking for their miracle. Kumuyi stood at the front, relaxed and unemotional, resting slightly on the pulpit, and looking around.

"Confess your sins," he urged, "become a new creature, and nothing will hinder the manifestation of a miracle. If there is anything between you and the Lord, settle it. Talk to the Lord."

And then, after a minute or so: "Forgive them, Father. Receive them into the family of God. Now, whatever your problem, I believe a miracle is on the way."

The people prayed. The atmosphere was electric with expectation.

Sometimes Kumuyi will receive "words of knowledge" while he is praying. He will become aware of particular needs in the congregation. Then he tells everybody to bow their heads and close their eyes – and he will specify a need as he has understood it. Then he will wait for the person concerned to raise their hand. Sometimes these needs are quite personal, which is why everyone has to close their eyes (it also helps them to pray with the pastor). The ushers need to keep their eyes open in order to watch out for the raised hand – not all areas of the building are visible from the pulpit and, of course, the word may apply to one of the people standing outside (where there are also ushers).

The first word this evening was: "There is a man here, thirty years old, who is still wetting the bed. Raise your hand and I'll pray for you."

The ushers indicated that a hand had gone up: "God bless you. I command that demonic problem out, in Jesus' name," said Kumuyi, quietly and unemotionally, but there was a loud, "AMEN!" from the other people present, with applause and a sense of celebration.

"There's a twelve-year-old girl. For two weeks now you have been involved with a familiar spirit. Your friends are pleading with you to come to the Lord for help. But these other people are still coming to you and threatening you. I want to bring deliverance to you. Raise up your hand."

A little hand went up.

"Amen. God bless you. All those spirits: come out, in Jesus' name. There is no other power. You will be delivered. When those people come again, I pray the power of the Holy Spirit will drive them away. In Jesus' name."

"AMEN!" and applause.

"There's a parent here who has lost a child."

A hand is raised.

"The Holy Spirit will recover that child. Lord, you have revealed it. You are going to do something about it. Bring back that child. Child, arise now, wherever you are, and come back home. In Jesus' name."

"AMEN!" and applause.

Kumuyi went on to mention a range of specific needs as people started praying for themselves and each other:

"The woman who is pregnant and has been bleeding: that bleeding has stopped." (Applause.) "Now, everybody, lift up your hands. You will get something tonight. Whatever your problem, lay your hand upon yourself. There is someone with cancer. There is a child who has run away from school and is frightened. There is a young woman here, and there is a curse that no woman in her family will get married. All sicknesses. All evil spirits. Someone here has a swollen abdomen. Someone has an infection in the private parts of their body. There are barren women who want children. Thank you, Father."

As Kumuyi finished and the buzz of prayer died down, he was turning to go, when he came back to the pulpit, "There is a woman here. She was carried in here very weak. That woman will walk back home. Those around her, raise up your hands. Put your hands on her. I rebuke that sickness and command it to leave, in Jesus' name."

Great whoops of delight and commotion arose from one part of the auditorium as Kumuyi left the pulpit; and that was the end of the service. He had been on his feet for an hour and a half. In a quarter of an hour he would come down to lead the third Miracle Revival Hour that evening, and do it all again.

I went over to a spot near me where there was some noise and activity. An older woman was singing, dancing and praising God, while a younger woman next to her seemed not very sure of what was going on. When they had calmed down a little, the older woman told me (through an interpreter) that she had travelled down from Kaduna to look for her daughter who had been missing for the past four months. The daughter was a Christian, and had run away from home because her father didn't approve and was tormenting her. She had even ended up in hospital once. When her mother got to Lagos, she heard of Deeper Life, and came to pray for a miracle, sitting in one of the "language classes". When she heard the pastor's word of knowledge for a parent who had lost her child, she somehow knew it was for her. She raised her hand, and the pastor prayed. When she opened her eyes, she saw her daughter sitting two rows in front of her! The girl had run to Lagos, and had been attending Deeper Life Bible Church for some weeks.

A couple of the young leaders in the church had arrived by this time. They asked the mother if she wanted to take the girl back. She said she did. So the daughter was told to go with the mother, but we spent some time in prayer then and there that there would be no more trouble with the father.

Over the next few days, I went on to visit three women who had stories to tell of deliverance through Kumuyi's ministry.

4

Good news for the poor,
release for the oppressed

I met three women who had been deeply affected by Pastor
Kumuyi's ministry in dealing with problems which have
a supernatural dimension. Rabi Olaiwola found herself at
a Miracle Revival Hour through the evangelistic work of
Deeper Life members in the area of Lagos where she lived.
Dorothy Okpotaku came to faith through the witness of one
of her cousins in another church, but joined Deeper Life after
having a dream. Sherifat Saibu was introduced to Deeper
Life by her elder sister.

As I talked to members of Deeper Life, it seemed that
most had been persuaded by the simple proclamation of
the Gospel. It did become obvious to me, however, that
when it came to deliverance, I was meeting many more
women with testimonies than men. I asked Kumuyi what
he thought about this.

"I think more women get involved with 'familiar' spirits,"
he said. "The evil spirits inflict some things on the
womenfolk. Maybe they count women as enemies and
want to injure them for one reason or the other. Although
men too have similar problems, from observation we have
seen it more among the women than among men."

"I'm not afraid any more"

In Kirikiri township just outside Lagos I went to visit Rabi
Olaiwola. The road was a bit broken and bumpy, but we
jolted along and found the concentration of single-storey
buildings around a main street, next to a Navy barracks.
The road ran down to a coastal inlet and was crowded with
street traders, construction workers, and children coming
home from school. Just a little bit back from the coast,
another road runs parallel to the main street. There we
found a double-fronted, single-storey house with a rusting
metal roof. The green paint on the outside walls was a little
flaky and faded. We crossed the storm drain by means of
some planks of wood. There were signs of cooking outside
– piles of charcoal ashes, and some large pots.

Through the front door was a dark, wide corridor, painted
red, with rooms going off to left and right. The back door
was open at the other end of the corridor. A voice came
from the first room on the left: "Good afternoon! Welcome!
Thank you for coming!"

Sister Rabi was pleased to see us.

There was a curtain over the open doorway so that the
room could be kept cool with the worst of the insects being
prevented from entering. I lifted the curtain and walked
into the small bed-sitting-room with a slightly musty smell.
There was a bed, with some bundles of clothes at one end on
the floor, a small wardrobe and a fridge, some pots and pans,
one armchair and a small settee. I was given the armchair,
my colleague from Deeper Life sat on the small settee, Rabi
Olaiwola herself sat on the bed and later her sister, Theresa
Osinge, came to sit next to her there.

Rabi had been born and brought up a Muslim, and
had been devout in that religion. She had observed all
its practices and sought to worship God. She is an *Alhaja*
(someone who has made the pilgrimage to Mecca) and had
been on the *hajj* (pilgrimage) not just once, or even twice, but
twenty-two times. She explained that ten times she had been
on the main *hajj*, and twelve times on the lesser *hajj*. As a

pious Muslim, she would not hear anything of Christianity. When Christians came to her with the name of "Jesu" she would drive them away, shouting, "Take the 'J' from your 'Jesu' and you have '*esu*' ['devil']!"

She has six grown-up children: five daughters and a son. Her first daughter met a Christian man when she started work, and they later wanted to get married. The *Alhaja* would have none of it: "I would never let her marry a Christian. But when she insisted, I refused to go to the wedding, and I stopped all the rest of our family from going as well. We would have nothing to do with Christians."

Rabi's sixth child, her fifth daughter, was born in 1970. But as young as the age of five, this girl turned to the occult and became involved in witchcraft. Not for the first time in Nigeria, I began to feel I was entering a different world, a different area of experience. Rabi was describing what I had read about of Europe in the Middle Ages, in ancient legends, or in science fiction. I was entering a web of belief that described a different kind of reality from my everyday experience in England. It was strange – but not incredible. All those around me were testifying to the reality of these things. Every township or village, every street it seemed sometimes, had its herbalist or native doctor. And these things are not hidden, as they might be in the West, but the herbalist will have his house signposted in just the same way as the medical doctor's surgery, open for business. Most of these local healers and diviners would consider it foolish to think that any problem does not have a supernatural dimension, believing that there are spiritual forces at work. That does not mean that these people's intentions are necessarily evil; but Christians are warned in Scripture not to have any kind of contact with spirits or those who deal with them.

But it wasn't frightening. It wasn't like the horror films! Perhaps I am foolish, and should have been frightened. But I felt strong in my European detachment – even disbelief – from whatever was being described. I also felt strong in the fact that these people were testifying that these evil forces had been overpowered. We were strong in the Lord's protection.

Rabi's young daughter began attacking her. She remembered particularly how in 1975 this daughter had "cut" (or cursed) her mother's left leg so badly that she has the marks on her foot to this day. Even though the girl was sent from Nigeria to be educated in England, she continued to practise her craft there. She took great delight in the fact that the house where she was lodging was near a cemetery, which she could use at night.

Rabi explained how she came back to Nigeria after a pilgrimage to Mecca in August 1986. When she arrived home in Kirikiri, a woman accused her of stealing some gold jewellery – but she knew she was innocent. She started going round the diviners and herbalists nearby to get a charm to make the real thief confess. Eventually this youngest daughter confessed that she had implicated her mother in the crime. It was the woman's sister who had stolen the gold.

"For these thirteen years," Rabi claimed, "this girl has turned my life from prosperity to poverty. Over the years I have had to sell all my property to try to pay for all the treatment I have needed. My body became swollen all over with boils and sores. They told me it was leprosy. Also I have had high blood pressure. I used to take lots of drugs just to get to sleep at night, including Valium. My daughter used to tell me that she was causing all these things."

But there were some Deeper Life members in Kirikiri. One day in January 1988, a small group of them were visiting neighbouring houses, inviting people to "come to our church and meet Jesus." They came to Rabi's house, but she threw them out. However, she overheard one say to the other outside, "That woman will soon be doing the will of God." She didn't understand what they were talking about.

Three days later they came again, and before she knew what to think, she found herself saying, "I will fast for three days, then I will repent and seek Jesus."

She was shocked at what she had said, and couldn't
understand what was happening. By that time, she told
me, she was "almost dead from poverty and hunger. If I
was walking only one hundred metres I would need to sit
down and rest three times. If I didn't beg, I couldn't eat."

So in desperation she went to the Deeper Life Bible
Church one Thursday for a Miracle Revival Hour, taking
her daughter with her. Pastor Kumuyi was preaching, then
during the prayers, at just the moment when Rabi happened
to be holding on to her daughter, he said, "There is a woman
here, holding her daughter. Leave that child alone, and she
will be delivered." Then he prayed for the girl.

The next Thursday Rabi went again. She sat somewhere
else – she didn't want the pastor or any of the ushers to
recognise her. At the prayer time at the end of the service,
the pastor said, "There is a woman here who has been
paying herbalists to get rid of evil. She has a daughter
under twenty years old who is a witch. She is so ill now,
she doesn't know whether she's alive or dead."

Rabi knew it could only be her – she raised her hand, and
the pastor prayed for her.

By now, Rabi couldn't wait for Thursdays to come
around. She knew something was going to happen. The
following Thursday (she sat somewhere else again) during
the prayer time the pastor had a word: "There is a woman
with leprosy. She has no money left to go to the hospitals or
even to native doctors. Today is your deliverance day."

Some other people had raised their hands as well as Rabi,
but because she was near the back there were pillars in the
way, and ushers standing around, so she could not directly
see the pastor. He said, "I can't see you. Where are you? Can
the ushers move so I can see you? I'm waiting for you."

Rabi told me she didn't know how she dared, but she
jumped up on the bench and shouted, "Yes, it's me!"

The pastor said, "I have been waiting for you. I have
found you. The angels are coming with your miracle.
Receive your healing, receive your healing. Even now it
is instantaneous healing."

"I just didn't understand what he meant," Rabi said, "but when I got home I saw that my skin was all covered in a thin film, like nylon. I carried on normally the next day, wanting to see what would happen – but everything seemed the same as usual. Then the day after that, when I was washing, the film came off and my skin was completely smooth and clean. I rushed out of my house, on to the street. I knelt down on the street and shouted at the top of my voice, 'Praise Jesus, he is God!' And not only is my skin completely cured, but since then I have been able to sleep peacefully at night."

This all happened in February 1988. Eight months later, she was testifying to me that there had been no recurrence of her problems.

Theresa Osinge picked up the story: "This is all true. She was all covered in sores, but now there's no sign of them – look at the miracles of God! My family are strong Muslims – even though I have become a Catholic – and they told me she was mad. Everybody knew she had been a strong Muslim. She used to need glasses because of eye trouble, but now she can read without them. When I first saw my sister after this I was just speechless."

Sister Rabi confirmed that since that day when she gave her life to Christ, the Lord has continued to prove to her his miraculous protection of her life – not least in the fact that she had recently survived two serious road accidents involving vehicles she was travelling in. But the Lord had also been active in her relationship with her youngest daughter.

Rabi and Theresa called what was troubling the girl *"ogbanje"* which is apparently a common name for an evil or "familiar" spirit. The girl has now confessed to her mother that she cannot harm her any more. Whenever she wants to attack her she can only see fire all around her. Rabi said, "I'm not afraid any more. Now I just argue with the native doctors, and tell them they are powerless. Jesus is my God!"

I asked whether the girl had been delivered from evil, and they explained that each time they deliver her she will "re-equip" herself afterwards. She even sometimes attends Deeper Life Bible Church with her mother. Whenever she enters the church she will "leave it outside", and then re-equip herself when she leaves.

At a Thursday Miracle Revival Hour the pastor had said, "There's a woman here with a daughter in witchcraft." Rabi raised her hand, and the pastor commanded the evil influences: "Come out. God wants you out."

Rabi testifies that she is now completely free of any evil influence from her daughter. Theresa had met the girl recently and she had confessed all these things to her:

"That girl has some strong powers. One night when she was staying with me I heard some sort of noise. I got up to check what was happening, but I couldn't see anything. Suddenly something knocked me down, and I twisted my foot. I didn't know what was going on, it was so painful. You can still see where my foot was twisted and bruised. I cried out, 'Jesus, what is happening?' I went to the Reverend Father the next day. He told me to remember my catechism, and to have faith in God. But that girl has strong power. I asked her why she had done all this to me and her mother, and she said she was not alone, that others were tempting her. Also that she disliked her mother because she did not give her enough freedom. But I told her we should be happy for her mother because of the healing she has received. I said she should believe in Jesus Christ."

Rabi brought me up to date:

"At the beginning of last week the girl came here and told me she was pregnant. I prayed for my Father's blessing on the girl and on the child. The man that got my daughter pregnant wanted her to have an abortion, but I told him I could not allow that. I am a child of God. I said I would pray for him, and that if he did not repent and marry my daughter, or at least provide for the child, then I would look after the child myself. My daughter was angry and said she would imprison the spirits of my other five children in the iroko tree behind the house here. I prayed for thunder to destroy that tree. Just fifteen minutes later a thunderstorm started and began blowing around violently. The girl was frightened and said she was sorry. I laid my hand on her head, asking the Lord Jesus to burn all the evil out of her. She fell down on the floor. But when she got up she said, 'I'll go and get another demon.' I replied, 'Jesus is in me, and I'll have no demons in my house.' I commanded the demons to hell. She ran away with the man."

The day before my interview with Rabi and Theresa there had been special services in the Deeper Life Bible Church because it had been a public holiday. At the end of one service Rabi had wanted to stay for the next, but she heard a voice saying, "Get out."

She moved to another place in the church, but the voice said again, "Get out."

For some reason she thought, "Lord, do you mean if I go out I'll see my daughter?"

But the voice just said, "Get out."

She went home, and later in the evening one of the Deeper Life members came to her house with what he thought was a word from God for her, that her daughter would come back and sleep with her that night, And, indeed, later that night the girl did come back, having been away for nine days, and slept with her mother peacefully.

"My God is a great God," Rabi proclaimed. "All my old life is finished. Jesus is with me now. I love that Deeper Life Bible Church. I go to the Monday Bible study, the Sunday worship, the Miracle Revival Hour, my House Caring Fellowship. I never miss anything. I always go. When I come home from a service I just want to read the Bible half the night before going to sleep."

She told me that she had had the chance to meet the pastor and tell him that her problem now was poverty. Now, even though her family will not receive her, things are getting better. For the past few months she had had no room to herself at all – she was just sleeping on the floor while a tenant had the bed. But now the family (who own the house) have given her five rooms there which she can use and let to tenants. With that help she has been able to start cooking and selling food in the street. "I'm not begging any more."

As we stood up to leave, Theresa and Rabi were rejoicing together in the miracles they had seen over the past few months. It was a privilege to be able to rejoice with them, but I also felt a foreigner in a strange world.

A handkerchief

Something else that I found strange was the business with the handkerchiefs. Handkerchiefs?

People in the Deeper Life Bible Church may send a letter with a handkerchief for Kumuyi to pray over. One of the leaders I met in Lagos was quite indignant, though, over non-members who took advantage of the scheme. "Some people just want to be healed or delivered without coming to church to hear the Gospel and be saved as well," he complained.

When I first heard about people using handkerchiefs in this way, I was immediately rather cautious, fearing that this may be precisely the type of occultic practice, tied up with witchcraft and superstition, which Deeper Life were supposed to be making a stand against: putting faith in things that can be "used", rather than in the Lord himself working by his Spirit. I asked how this practice had developed.

I learnt that the first time an "anointed handkerchief" was used in Deeper Life was in 1985. A woman was in hospital in Aba (Imo State) with an issue of blood that would not stop, and one of the nurses there heard that pastor Kumuyi was preaching in Aba that week. The nurse just took one of the woman's handkerchiefs to the pastor for him to pray over. She took it back to the woman, who then recovered. Deeper Life were unsure at first exactly what was going on, but then they found that this was a manifestation of something which had occurred in New Testament times!

> God did extraordinary miracles through Paul . . . hand-
> kerchiefs and aprons that had touched him were taken to
> the sick and their illnesses were cured and the evil spirits
> left them. (Acts 19.11,12)

It seemed that the New Testament could allow such things,
and that they were indeed used by God to glorify himself.

I went to Surulere to meet sister Dorothy Okpotaku.
I found her in a comfortably furnished one-bedroomed
ground-floor flat. She had obviously done well in business, had travelled widely, making friends and contacts,
and attaining a standard of living above the average. A
competent and confident woman, she was nevertheless,
like all of us, vulnerable to spiritual attack. She spoke to
me slightly nervously, and became confused at one or two
points, reflecting how life had been difficult for her in recent
years. We sat in a large, pleasant, square room, light and
airy with windows along two walls which formed one corner
of the building. The communal concrete yard outside was
a place to hang the washing, and to park the car. Dorothy
is a member of a Deeper Life House Caring Fellowship,
which she helps lead sometimes, and also helps as an usher
in the church services. Some Deeper Life members had been
praying with her since she joined the church, and she knew
there were things about her life which she had to change. It
is difficult to work as a trader without getting involved in
bribery, so she had given up that business. Just that week
she had been to the bank for a loan to start a restaurant.

Dorothy, who was born in 1960, developed asthma in
infancy, and it has plagued her ever since. She remembers
being taken when a child to a local traditional healer who
prepared a herbal concoction in a pot for her to drink. It
didn't do anything. Later she tried acupuncture. Some other
people advised her to move to another part of the country
where the climate would be different. She was taking tablets,
giving herself injections, and always needed to have an
inhaler with her. After finishing at school, she went into
teaching for a while, but then left that to start trading. Her

business was successful, and she travelled outside Nigeria a lot.

In October 1986 a friend recommended someone to be her house girl, and the girl moved in. But Dorothy soon began to realise something was wrong. One night, at two o'clock, she was woken by a tremendous crash and ran into the sitting room to see the glass shelves of her wall unit shattered for no apparent reason. Two of the shelves were beyond repair. She showed me the broken pieces of the remaining shelves which were still big enough to use.

After that Dorothy would often be woken up by noises of banging and crashing in her apartment – but when she looked, there was nobody there and nothing had moved. She could not understand what was happening. She was frightened. To make things worse, her new house girl slept peacefully and said she never heard anything. Dorothy had started to suspect the girl of having an evil influence when she had a vivid dream:

"I saw the person who recommended the house girl to me, but this time my friend gave me a python. I kept the python, looked after it, and fed it on smaller snakes. Then I saw some soldier ants. They came in and ate up the python and the other snakes, but didn't come near me.

"I liked the girl," Dorothy went on to explain, "but things were so dreadful when she was around. Even the food she prepared for me made me ill."

In November 1986 a cousin came to see her and invited her to a Four Square Gospel church. At the end of the meeting there was an "altar call" and Dorothy stood up – she committed her life to Christ.

"Each night I prayed about the terrible things happening in my flat. They were a real burden to me. I decided to invite the girl to come with me to the church. She refused, packed her bag, and left. I haven't seen her since. I couldn't sleep at first that night, but by about 4 a.m. I felt at peace."

The day after the girl left, a snake came into the flat, something which had not happened before, and has not happened since. Dorothy shouted for her neighbours, and they helped her drive it out and kill it.

She joined in with her new church, became a house group leader, and was actively witnessing her neighbourhood, seeing people come to Christ. Her sister attended Deeper Life Bible Church, but Dorothy was happy where she was until one afternoon in early 1988 when she fell asleep and had a dream. There were a lot of people filling a large space. She asked, "Where are we?" "Deeper Life," they replied. She felt as if there was fire closing in all around her. She was afraid. She cried, "What shall I do?" They answered, "Go to Deeper Life." So she left Four Square and joined Deeper Life.

It is widely understood in most cultures other than Western that, sometimes, your spirit may leave your body (to observe, to do good, or to do harm). This would normally happen while you are asleep. Dreams are often perceived, therefore, as recollections of the activity of your own spirit, which are as real as anything you may do in your body when you are awake.

Dorothy continued her story. "My asthma was still bad, and I was suffering from terrible migraine at the time. I had also just started a serious pain in my stomach, which two doctors had diagnosed as appendicitis. I was booked into hospital – the minimum fee for the operation was going to be N750. I started coming to Deeper Life and decided that I didn't want to take any drugs for my conditions. One night I was almost rushed to hospital, but I persisted in looking to God. To make matters worse, sometimes I would come out in the morning and find *ju-ju* on my car bonnet or roof. Once I stayed nearly all day at the Deeper Life 'Prayer Warriors' (where you can be prayed for personally after any of the services at the Deeper Life Bible Church), but nothing happened. Eventually my sister took me to Biodun Kumuyi – the Deeper Life Women's Co-ordinator. After she heard my problem, she suggested sending a handkerchief to the pastor. So I addressed a letter to the pastor, and enclosed one of my handkerchiefs. I was told I would have to wait two weeks. In fact, it was three weeks before the handkerchief was returned to me with a letter saying that the pastor had prayed over it. I can remember it was a Tuesday, and I was very excited. I placed the handkerchief on my chest, and I just knew my battle with asthma was won. I didn't tell anybody – but I kept the handkerchief. If I had an asthma attack, or migraine, or pain in my stomach, the problem would stop without drugs. As I became stronger in the Lord, whoever was putting *ju-ju* on my car must have got frightened, because those things stopped appearing. Everything stopped troubling me within a month."

That was in May 1988. I met Dorothy the following October and there had been no recurrence of any of the problems. I met dozens of people – many more than those who appear in this book – with testimonies of conversion, deliverance, healing, and provision. Often in one person there would be evidence of God's activity in different areas – sister Dorothy was testifying to conversion, deliverance, and healing. Oppression by evil spirits and demonic attacks were often the needs which drove people to Deeper Life. One person explained to me:

"Africa is the Devil's continent. Evil is so much more active here than in other places. So we need miracles of deliverance. The people are so poor, they cannot afford medical help, so we need miracles of healing and provision. In the UK you don't need those things because you have the National Health Service."

Release from a curse

I went to visit a nineteen-year-old woman who had testified in the Miracle Revival Hour on September 29th, 1988, to miraculous healing and deliverance. On the way we gave a lift to a Deeper Life member who needed to get to a clinic because she had an eye infection that needed treatment. Expectancy of miracles does not rule out our own responsibility to act, although it is sometimes difficult to have faith in God for a healing and then at the same time

take medication. To take medication seems as if you are not
trusting God. It is easier, though, not to take medication
if you are too poor to afford it in the first place, which is
probably the case for the majority of Deeper Life members.

I met Sherifat Saibu and her elder sister, Esther Omowumi
Akinwale, outside their house in Gbagada. Esther, a young
widow, works as a street trader, cooking and selling food
to passers-by. She rents one room in the large house.
Sherifat led us down the dark corridor with cement floor
and walls into their basic but clean room with just a
bed, a couple of chairs, and one small wardrobe. This
room – maybe three metres square – was where Esther,
Sherifat, and Esther's two small boys lived. There were
three posters decorating the otherwise blank walls. One
proclaimed: "God will give you your miracle." There were
some small sacks of grain in one corner, which Esther uses
as the base of what she cooks and sells outside. It is a
hard life, but a home where the sisters know that God
loves them and in Christ can meet their most serious
needs. The light of Christ was in their eyes, and in their
smiles.

Sherifat was born and brought up in Ikorodu by her
nominally Muslim parents. But when she was five years
old there was an argument in the family, and her father's
other wife arranged for Sherifat to be cursed with a charm
inflicting epilepsy. From that time she started to have
epileptic fits frequently – usually every day, sometimes as
often as seven times in one day. Her parents took her to
many different places to try to get the epilepsy treated. They
went to herbalists and local traditional healers , and bought
some tablets from London, but there was no improvement.
One time, she remembers, despite their being Muslim, being
taken to a "white garment church". The parents were told
to buy a goat, and to use its urine for medication. They
were then told to kill the goat, and Sherifat had to eat it.
As there was no improvement, the parents were told to buy
and kill a pig, and Sherifat should also eat that. There was
still no improvement.

By that time her elder sister had married a churchgoer, even though she was supposed to be a Muslim. She became a Christian through the ministry of a church in Yaba where she was living with her husband, and took the name Esther. She told me she had joined that church in 1980, but she wasn't sure now whether she really understood their message.

Sherifat used to come and stay with Esther in Yaba during her school holidays. As she was still not cured of the epilepsy, Esther persuaded her to come with her to church. They told Sherifat she was a witch, and fettered her legs and hands and kept her in the church. She was made to fast for seven days and nights. Esther tried to bring her food and water, but they would not allow Sherifat to eat or drink anything at all. At last Sherifat was released – and there was still no improvement in her condition.

It seemed that Sherifat and her family had run out of places to go for help. Because of the epilepsy, life became increasingly difficult for Sherifat at school. She told me that all the teachers and students would run away from her when she had a fit. The maths teacher, she remembered, would not let her attend her class at all. Because of these problems, and because her parents had run out of money, she had to leave school before she could finish the course. Her parents had by now spent everything they had to try to get the right medication. They used to do quite well in the market, but now they were poor through trying to get Sherifat healed.

During this time Esther was widowed. She had left the church where she was converted after the way they had treated her sister. Then one day she was in a bus in which some Deeper Life members were singing and clapping. She had heard a little about Deeper Life before, so was interested. She decided to stay on the bus and go with them to their church. "When I got there," she said, "I saw that somebody was really preaching."

That was when she moved to Gbagada and joined the Deeper Life Bible Church. Now she is a House Caring Fellowship leader and an usher.

She started praying that God would take control of Sherifat, "I begged my mother to let me take my sister to our church, but she said it was impossible to do any good there, because Deeper Life don't 'use anything'."

Sherifat picked up the story:

"My sister had moved to Gbagada and brought me to Lagos in 1987 after I left school. She had become a member of Deeper Life and wanted to take me there. I refused to go. I said I had been to different churches and didn't want to go to any more. My sister said this one was different – it was not like other churches I had been to. She told me God would answer me if I had faith and believed."

So Esther took Sherifat to the church. If you want to see Pastor Kumuyi you need to make an appointment through your Zonal leader. They collected an appointment card, but when they got there, the pastor was not able to see them. Sherifat started crying, "I won't go unless brother Kumuyi prays for me."

Some ushers calmed her down, and told her not to worry, that she could collect another appointment card. But she told me, "I didn't want to go again after that."

However, Esther kept on praying, and in 1988 – on April 14th – they were able to get a card, and Sherifat agreed to come. By this time her mother also was interested and wanted to come too to explain the history of the illness to the pastor. It was a Thursday and they came together to the afternoon Miracle Revival Hour at five thirty. After the service they went to wait for the pastor with the other people who wanted to see him. The ushers explained that when it gets to eleven o'clock no more people can see the pastor. Time dragged by. At eleven o'clock the ushers called together those who were still waiting to say that they would have to get another appointment card.

Sherifat began crying, "I won't go home unless you pray for me today."

This time she wouldn't be pacified, and Esther and her mother started crying too. Sherifat went on with the story:

"Brother Kumuyi heard me crying and told the ushers to bring me inside. He prayed for me for less than a minute – he simply commanded the problem to vanish away, in Jesus' name. Since then I have had no problem. I'd had a very severe fit on April 12th, but since brother Kumuyi prayed, I haven't had a fit at all: that's five and half months. We're so happy. My mother even wanted to come to the pulpit and give testimony with me. I'm now a Christian, and a member of the Deeper Life Bible Church here in Gbagada. My parents still call themselves Muslims, but they have both started attending the church. The woman who charmed me when I was five years old appeared to me in a dream soon after brother Kumuyi prayed for me. She was asking me for forgiveness, I told her that I had forgiven her."

Esther and Sherifat are now continuing to serve God in Gbagada. Sherifat has enrolled as a student on a secretarial course. God worked in her life in different ways, and it affected not only Sherifat, but also the other members of her family. The Deeper Life ministry at its best and most effective is not blind to the forces of evil, and speaks into situations created in the web of human relationships: dealing with the whole rather than one bit of an individual's experience.

I asked Deeper Life leaders whether there were any instances of Christians being converted to Islam. They laughed, considering this impossible for someone who was truly "born again". (To that extent, I wonderd how truly Muslim Sherifat and Esther had been.) Deeper Life are certainly confident that they know the truth and it is that sense of definite and clear truth which attracts the majority of their members. Most of them are "transfers" from other branches of Christianity, some already "born again" who prefer Deeper Life, others who convert from nominalism to true faith through Deeper Life's ministry.

From sister Sherifat's story, and the way some "African churches" treated her, it is easier to be sympathetic towards

Deeper Life's reluctance to become too "African" in their worship. Deeper Life is now established across Nigeria, each church following the same pattern of worship as at Gbagada – Sunday worship, Bible study, and Miracle Revival Hour. But the beginnings of Deeper Life is another story . . .

5

History and growth of Deeper Life

Any history, particularly a short one, distorts the past by being selective in what it records, and reflects the bias of the author and his or her sources. This chapter is no exception! But there do seem to have been significant turning points (or growth points) in the development of Deeper Life. In 1973 Kumuyi started a Bible study group in his sitting room. By 1979 a new religious movement was forming with its own distinctive image. In 1982 that movement formally became a Church by starting to offer Sunday worship, although setting a distance between themselves and other churches by not seeking to join such bodies as the Christian Association of Nigeria until 1988. Then in 1984 two steps: a new emphasis on miracles, and a more developed, strategic missionary vision for Africa. The recollections of the past in this chapter are centred around these milestones.

FROM A SITTING ROOM TO THE REST OF THE WORLD

Flat 2

Brother Akinwande is currently District Co-ordinator for

Deeper Life in Agege, Lagos. He explained how Kumuyi began to become well known in 1973:

"My parents didn't go to church. My father is an idol-worshipper (there is a shrine in our village where people leave little gifts and sacrifices of money or meat). My uncle and my brother attended the Methodist church. I followed them to the church on Sundays, but it didn't mean much to me. I joined the Scripture Union when I was at school, and in 1972 at an SU retreat in Oyo State there was a message about Samson and Delilah. I repented and gave my life to the Lord Jesus Christ. While I was there I made friends with someone from Lagos. I visited him there in 1973, and he told me about Kumuyi's Monday Bible study at the university. I went along, and it was as if I had never heard Scripture interpreted meaningfully before."

Kumuyi had started a small Bible study group at his home – Flat 2 at the University of Lagos. The fifteen members of the group met on Monday evenings. I asked Kumuyi why he had started the group when there were already other groups on the campus:

"Because of my involvement with the Scripture Union, many people were calling me to come and give a message here and a talk there. Some others also came for counselling. Some of these seekers were already members of different churches. Others were new converts. Those who had witnessed to these new converts encouraged them: 'If you need further help, you can see the man at the university.' Some of the people who were intellectuals would argue with those who witnessed to them. Such simple-minded people sent the intellectuals to me for help and answers to their questions. In this informal way, people kept coming to me. Later, I felt they were taking too much of my time, because I still needed to lecture and to carry on research work. So I said, 'Let's all come together one evening in the week and we will study the Bible. If there are any questions that are not answered after the Bible study, you can see me personally for counselling.' That's how we started the Monday Bible study.

"The Scripture Union is for students of secondary school,

so as a teacher I would just be called a 'senior friend'. There was a Christian Union on the campus, but the people who were coming to me were outside the university community. They knew about me because of my involvement in different places. They couldn't really be accepted into the Christian Union (the students' fellowship group on the university campus) because they were not students of the University of Lagos. Neither could they be accepted into the Scripture Union because they were adults. The Monday Bible study was therefore the legitimate fellowship they had for the study of the word of God."

Within a short time Kumuyi was being invited as a guest speaker to other universities in Nigeria, and was attracting a following from those who turned to Christ through his ministry, as well as members of various denominations who valued his teaching of straightforward Bible exposition. He called his work the "Deeper Christian Life Ministry".

Daisi Akinyelu is currently a full-time employee of Deeper Christian Life Ministry, responsible for the Deeper Life Campus Fellowships nationally. He was impressed not only by Kumuyi's teaching gift, but also by his character:

"I was brought up an Anglican, and was secretary of the SU in my secondary school in 1972. I was born again at that time through the evangelistic efforts of undergraduates from the then University of Ife. Through their counselling I realised my sins, and by the grace of God I was born again. I kept on in the Anglican church, and the SU. When I went to the University of Ibadan as a student, I joined the Christian Union. W.F. Kumuyi was invited to a three-day CU meeting in 1974. He taught with clarity and precision. You could see sincerity in him – this was someone who was living by what he preached. He was staying with a friend of mine, and I thought he was a student like me. When I learnt he was a lecturer, I understood his humility."

In his spare time from being a chartered accountant in Lagos, Philip Olasupo Oluwi is Mushin District Co-ordinator. He told me how he found the Monday Bible study in 1975:

"I was brought up in a religious home – usually going to an Apostolic church. I became born again in 1970 without being preached to. The Apostolic church was preparing for a revival – the young folks were taught to pray. I noticed a particular individual there whose life was totally different. They were asking for the baptism of the Holy Spirit. I knew I couldn't have it. I knew I was a sinner. I went home and really prayed. My dad and others in the family knew something was happening to me. There had been a transformation in my life. But nobody followed me up. Nobody really taught me the word of God; so I didn't grow. Eventually I came to Lagos and lived with a colleague who had been a fellow-student with me at the polytechnic. I knew I was born again, but I was anxious to have a deeper knowledge of God. All along I wasn't satisfied with what I was receiving from the churches. A friend told me about the Deeper Life Bible study. He told me that it would surely meet the desires of my heart, so in January 1975 we went together to Flat 2. After the Bible study that night I knew I had arrived at where I really wanted to be. There was a deeper teaching of the word of God. There were about 500 people attending the Bible study at that time. Seats were arranged all around outside the flat, and we could listen to the loudspeakers. I joined, and later led, a Deeper Life evangelism team. As we got reasonable numbers, we started a local Deeper Life Bible study group. The material that was taught at the central Bible study on Monday was reproduced and distributed for local Bible study groups to use on another day later in the week. It was to provide an opportunity for study for those who could not come to the centre."

The first "Retreat"

In the December of 1975, the first Deeper Life "Retreat" was held at what is now the Federal College of Education (Technical), Akoka, Lagos. Deeper Christian Life Ministry provided food, books, and accommodation. Participants had only to find their own travelling expenses. L.P. Nnadozie is now Deeper Life District Co-ordinator for Ikeja, Lagos. He explained:

"The retreats were a period of concentrated study. We were taught, we studied the Bible, and had time to pray. We were encouraged to join the local Bible study fellowships, and to be active in helping our own churches."

One thousand five hundred people attended the December 1975 retreat. I asked Kumuyi where the money came from!

"Well, in the early days we had offering boxes in the meeting place, so those who came to the Monday Bible study would just drop in whatever they had. I was a lecturer at the university then, and a substantial part of my salary went into the work. I wasn't married, so I had less responsibility. Then whenever we were to have retreats we made announcements and told our members that we needed to keep the retreat free so that nobody missed the opportunity of hearing the Gospel because of financial hardship. They always responded to the announcements by giving. And with that we held our retreats. We used schools for our accommodation. The first retreat we held was at the Federal College of Education at Akoka. The second (April 1976) was at the Baptist Academy, Obanikoro. The premises of these schools were given to us free. We provided the food and other necessary materials."

New Deeper Life Bible study groups outside Lagos

But Deeper Life was far from being a one-man ministry. From the early days, as numbers grew, various people in the fellowship became "workers" for Deeper Life (although they would remain in full-time employment elsewhere – all along, money has been spent on financing outreach rather than salaries). The workers would help in the practical organisation of meetings, also leading the evangelism teams, local Bible study groups, and small groups at the retreats. The workers had a regular training session on Sunday evenings.

In 1976, Deeper Life fellowships also started in Ilesa and Osogbo (Oyo State) and at Omoku in Rivers State. I asked Kumuyi how this came about.

"It was informal. Some of the brethren, after hearing about evangelism and bringing other people into the saving knowledge of the Lord Jesus Christ, became concerned for their home states. They came to me with the burden to start Deeper Life Bible studies in their own locations. I would say that was all right, but that they should seek employment in those places so that the fellowship would not have to pay them. Thus they went, settled down, and opened their homes up to Bible study. The Bible study materials we had been using in Lagos, which they had filed over the years, were adapted for their individual needs. That was basically how we started most of the first meetings in other states of Nigeria."

In Lagos, the work continued – reaching out with evangelism teams and events and, increasingly, literature. The December 1976 Deeper Life retreat was held in Enugu, Anambra State – with 3,000 participants – a completely different part of the country from the first two retreats.

In 1977, the Deeper Christian Life Ministry really began to snowball, with fellowships formed across the south of the country – in Ogun and Bendel in the west, Imo and Anambra States in the east.

I met a senior police officer in one of the towns in Imo State. I was ushered into his office, overlooking the police car park, and squeezed into the schedule of this distinguished and busy gentleman. He was proud to be a member of Deeper Life, although he had been born and brought up in a strong Anglican family. As I sat across the desk from him, he explained how he had been suffering from high blood pressure for over five years. Over the years, different doctors in his various postings had prescribed a range of drugs, but he still felt weak most of the time and got easily tired. At one

point he was feeling so ill that he told his doctor to forget
about the drugs, and to just let him live or die by himself.
His wife had attended a Deeper Life programme in 1987,
and in October that year she took her husband to the Friday
Miracle Revival Hour at the local Deeper Life Bible church.
He was persuaded by what he heard, asked for prayer, and
stopped taking the drugs. Brothers from Deeper Life came to
pray with him every day. He has now started to feel well, and
when I spoke to him, he had not taken any drugs for over a
year, with no ill effect. Indeed, he felt as well as he had done
before his health problems started.

At virtually the other end of the social scale in the same
town, I was introduced to Juliana Okonkwo, who lives in
a comfortable but small room with her children. She didn't
speak English very well – or at least she felt too embarrassed
to speak her English in front of me – so a friend from Deeper
Life acted as interpreter for us as she talked to me in Igbo:

"I had two boys – the second was born in 1979, but after
that, whenever I conceivèd, the Devil came and disturbed
me, and I would have a miscarriage. A dreadful object with
the face of a human being but the body of an animal would
come and frighten me in my dreams, and the day after, when
I woke up, I would abort. This happened three times: in
1980, 1982, and 1985. I and my husband joined Deeper
Life in 1985. I went on the Deeper Life retreat at Owerri
(Imo State capital) in December 1987, and after that retreat
I conceived again. I told our local Deeper Life pastor about
the dream I used to have, we prayed together, and I didn't
see that devil again. When I went to the hospital, the doctor
told me I would need an operation. I wrote a prayer request
to the church that I would not need an operation. They
prayed for me, and I didn't need an operation. I delivered
this little girl safely all by myself at hospital. We have named
her Chinyere ('God's gift')."

The ministry also spread north to the more Muslim
Kwara State. Retreats were held at Ibadan (Oyo State)
in April 1977 (3,000 attended), and at Onitsha (Anambra
State) in December (4,000 attended). In Lagos, people

were not only filling Flat 2, but also sitting outside, and on the road, and in the fields around. The Monday Bible study moved to use the premises of the Redeemed Christian Church of God. The Sunday evening workers' meeting was moved to Thursday evening, and became an Evangelism Training School, using a Pentecostal Assembly building. Thursday evening was for more in-depth teaching, strengthening the already existing evangelism teams, and forming specialist hospital, prison, and schools visiting teams. Kumuyi worked tirelessly, and by his example encouraged his followers to do likewise.

Deeper Life outside Nigeria

In other countries in Africa word was getting around.

In 1978 Kumuyi attended a School of Ministry in Kenya. There were many Africans represented and one of the Nigerians who knew Kumuyi spoke to all the other Africans telling them that they should co-operate and help one another. They should learn from each other's experiences, he said, and emphasised that distributing resources is not only applicable to money, but also to knowledge. He assured them that they knew how to evangelise their people better than Western missionaries because of their own experience. So they gave one another invitations, and Kumuyi visited Ghana. The 10,000 participants at the Deeper Life retreat in Ilorin (Kwara State) in December 1978 were joined by some Ghanaians who wanted to see for themselves what was really happening in Nigeria.

Then in 1979 Ghanaian Christians invited Kumuyi to lead a crusade and they started a Deeper Life Bible study fellowship in Kumasi with about thirty members. Whenever there was a Deeper Life Workers' Retreat in Nigeria, Ghanaians would come. Eventually they asked Deeper Christian Life Ministry to send them somebody.

"So we sent somebody," Kumuyi told me. "Then when we saw the progress of the work in Ghana, we felt we should help other African countries. That's how we started our international ministry – it was not by deliberately sending out people at first."

CONSTRUCTION AND CONSOLIDATION: RELATIONSHIPS, BUILDINGS, AND IMAGE

Brothers – and sisters

By this time Deeper Life fellowships had also got under way in Ondo and Cross River States in the south; and Niger, Benue, Plateau, Gongola, Borno, Kaduna and Kano States in the north. Retreats were held in the east (Owerri – Imo State – 6,000 attended), in the north (Kaduna – 3,000 attended), and in Lagos (6,000 attended).

One person at the Owerri retreat in 1979 was brother Samuel Kolawole Osinaike, who is now Deeper Life District Co-ordinator for Gbagada, Lagos.

"At the Owerri retreat one sister preached about the use of the tongue. I can't forget that message," he said. "I discovered that in Deeper Life the word of God being taught was real. Also there was no differentiation between social classes or social strata. That was important for me."

To over-simplify, most Nigerians like to know who are their superiors and inferiors. If you are above someone, he/she must do what you say. If you are below someone, you must obey. In Deeper Life, all are brothers and sisters, and that has made a real impact as something unusual and different, but which is obviously scriptural. Also, to allow women to be involved in leading is quite rare in a Nigerian institution. It is often difficult to apply the Gospel to one's culture, as it will sometimes make painful demands upon us. We none of us like to give up that little bit of status which we have achieved – or which we have received. Furthermore, what may be an easy application for one culture may be very difficult for another. We also need to be aware of what biblical principles are at work: a necessary application in one place may not appropriately reflect the original principle in another. This is the heart of the struggle which the African churches face in developing a faith which they learnt at first from Europeans and North Americans. The role of women in the Church is an issue in Britain – it is not so in Nigeria. Nevertheless, Deeper Life have made strides in accepting the ministry of women, so I asked Kumuyi what he felt about the role of women in the Church.

"Really, it depends on the calling of an individual, but a closer look at Scripture shows that there is more on the side of men being called into some roles and responsibilities. The leadership role of the women in the Old Testament was mainly among the womenfolk and also in the home. Deborah and Huldah in the Old Testament were exceptional. In the New Testament, apart from the twelve apostles of the Lord Jesus Christ, I understand that among the other apostles mentioned in Romans there are one or two women who the Greek would seem to suggest very strongly were ministering in the capacity of an apostle. I'm not a Greek scholar, so I cannot say yes, I cannot say no.

"But what I have seen is that women have an important ministry to women. In our own church this is because there is a lot that the women need to learn which we cannot teach in the regular services. Women's ministry can take care of a lot of that. Then in personal evangelism, it's easy sometimes for women who have known the Lord to reach women. If they were totally useless in the church, then how would they learn the boldness to communicate with people outside? So we have felt that the church is the training ground for all of us – men and women,– to get involved, so that we can be of help in evangelising the world outside the church.

"All over the world, I think, there have been more women missionaries than men missionaries. So the whole Church seems to believe that the women have a role to play in evangelistic and missionary work, talking to those who have not known the Lord. Sometimes this missionary work demands more sacrifice, more wisdom, and more spiritual strength, than the pastoral work in the church. The pastor who talks to a regular audience does not need as many gifts as the missionary who goes out 'into the field'. I do not see that Scripture goes against women ministering. I would see from the Scriptures that there is more for the men, because the women have a lot of things to do at home. We still want them to take care of the family and the children. We wouldn't want their ministry in the church to conflict with the training of their children at home. So we just try to strike a balance. In the early days our single women led Bible studies, but now that they have been getting married, we have slightly changed so that they can fulfil their roles at home, and work with their husbands, rather than working alone."

Within Nigerian society as a whole, this approach to women's ministry is really quite forward-thinking (or Westernised?). Releasing the women from burdens at home is a question not only of realisation by the men, but also desire on the part of the women – neither of which are there (yet!). Dependence on the Bible in working out church practice is clear. I would like to have seen a greater allowance made for the cultural norms of the people of Bible times within which God worked. In the same way, though, God is working through the cultural norms of Nigeria today.

Deeper Life's women's work began in a small way in 1976 with a special day's programme of Bible study especially for the sisters. But it was not until much later – the end of 1987 – that Deeper Life in Lagos started women's meetings every month, with a particular focus on the role of the Christian wife. A Women's Representative has been chosen from each of the forty-nine Zones. Biodun Kumuyi heads up the work as the Women's Co-ordinator. She teaches the women leaders on Bible study on such characters as Miriam and Ruth, but also practical matters such as setting tables, making the home comfortable, intimacy with God even though they are busy, and accidents in the home.

The Zonal Women's Representatives therefore relate pastorally to all the women in their Zone, under the leadership of the Women's Co-ordinator and the (male) Zonal Leader. I asked Biodun Kumuyi why this work was useful:

"There are many things the pastor cannot teach direct from the pulpit which are relevant to women. For example: 'What husbands expect from their wives'. We can teach them how to settle differences, and deal with problems of communication in the home. Another topic we have tackled is 'love and discipline in the home'. Soon we hope to try to teach them how to lead their children to the Lord. We hope the children will see a difference in the home because of the work we are doing with their mothers.

"Sometimes we help them with domestic matters – we may teach them a new recipe or menu. Just recently we taught them how to mix buns. We try to encourage the women to help and contribute to the financial responsibility for the home, and some of the women have now started selling buns. So the husbands are happy that their wives are bringing something in. We now have testimonies of the women's appreciation of these meetings, because we can be practical. Some women have lost their children because of little accidents. But now, after our session on 'Avoiding Accidents', the Lord has helped them and their children to be safe in the home. We give straightforward advice about not leaving knives around, or poisonous medicines; or not to put too much water in the bath to prevent the risk of drowning. The women have needed to hear these things. These meetings have helped to get women more involved in the life of the church."

Building work

In October 1980, IBTC (the International Bible Training Centre) was started by Kumuyi at Ayobo, just outside Lagos. He had realised that there were many independent churches in Nigeria, and also in other parts of Africa, that did not have a regular seminary training for their people.

The people did not have the money to travel overseas and they did not even have the education to be able to cope over there. Deeper Life felt they could do something for these independent churches by training their ministers, or ministerial candidates, and then sending them back to their churches.

Just one national retreat was held that year. It took place in the new IBTC – and 40,000 attended. Numbers were outstripping resources: the Monday Bible study and Thursday Evangelism Training School were also so large by now that Deeper Life needed their own building in Lagos. It was not until now that they began to build their own premises, as the primary call on their finances had always been outreach. They bought some land in Gbagada, and built a simple hall: concrete floor and walls, with an iron roof and plain wooden benches. Because the building was in a dip, storm drains ran through its centre. At the time I visited (October 1988) this was still the central Deeper Life building, although it had been extended a number of times.

Numbers continued to increase – 45,000 went to the 1981 retreat at IBTC. Now the work in Ghana was established, exploratory work was beginning in other African countries. Sister Grace Adebayo, for instance, went to Liberia during her holidays with another sister, to visit ministers and churches, to tell them about Deeper Life and IBTC. By the end of the following year, a permanent missionary had been established there.

Lifestyle

Deeper Life grew through the straight preaching of an Evangelical (and Pentecostal) Gospel, in a thorough attempt to understand and fully apply Scripture. This worked out in various teachings and publications relating to personal behaviour. Conversion to Christ does affect the whole of our lives, and members of Deeper Life are committed to placing themselves unreservedly under the demands of the Gospel. For example, in the early days of Deeper Life it was unacceptable for women to wear trousers, jewellery, or make-up, and they would always have their heads covered when in church or at prayer. Men were to wear simple clothes: unflared trousers (despite the fashion of the time) and plain shoes (acceptable heel heights were specified). Born-again Christians would not watch television or drink minerals such as cola or lemonade, but only fruit juice. Marriage was not really acceptable for the truest disciple of Christ – although this teaching was modified after Kumuyi's marriage to sister Biodun in 1980! All this has led to charges of legalism, which are still made. These accusations regarding the past are no doubt true, but certainly in Lagos, and in most of the other places I visited, I did not hear such strict lifestyle regulations being preached any more. Kumuyi commented to me:

"I think that most of us are creatures of our background and early environment. When I became born again, the church of which I was a member emphasised all these things as part of one's Christian life. Then too, I read much of John Wesley in my early years of Christian life. I always knew that you are saved by grace through faith. But then that we are 'created unto good works' (Ephesians 2.10). That means, as an evidence that I'm born again I should show it by the lifestyle that I lead. If my life does not conform with the Bible standard, and I am 'living in sin' (Romans 6.2), it is an evidence that I do not have what I profess. I am saved by the grace of God, but the good life is an evidence that my testimony is real.

"When we started the Bible study, for me it was strange – women wearing slacks and using jewellery and lipstick. So I would teach them that a born again Christian sister does not dress that way. Being born again affects everything that you do in life.

"Then you have seen the lifestyle in Nigeria: the bribery, corruption, unpunctuality, falsifying accounts (when you get to a place of work at 8 a.m., you write that you got there at 7.30 a.m.). Now the only way for me to correct all these things was to say, 'If you say you are a Christian, indicate the exact time you get to the office. If you resume at seven thirty, put seven thirty. If you get there at nine, put nine. If you resume at nine and you put eight, you are lying, and a Christian should not lie.' That way the lives of the people became changed. And so we were known as people who were legalistic. We would say that if you are a Christian, then you couldn't do this, you couldn't do that; if you were cheating your employers before, you will restore the money. We just counted that, and even now we still count that, as an evidence that you are born again. We don't count that as trying to buy your way through into the Kingdom of God. I think the interpretation of the other people is that we feel that you get yourself qualified to get into the Kingdom of God, but that's a misinterpretation of what we stand upon. It's the grace of God evidenced by the good life.

"At the bus stop, or anywhere, people in Nigeria normally wouldn't queue, but just push. This was worse before the country started the 'War against Indiscipline'. But even with the 'War against Indiscipline' there is still a lot of this. But we would teach our own members that if you say you are a Christian, take your place, 'do unto others as you want them to do unto you'. Somebody got there before you, therefore queue up.

"On the issue of marriage, all the things others said about us were true. I read much of John Wesley who had a bad marital life. I also read Charles Finney, and a lot of others. So I would teach that marriage was acceptable, but that they would have difficulties, and it would limit their time. We wanted the evangelism to go on, and Jesus could return at any time. But even before I got married we were piping down, because I saw that more adults were coming to the Bible study. You see, when the membership was about ninety per cent single, young people, there was a style of preaching that was acceptable. When the membership became thirty or forty per cent adult, then I had to change my style.

"Since I got married, I would say that the only change is that we now have seminars on marriage. We tell people how to find the will of God, readjustment, and other things. We were doing a bit of this even before I got married, because I remember at our retreat, in 1979, we had a seminar on 'Knowing the will of God'. However, we do more of it now than at that time. Some of the allegations are true. But things changed over the years, because of increasing maturity. When I was a child, I spoke as a child, but now that I am an adult . . . !"

Some of these early teachings persist, though not in such a stark form. The desire of Pastor Kumuyi and his followers to be thoroughly Christian and uncompromised with the world may, on reflection, have led them into a legalism which was excessive. The acceptability or unacceptability of women wearing trousers, or men wearing shoes with heels, is an issue which changes not only with culture, but also over time. Nevertheless, they tried. We would do well in Britain to allow the Gospel to challenge our lifestyle more deeply, in whatever ways may be appropriate to our cultures.

One of the people I met in Kano one Sunday afternoon was Raphael Okoye-ukonze – an Ibo from Anambra State in the east of the country. He was living in that part of Kano which is known as "Nomans land". He is a member of a Deeper Life House Caring Fellowship and has been a successful businessman in sports equipment, running his own company. His house in Kano was quite large and comfortable. His story is one of a changed life in response to the Gospel.

"My parents were Roman Catholics, but I was never very religious," he told me. "In fact I was a great sinner. I was well known amongst Ibos in this town because I was a traditional ruler in my home area. But I did not know God. I encountered the Lord when I was returning from Japan one time. A lady in the aircraft gave me two tracts. I only took them because I was interested in the woman! Later, one night, I read the tracts, and I couldn't put them down. I kept re-reading them. The next day I was restless –

I thought they must have given me some poison, or put some kind of curse on me. I happened to have a friend who I knew was a member of Deeper Life. I called him. They prayed for me – and preached to me. I repented and received the Lord Jesus Christ in November 1985. Before then I always had money, but I didn't have any peace. Now I have peace, my business is moving, and my family is flourishing. I now believe that I am saved. I'm enjoying all the promises of God. I am transformed.

"In Kano here I was the leader of my people. I told them that I had become a Christian, and they accepted my position. I have renounced my title, as there were some things I would have to do as leader that I did not feel I could do any more.

"At that time I had two wives, so I had to send the second wife away. I gave her and the two children a good house for them to settle in, but we could not continue living together.

"And I used to cheat people to get money. Now I have diversified my sports business, because I am refusing to get involved in any kind of bribery. To sell N100,000 worth of stock to a dealer, I might have to pay the dealer personally another N40,000 or someone else would get the order. I can't do that type of thing any more – so I lose orders. I now refuse to give bribes, and so I have now diversified into trading successfully with beverages – the sports business is still going on, but it can't flourish as before without bribery. But the other side of the story is that just recently, someone who works for me was converted in Deeper Life. Before then he had been stealing from me, and he made restitution. He returned to me stock worth N23,000 which he had stolen from the firm.

"I also used to drink a lot. Before I became a Christian in Deeper Life I and my business associates would spend more on drink in one weekend than a term's school fees for one of my children. Now I don't have anything to do with alcohol. It was difficult to adjust at first, but it's OK now. My wife was very discontented at first, but now she is coming round to the idea!"

We continued talking and laughing in the cool of Raphael's sitting room as we explored together how the changes in his lifestyle, although difficult to start, and sometimes difficult to continue, actually made his life better and happier. Later that evening we went on together to the House Caring Fellowship where he is a member, and he told the other members of the group how he had been praying for his home town for the last three years, since he had given up being traditional ruler after coming to faith in Christ. He reported to the group that the previous weekend he had visited his home town to celebrate the opening of a new Deeper Life Bible Church there.

A NEW CHURCH

The Deeper Life Bible Church

Through the 1980s Deeper Christian Life Ministry continued to see significant developments, the most important of which was probably becoming a Church in 1982. Sunday worship started, and although it was still possible to attend the Bible study and evangelism school whilst being a member of another church, the emphasis was now on being fully and primarily committed to the Deeper Life meetings and activities. In one sense Deeper Life already was a Church, in so far as it was a body of Christians, but the purpose of the Deeper Life meetings up till then had been training and equipping Christians, wherever they worshipped on Sundays. The new denomination was called the "Deeper Life Bible Church", while the non-denominational ministry continued its work with other churches and groups.

With the formation of the Deeper Life Bible Church, further developments took place early in 1983. Lagos had already been divided into eighteen Zones, each with Zonal Leaders, and within the Zones, there were Areas with Area

Leaders. Up until then there had been the evangelism teams and local Bible study groups. This local structure within each Area was changed into local House Caring Fellowships whose purpose included evangelism and Bible study, as well as caring and fellowship. The evangelism teams had been mixed, but the House Caring Fellowships were set up separately for the brothers and the sisters. This was an important development in that it allowed women to find a fuller voice in the fellowship. In a mixed group, the women would tend to keep quiet. Each House Caring Fellowship has a leader and an assistant leader together with ten to twenty members. As the group grows it splits, with the original leader taking some to a new location, while the remaining members stay in the same place with the former assistant as their new leader. As the church grew, so the number of Zones multiplied, and they were grouped into Districts, more or less on the geographical pattern of the original Zones.

Mojeed Lasun Akande was then Zonal Leader for Suru-lere – for which he is now District Co-ordinator. He explained that in 1983, "We would have Zonal crusades, simultaneously in all the Zones, led by the Zonal Leaders. People were drawn into Deeper Life. But most of the growth came through the House Caring Fellowships which were multiplying rapidly."

By 1988 there were well over 5,000 House Caring Fellowships in Lagos. Although there is no doubt in my mind that it is the personal character and ability of Kumuyi which strengthens and keeps people loyal in Deeper Life, the initial contact is almost always by personal invitation.

Parallel with the House Caring Fellowship system is the International Friendship League (IFL) which is a group with the same purpose, but whose membership is composed of professional and highly placed Deeper Life members to enable, perhaps, a more intellectual discussion in the Bible study. There are also IFL social and evangelistic events which attract professionals more than the crusades and house-to-house evangelism. By 1988, in Lagos, there were over 600 members of IFL.

As the work continued to gather pace, Kumuyi finally resigned from his lecturing post at the University of Lagos in April 1983, to devote his full energy to Deeper Life. By 1988 he was still not drawing a salary from Deeper Life, but only claiming modest expenses.

Not everything for Deeper Life has been a success story, and Kumuyi has been strong enough to abandon projects which failed. A lot was invested in IBTC – but it closed in February 1983. There were enough students – from East as well as West African countries – but Deeper Life could not afford to develop the facilities as much as the students demanded without having to charge fees, which the students couldn't afford. Now IBTC is used for various meetings, seminars, retreats and conferences. The current hope is to develop it into a conference centre for both the demands within Deeper Life Bible Church and the Ministry outside to other churches.

MIRACLES AND MISSION

A new ministry to people in need

The Thursday Evangelism School was changed into a Thursday Miracle Revival Hour in 1984. I asked Kumuyi what led to that change:

"We had been emphasising the evangelism training, reaching out and talking to people. But I took time off and analysed the congregation. I realised that most of the people were single, young people. This meant we were reaching the young people, but I wanted to know why we were not reaching the adults. I saw that the felt and known needs of adults were more on getting healed, having a happy family, having job satisfaction, and a lot of other things. I felt that in the New Testament these needs were addressed. So I thought, 'We'll still evangelise, but we'll couch our message in the language that will meet the felt needs of the people.' We therefore changed our Thursday Evangelism Training to 'Miracle Revival Hour'. The people, especially adults, started coming, and they were being healed and saved. We saw more people pressing forward to want to know the Lord than we saw before. When our emphasis was on personal evangelism, we were not getting people of traditional religion and other religions as much as we do now that we are addressing their felt and known needs."

I then asked whether he had seen "miracles" in Deeper Life before, or how his ministry changed after starting in this direction:

"Since I became born again, I have known that Jesus can heal. I know that God has the power to do all things. I also believe that if someone is sick, he or she can pray and be healed by God. But most of the healings that we witnessed at that time were gradual. You pray, and others pray for you, and eventually you are healed. I started studying the Bible. In October 1982 I attended a conference at Caister, in the UK. I saw others minister to the sick, and it was a little bit new to me. So as a result of my reading and praying, in February 1983, I mentioned someone's problem while praying in church. The Lord revealed it to me, I prayed, and the person was delivered, and came to give her testimony. The incident encouraged me to know that the gift was there but I needed to develop it. So eventually we started seeing some of these things in a little measure, and it has been growing since then!"

I asked if the miracles were always in response to a "word of knowledge" like that.

"No. Just yesterday, a woman gave a testimony. She was brought to me, I prayed for her, and she was healed. There wasn't any word of knowledge, she identified the problem herself. During crusades I generally group the problems of the people together. I say, 'If you have this kind of problem I will pray for you,' and then miracles take place. This is not by word of knowledge. My first experience of deliberately praying about short legs took place in July 1988 at the Benin Miracle Service. I never had any inspiration to do so before that time. But at that Miracle Service I said, 'If you have a short leg, or short hand . . . ' The Lord so ministered to me that I felt it was a gift of faith, and I said, 'The people should go there and open their eyes, and see the legs grow out.' I'd never done that before. They opened their eyes and as I was praying the legs were growing out. They started clapping and rejoicing. So it's not all the time that miracles take place by word of knowledge."

In Niger State, to the west, the impact that a visit from the General Superintendent can have was seen in June 1988. The normal attendance at Sunday worship at the central Deeper Life Bible Church in Minna, the state capital, is just over a thousand, while maybe another 1,700 attend the other thirty Deeper Life Bible Churches in the state. But when Pastor Kumuyi came to conduct two Miracle Services on a Friday and Saturday, the recorded attendance was 25,000!

The positive response and the high level of expectation that the people give the "words of knowledge" surprised me at first; but the local diviner has an important place in the life of most African communities. People are used to the idea of information being made available through supernatural means. I now wonder whether the gift of prophecy referred to in Scripture and being experienced in some churches (though not apparent to me as such in Deeper Life) is likewise God's supreme manifestation, in the Church, by the Holy Spirit, of what the diviners are claiming to possess. (Read, for example, Isaiah 44. 24-6 and Micah 3.5–7).

A missionary movement

By the end of 1983, missionary work in other African countries was well established. From the expansion at that time, permanent Deeper Life missionaries from Nigeria are now established in Burkina Faso, Ghana, Côte d'Ivoire,

Kenya, Lesotho, Liberia, São Tomé and Príncipe, Sierra Leone, Swaziland, Tanzania, Uganda, and Zambia.

Originally missionaries were sent from Lagos, but now financial, strategic and pastoral responsibility for the different African countries has been placed upon the seven districts of Lagos and the Deeper Life in the other states of the Federation of Nigeria; approximately one country per district or state.

Sierra Leone

One evening I met Felix Akinola. He was leaving for Sierra Leone at five the next morning, but he was happy to talk late into the night with me, saying, "It is my work!" I don't think he knows about having a day off.

Felix gave his life to the Lord Jesus Christ in 1975. He had been brought up a Baptist, but it was through involvement with Deeper Life in late 1974 that he was "born again". In 1984 Deeper Life sent him to Sierra Leone. He started in the coastal peninsula where he was living, in Allen Town. After two months, about fifty people were meeting regularly in two sitting rooms in different parts of the town. Then Pastor Felix moved up to the capital, Freetown. It was difficult to find accommodation: land there is scarce, and he also had transport problems, so he could not properly pastor the fellowships he had left behind in the peninsula. They continued to grow, however.

Once again, in Freetown he started in a sitting room. The numbers became so large that they moved to using a school hall – but the caretaker was not always friendly and would sometimes lock them out. So they met outside! In 1985 he managed to get accommodation for himself where he could squeeze a hundred people into his dining and sitting rooms. He started to hold crusades in the town, just speaking in an open place one evening, having used handbills, posters and radio announcements to advertise the event. Two hundred people came to his first crusade; now he can expect over five hundred if he is led by the Spirit to hold an open evening meeting like this. At these crusades, Felix has seen many miracles of healing and deliverance. He spoke of one man, a diabetic, who had been healed at a crusade. He had seen his doctor five times since the crusade to check, and there was still no sign of the illness. A woman who had been cursed with an evil charm on her foot – Pastor Felix told me you could see where the charm had worked, and she had been afflicted by this for three years – was completely delivered at a crusade.

Felix went on to describe a spirit which is common in Sierra Leone – popularly called the "bush devil". It is also called "night husband" or "night wife" as it will come to a woman or man in the night and claim them for itself. It causes infertility, or hinders marriage in some other way. It causes breakdown in marriages, stopping husbands and wives from loving each other. This spirit can also hinder promotion prospects or business success. "But," said Felix, "when we minister in the name of Jesus, they are delivered." He told me of one woman at a recent crusade who had been tormented by the "night husband" for thirty-eight years. The spirit was cast out.

To a Westerner it might seem fantastic that such a spirit exists. To an African, it might rather seem fantastic that such a spirit could be driven out so easily. But there are many, both in the West and in Africa, who will testify to the power of evil spirits, and the victory of Christ over such things. Surely it is significant that the symptoms vanish when what is perceived to be causing them is cast out, or exorcised. The majority of Africans need no persuading of the reality of evil and personal attacks by evil spirits (although the point can be reached where everything that goes wrong is blamed on an evil spirit). The Good News is that Christ has won the victory, which we can claim.

"It is not we who help, it is the Lord," said Felix. "There isn't any problem the Lord cannot help. There is no problem he cannot solve. All power has been given to him. When any person approaches God for a miracle, they must believe.

Someone may believe for salvation, but doubt for a miracle. Without faith we can't please God. God wants us to believe in him, that he is Lord of all ability."

I pressed Felix on whether there might be failure, or misunderstanding, or some sovereignty in God which may mean a healing or deliverance would not take place, but he was genially adamant that if we believe God for a miracle, it will happen. The onus for success is therefore on the faith of the believer. I found an equally hard line on this among a number of the other leaders in Deeper Life, but among some of them, including Kumuyi himself, I found a slightly more sympathetic approach (see p. 151).

Four years after arriving in the country, land was still a problem for Deeper Life in Sierra Leone. They are waiting to build their own church in Freetown, where they now have about 180 members. In the peninsula there are now three fellowships, numbering 50, 120, and 160. Deeper Christian Life Ministry recently held a Church Growth conference for ministers of other churches in Freetown, and 150 attended, without there having been any formal publicity. More such conferences are planned. (These conferences are held all over Africa, with two people from Lagos working full time setting them up and teaching at them.) Felix explained that although there are miracles, the main reason why the church grows is through personal evangelism ("the most effective method"). I asked Felix if there was any vision for reaching further into Sierra Leone. He said he was now hoping for this – he was waiting to be led by the Spirit to lead a crusade in Bo. There was one member from the Deeper Life Bible Church in Freetown whose company had transferred him to Bo, and he had already started his own Deeper Life House Caring Fellowship there. Thus the same pattern of growth is operating as when Deeper Life first spread outside Lagos. An individual moves, finds work, and out of his or her own conviction and commitment starts a Bible study group.

Zambia

A few days later I met Pastor John Amoni. He had been to a Catholic church as a child, but stopped attending when he went to secondary school. While he was there, though, two of his friends were converted, and he noticed that there was a new calmness in their lives. He was challenged by their orderly lives and converted through their witness to him, but did not start going to any particular church. He enjoyed fellowship meetings, but his family did not approve, and sometimes when he got back from a meeting he would find himself locked out. He started going to an Assemblies of God church.

Eventually he became an accounts clerk at Yaba Technical School in Lagos, and in January 1978 he started going regularly to the Deeper Life Bible study and Evangelism school. He joined an evangelism team:

"I had the urge to reach out to people. When I finished at Yaba I just felt I should go into full-time ministry, but I was concerned about how I would be able to support my family. I had a brief discussion with the General Superintendent which helped to settle my mind in this area. So I joined the staff at the Deeper Christian Life Ministry headquarters, labelling cassette tapes and helping with the accounts. I knew I should be serving God more fully, but I didn't know where. At the end of 1983, the GS called me and told me it was time to go to another location: Zambia.

"On the last day of 1983 I arrived in Lusaka. I had nobody to go to, and nowhere to stay, but there was a diplomat in Lusaka who had been a member of Deeper Life in Lagos, so I went to stay in his house at first. I started a Bible study, and began to try to get Deeper Christian Life Ministry registered with the authorities so that I could get a work permit.

"The Deeper Life fellowship in Lusaka grew to forty-five members, but I had to leave in July 1984 because I had not yet been able to get a permit. Registration was finally granted in November, and this time I arrived, with a work permit, on the last day of 1984! But the fellowship had dwindled to fifteen while I was away.

"There are transport problems in Lusaka – no commercial vehicles are allowed to run after 7.30 p.m. so it is difficult to hold evening meetings. We started meeting for Bible study on Saturdays in the Salvation Army hall. When we got to seventy-five members we moved to Kamwala Secondary School in Lusaka. In April 1985 I led an Evangelism retreat attended by 500 people. I remember particularly someone came into the retreat to beat his wife because he didn't want her there."

I asked John what exactly had happened, and he explained that the man had beaten his wife in the middle of the meeting. It is a commentary on the normal African attitude to the marriage relationship that the 500 participants allowed this to happen without attempting to restrain the man.

"After he had beaten the woman, we were all weeping," John said. "It was an experience that shook many people. We just prayed that God would change his life. Two months later the man came to see me, carrying a Bible, to apologise. He had been upset after what had happened at the meeting and eventually had started to read his wife's Bible, so his life had changed.

"Now we regularly hold crusades, retreats, and seminars. In Lusaka we have 400 regularly on Sunday mornings, and 250 at the Saturday Bible study. Most of the non-believers who experience conversion through our ministry have been troubled by evil spirits. They try to go to a witch doctor to expel the spirit, but without success. We are able to cast out the devils and preach the Gospel. Such people don't like to leave us, because they know where they got their deliverance from. For example, in August 1988 we gave sixty people water baptism – that means those people had not been members in any other Gospel church before coming to Deeper Life. We have planted Deeper Life Bible Churches in eight other locations in Zambia – two of these are led full time by people working voluntarily, the others are led by people who have left Lusaka to find employment elsewhere, and started Deeper Life work where they went.

"When you start work in a different country, you need to learn the rules. In Zambia you need a police permit for any public meeting of more than ten people. When I first arrived in Lusaka I just preached everywhere. I used to preach in the buses, but I was told I couldn't do that, so I resorted to personal evangelism, and that's how we grew."

. . . and throughout Africa

Apart from the places where churches have been planted, exploratory visits have been made to most other western, central, and eastern African countries, with a view to establishing permanent work if welcomed by the governments and fellow-Christians there.

I met brother Emmanuel Umoh who was about to spend his annual leave visiting Tanzania to explore the possibility of working there. The previous year he had been to Sudan – where he really learnt to depend on God:

"God was fighting for us. When we got to Khartoum at around 2 a.m., we didn't know where we were going! We took a taxi and went to the Nigerian Embassy, and they welcomed us. We wanted to go south to Juba where we had heard the churches were active, but we couldn't get there because of the war. We went to the Sudan Council of Churches, and met their Director of Evangelism – he showed us around, and I almost wept at the needs of Sudan. The SCC asked us lots of questions, and I told them that God was doing many mighty things in Nigeria, and we didn't want to keep it to ourselves. I told them we worked by faith and lived by prayers. They invited us to preach in different churches there – I remember going to the Episcopal, Catholic, and Coptic churches. They wanted us to stay. We were there only three weeks, and there were so many churches asking us to visit them. We promised them we would surely come back."

I find it remarkable that the missionary strategy of Deeper Life has developed so fully, so quickly. Within Nigeria there is a Deeper Life presence in every state, with its State Overseer. Thus there is a missionary structure which reflects the country, and where the people are, rather than a pastoral structure according to where the members are already grouped. Equal weight is put upon each state, and some of the best people are sent to the farthest-flung places. Deeper Life have had the advantage of starting from scratch, but other Christian groupings could do worse than seek to follow that example of structuring according to local political and administrative boundaries. Outside Nigeria there has been the same strategy of one missionary per country, whether the work has been initially "successful" or not. It may appear naive just to travel to a country and try to start something – but on the other hand it seems an excellent piece of missionary training to send the potential missionaries themselves to make an exploratory visit of their own before they resign their current employment. It is a good way of giving the individuals a grasp of the enormity of the task involved, and also of confirming – or bringing into question – God's call upon them.

I think it is worth noting that the tendency in Western missionary agencies is towards short-term service – maybe less than two years, while even two weeks is considered acceptable and worthy of God. Popular Western trends suggest that mission can be accomplished in a long vacation, whereas Deeper Life missionaries are placing their lives in service to the communities where they are sent, taking up permanent residence. It is also worth noting that these Deeper Life missionary efforts have involved contact with local Christian groups, and although the outreach is specifically Deeper Life, it is also made in a spirit of partnership in the Gospel.

"But we feel that only helping other churches is not sufficient in reaching the unreached," Kumuyi explained to me. "In Nigeria alone we have about 18 million nominal Christians, who only go to church at Easter and Christmas. With all that the churches are doing, we have still not reached out to these people. We have also discovered that even if we give out strategies and methodology on reaching the unreached to some of these denominations, they do not have the resources to reach out to them. Sometimes they have the resources, but they are inward-looking. They want to solve problems in the church. But problems will always be there! So because of that lack of vision, we have felt that our role is not *either* strengthening the other churches *or* planting Deeper Life churches, but *both*. Furthermore, most of the established churches have their branches and headquarters in cities like Lagos, Ibadan, and Port Harcourt. The rural areas are by and large neglected, and we have at least sixty per cent of the nation still living outside the cities, so we have felt that planting churches would be part of the answer, although not the total answer. We really want to strengthen the work in the rural areas, because that is an aspect of the work that has been neglected by most of the established churches. Some of the churches are represented in rural areas, but the ministers are not catered for or trained, so the church is not really as strong as it should be. Those who go for training prefer to go to the West. They travel out, get trained, and when they come back, because of the lifestyle in the West, they can only fit into the cities in Nigeria. To go to the rural areas after graduating from a seminary in America or Britain is very, very difficult.

"When we send missionaries to other countries they generally go to the capitals because to get registered and recognised you need to be in the capital. What we have done now is to attach one African country to a state in Nigeria. I hope that the states will send people to hold crusades and other programmes. Eventually many of these people will catch the vision to stay in those countries. But we do encourage our missionaries not to concentrate in one city. We tell them to go to different provinces and rural areas. Thus they will be able to strengthen the church there."

Deeper Life's vigorous growth from a small group in the mid-1970s to a major international Christian ministry and denomination in the mid-1980s has not, though, been without controversy. We now turn to some of those more painful aspects of Deeper Life.

6

Commitment and controversy

By 1977, Deeper Christian Life Ministry had become very
visible, with their emphasis on Bible study, evangelism,
and being active in the churches. Some churches welcomed
Deeper Life's contribution, while others began to be more
cautious.

As his ministry was obviously being confirmed in terms of
the response of the people, I asked Kumuyi why he had not
sought to enter the ordained ministry in any of the existing
churches:

"I never really thought of joining an established church.
From the way we were operating, we had converts through
our involvement with the Scripture Union. In the Scripture
Union the vision was that we should make ourselves
available to all the churches. I even felt that it would be
disadvantageous staying with one church. This was because
the Pentecostals will reject you if they know you are with the
Evangelicals, and vice versa. So I felt it was advantageous to
help everybody, every denomination."

Problems in the churches

But despite this desire to help on a broad basis, churches
were beginning to complain about Deeper Life, and Kumuyi

was having problems in his own church, the Apostolic Faith
(originally from Portland, Oregon, USA). He described what
it was like in those days:

"I think the faults were on both sides, that is, on the side
of both Deeper Life and the other churches. In 1973, when
I became a lecturer at the University of Lagos, I just had a
concern to teach young people because I had been involved
with the Scripture Union and young people's groups. We
were teaching these young people to be born again, and to live
consistent Christian lives. We also emphasised evangelism
in those days. Now the church I was going to at that time
did not accept the way we carried out personal evangelism.
They felt that young Christians who evangelise might fall
into false doctrine. They encouraged you to invite people to
the church services, and believe that they would be saved.
I didn't agree with that, and so I was the target of the
preaching there a lot of the time. They would allude to
'the young man who is going astray'. But I kept on going
to the church, and a lot of people who were coming to
the Bible study went to different churches – some to that
church, some to Pentecostal churches, Evangelical churches,
and some remained in the 'orthodox' churches like Anglican,
Methodist, and Presbyterian.

"Then we had retreats. After the retreats, Deeper Life
members would go back to their own churches and evangelise those people who they felt were not born again. That
approach may have been wrong, it may have been right; but
that's what they did. They felt the people in the churches
were not receiving clear teaching on the new birth; and that
their lives did not show clear evidence of the new birth,
although that was a subjective judgement. But that was
their reason for evangelising them. They also taught them
about what they believed was consistent Christian living –
holiness, and other practical issues like 'do not smoke, do
not drink'. Now as young people they had zeal, and it was
good. But sometimes they were wrong in their emphasis, so
I would correct them at the Bible study – but the churches
did not know about the correction, because they were not

at the Bible study! Eventually some of them were driven out of the churches. For example, one denomination gave a general type of statement at their headquarters: 'Anybody who attends any other Bible study outside of the church's, especially Deeper Life Bible study, will be driven out of the church'. The brethren who attended the Bible study therefore left that church and went to another church. But the story repeated itself; other churches also drove them out. Eventually my own church sent me out too. I didn't want to tell you all this earlier on, because I didn't want to sound negative about the local churches. The local churches are doing good work; it's just that there are differences in our convictions. I think, to be consistent, I would rather say that the way they felt was the only option they had. My Overseer called me and told me that he didn't enjoy what I was doing. He said I was not practising what the church taught me and that that might have some consequences. I explained my perception and admitted that if what I was doing would hinder the growth of the church and the Kingdom of God, I would patiently bear whatever they would do. And yet I couldn't give up my convictions on evangelism. Finally, the church took the decision to excommunicate me. In fairness to them, they bore with me for a number of years, but because I was 'incorrigible' from their viewpoint, they had to take that stand.

"Now, when they excommunicated me, I didn't join any other church. The church I had been going to preached on holiness, and restitution. I felt that if this church (which stands on the Bible) could drive me out, then any other church not standing on the totality of the Bible could do worse. I was driven out in 1977, and we just continued the Bible study. The people coming to the Bible study and who had also been attending that church with me, kept going. I made sure that they were not negative about it. I excused the church, saying that they were not committing sin; that they did the best they knew. Our difference was in our conviction.

"We also had differences of opinion on healing. They

believed that God could give sickness to a believer to discipline him, to make him a better Christian. I disagreed. They may have been right, I may have been wrong. I just felt that you couldn't do that to your own child. If your child wasn't doing anything wrong, you couldn't inflict sickness upon him or her. They felt that God thinks in a different way, and his ways are mysterious. They felt that if I remained in the church I could influence people and it was dangerous keeping me there. I think they were consistent with themselves. I don't agree that they were completely right, but I could justify them, or at least put a good construction on what they did. But in the Bible study we still taught very strongly what we believed. And we still allowed these people to go to the churches.

"In Deeper Life, I just taught the Bible, and maintained the doctrines of evangelism and divine healing. I taught that God is never the problem, Satan is the problem. He is the enemy. I taught simple, basic things, not complicated theology! I would also teach people very strongly to have real convictions, and still to keep on going to their churches.

"Some churches began accusing us of 'sheep stealing'. But I think what they didn't realise was that when we held retreats we would bring people together and would feed them for free, and give them free literature. Therefore many people were getting to know the Lord through Deeper Life. They went back to the local churches after these retreats, but those churches would not recognise that these converts came from Deeper Life programmes. They thought that they were their members, and eventually if they spoke unkindly about Deeper Life in their sermons, those converts would leave for another church, but they still kept coming to our Bible study."

Kumuyi's former church should not be discredited for asking him to leave, any more than most of the other churches in Nigeria. As I understand Deeper Life people to be saying, very few Nigerian denominations are tolerant of diversity of belief or practice. Responsibility for schism lies as much with existing groupings as with the new movements. It was primarily pressure from existing churches which led Pastor Kumuyi to start Sunday worship for Deeper Life members, thus forming a new Church, rather than remaining as an interdenominational ministry.

Creating a spiritual home

Bunmi Odetola (now one of Deeper Life's full time editors) explained, "The Deeper Life Sunday worship which started in 1982 was the best thing that could happen. We had this problem of going to worship on Sundays in places where we weren't recognised. Now the Deeper Life Bible Church is our home, and we are spiritually satisfied."

"Some of us desired that Sunday worship at Deeper Life should commence," added Oluwi, Mushin District Co-ordinator. "Those of us who used to preach in the buses and elsewhere were sometimes made to stand up in church and be publicly castigated by our pastors. Most of us really felt very happy when Sunday worship finally started."

I asked Kumuyi how he reached the decision to start Sunday worship – and thus form a new denomination – and, indeed, why he had even delayed in making such a move, when he had been without a "church home" himself since 1977:

"The churches had some points against us, and some of them were legitimate. For example, our retreats were generally in Easter and December. We chose those periods because of the vacations, but then those times are important for the church and many of our people would go to the retreats, and it would tell on their attendance at the church. So there were conflicts. Some of the churches were feeling that we should be a regular church so that they would know their members, and they would not just be catering for Deeper Life members who would not be there when they needed them for important church programmes.

"Then some of the people were not accepted as 'workers' [i.e. given responsibility] in the churches. Our members saw it as persecution but some of the churches felt it wasn't persecution because if they were to be workers they must have total allegiance to the church, which they couldn't have because they were partly here, partly over there.

"They also had problems with their tithes and offerings. Some churches keep records of who gives tithes and offerings, and they said that some of our members gave part of their tithes to Deeper Life and part to their church. The churches then felt that Deeper Life members were not really dependable and reliable, so they couldn't use them as workers. And yet they wanted to be useful. In Lagos at that time the Monday Bible study was more than 5,000; and all over Nigeria we had pockets and groups of people affiliated with Deeper Life.

"So some of the churches were driving out our people, and some pastors themselves even advised me that these problems would be solved if I started my own church. Then some of the members of Deeper Life were backsliding. When they saw this unhealthy relationship amongst Christian bodies, they felt they would not want anything more to do with Christianity. Some felt our methods were causing more harm than good. Others felt that we should be on our own and that there was nothing wrong in being a Church.

"I had been thinking and praying about this since about 1980 or so, as far as I can remember, but I kept quiet about it. I didn't tell even the leaders anything. In the first half of 1982 we had a meeting at IBTC with about 110 key leaders, and I just hinted to them, 'Suppose this were to happen, what would you feel?' Some of them felt we shouldn't because we had told the people publicly that we were not going to have Sunday worship, we were just going to have Bible studies, retreats, and evangelism. So if we changed, it would be as if we originally had intended to have Sunday worship, and we were therefore deceiving the people. So I kept quiet, and didn't explain any further. But I felt that when we started in 1973 we had only spoken according to the limited vision we then had. We didn't know then about the problems, about the consequences of the Bible study, about all this driving out. I felt that if we looked at these problems and we prayed and God allowed us to do it, it wouldn't be a contradiction of what we had said before.

"I think it was about August or September 1982 that I called some people in Lagos – because at that time the pressure was getting high from the people that were being driven out of the various churches. There was a particular case where the minister of a church asked who was going to Deeper Life. Some people stood up. Then he spoke about Deeper Life, that it was not good and the people were fanatical. He asked them who would still continue going to the Deeper Life Bible study, and some people kept standing. There was a couple in particular, and the pastor went up to the husband and slapped him. Then he said that the husband only had a wife as a result of his prayers, and that therefore he was breaking their marriage; that whatever he loosed on earth was loosed in heaven. (The couple did not accept this because they knew it to be a misinterpretation of the Bible.) The couple came to me and said, 'This is what is happening. We understand suffering and persecution, but why do we bring all this persecution on ourselves?'

"So on Monday, November 1st, 1982, I announced to the people that the next Sunday I wanted to tell them something special and that they should come to Gbagada. I prayed and got together with some of the leaders in Lagos and we saw that this was the only alternative that would at least give us some peace. So on Sunday, November 7th, 1982, I spoke to them, saying that we believed this was the solution to the problem, that I had prayed and this was how the Lord was leading me.

"The majority of the people rejoiced because they had been suffering the way I had in 1977. They were still in the midst of the problem so they felt it more than I did. So we started the Sunday worship. Some people said they would not come to the Sunday worship, but they would keep on coming to the Monday Bible study; which we said was all right. We held the Sunday worship to solve the problems of those who were finding things difficult with the other churches. Those who remained in the other churches continued facing real problems. Eventually they joined us because of what they were experiencing.

"Then a fresh wave of persecution began. The churches started to accuse us, pointing out that we had said we were not going to have Sunday worship. Over the years, these are the things that have brought Deeper Life members to want to say, 'All right, let's do what we want to do, without being hindered by what the other churches are saying.' Many of the independent churches felt injured, because some of them had even developed on Deeper Life. Anywhere we had a retreat, they would plant a church, because they knew that we did not have Sunday worship – they had some strategy! Now that we did what we did, it affected them very seriously, therefore they were bitter."

Rebuilding relationships

As soon as Sunday worship started in Lagos, the Deeper Life fellowships with larger memberships across Nigeria followed suit in a matter of months. All this is still recent history in the minds and experience of Deeper Life people and has led to an exclusivist stance. But this is softening now, particularly in the north, as Christians have come together in the face of Muslim opposition. Deeper Life has been part of that coming together, contributing to the broadly based Christian Association of Nigeria – but it was only in 1988 that Deeper Life actually applied formally to join the Association.

"Most of the time now we will be mild," Kumuyi claimed, "and at least the people in Lagos know that we accept other people as Christians. They knew that from the onset because I would say, 'We have different convictions, but we are all children of God. We believe that this is what we ought to do, this is our ministry and our vision. We should be strong in our conviction, and yet put the best construction on what other people are doing.' I believe that in the love and grace of God everything will eventually be cleared up as an answer to the prayer of the Lord Jesus Christ.

"We still help the churches," Kumuyi added. "When the Christian Association of Nigeria had a problem in 1987 we gave N100,000. We also printed 500,000 of our own tracts for them which they requested, and we printed free of charge. Last year (1987) I think we gave N10,000 to PFN [Pentecostal Fellowship of Nigeria]. When another Christian organisation was trying to build a mini-stadium in Lagos for use by Christians (we were all having difficulties getting the National Stadium for religious programmes), we gave N10,000. Also, this year, a church that has its headquarters at Ibadan wanted to hold a retreat, so we gave them ideas on how to get the unchurched to their retreat. Then they said that if they followed the programmes we described to them, they wouldn't be able to finance it, so we gave them N10,000.

"There are Ministers' Conferences too, in all the states in Nigeria. Interested ministers usually come together once a month in a forum where the Deeper Life State Overseer describes the strategies we are using, – the house fellowship system, praying for people, organisation, church administration, and so on. Most of them are pastors of independent churches who do not have the advantage of being exposed to the administration of the well-established churches. So in that way we still carry on the ministry of helps to the other churches."

At the end of that turbulent year of 1982, the December retreat at IBTC saw an attendance of 70,000. This was to be the last retreat for the whole membership at one time. Numbers had got too big.

Reactions to Deeper Life today

Kumuyi had been brought up as an Anglican. I went to meet the Anglican Archbishop of Nigeria, the Most Rev. Joseph Adetiloye. One of the things the Archbishop told me was that it was easy to start a church in Nigeria – "All you need is a Bible and a handbell and the people will flock to you." It is to Kumuyi's credit that he tried to stay non-denominational for so long, and that it was only when the pressure was so great that he created a new denomination. It is a rebuke to the other churches that they could not accept his kind of ministry when it was obviously what many people needed and wanted.

As I understood him, the Archbishop was saddened by the schism which has been happening amongst the churches in Nigeria. He is hoping that the Anglicans, who represent a united breadth of churchmanship, may be able to hold together, adapt and grow, and continue to make new converts and new members.

"The church needs renewal all the time," he told me. "We're planning a renewal conference – an 'Anglican Renewal Ministry' – because without renewal from God, people will pull down standards. Paul said that Christ 'gave gifts to men' (Ephesians 4.8), and these gifts are for building up the body of Christ. Some people have discovered that they have a gift, but haven't been able to use it within the body. We are trying this renewal ministry, so that if there are any gifts that we have neglected, we can bring them to the surface. We want to see, and are seeing, these gifts – for example, healing – used in our churches. If you have a gift of the Holy Spirit, it is for the unity of the church. We must do all we can to keep Christians united for the proclamation of the Word.

"Of course, we have made mistakes. Firstly, the Bible is very important to us – I tell my people how important it is to read the Scriptures and to pray every day. But we are more familiar with the Old Testament than with the New. We need to work harder at our Bible study. Secondly, we have lacked local custom and tradition in our Anglican liturgy. Our ancient prayers and 'collects', said by the saints over the centuries, have their dignity, but Africans are exuberant, and want prayers that strike them here and now. We must bring African music into the church – and let the people dance!

"Thirdly, one of things we haven't done well enough is our youth ministry. To be honest, I think we failed Kumuyi when he was so serious about Bible study."

Some of those who are most critical of Deeper Life's perceived exclusivism and legalism are Anglicans. One of the Anglican dioceses in Nigeria is centred on a major city in Imo State – Aba. I met the Bishop of Aba, the Rt. Rev. Dr Iwaugwu. After he had welcomed me with a huge hug he gave me some of his ideas on African spirituality and the new, independent churches. He emphasised that he knew about these new religious movements in general, but not much about Deeper Life in particular, so any criticism should not necessarily be taken as applying directly to them.

Firstly we discussed the importance of indigenous culture. He explained that when the early missionaries arrived from Europe, there was a clash between African and European culture – and Christianity was associated with the latter. The new faith was established, but did not destroy the original way of life. There were (and remain) needs which were satisfied by the old ways, but which the new (European) religion could not handle. He also described "the psychology of the African". Africans like to put their whole weight into whatever they are doing – they want emotional depth. They like to "dance religion" – to experience it and feel it. They also expect religion to solve every problem, "even things they should be able to do for themselves".

The Bishop confessed that there are areas of weakness in the traditional churches established by overseas missionary societies. He said:

"These new groups rise to fill the gaps where we are lacking. They supplement where we are failing. But I can't see any church that is fulfilling every requirement! Also, in an international, multi-cultural church there are constraints – you have to agree things and act together. In a small grouping, there are no such constraints."

I could see in Deeper Life some of the things Dr Iwaugwu was describing: the way they give authoritative teaching, directly address evil spirits, and encourage their members to expect solutions to their problems from God. Deeper Life members are not very emotional in church, and in all the Deeper Life Bible Churches I visited I never saw any dancing. Even in Britain people are beginning to laugh and cry in church, and in some places you can even dance! I hope that in the future Deeper Life may be able to release this natural expression of worship and relationship with God, without conceding to the pressures of occultic worship which such practices could be seen to be enabling.

The second factor we discussed was poverty. Deeper Life have attracted members from all parts of society, all across the country. Although many Deeper Life members are from the professional classes, it is probably true that the majority of them are poor. People need to feel at home in a church, and especially when they are poor, they need to feel important and cared for. Deeper Life have their House Caring Fellowships, but most of the larger churches of other denominations do not yet, so new, small churches start. The poverty of the people also works against an international church, because it can become an "élitist club" (to quote the Bishop).

"Some of our Anglicans," he continued, "are more English than Ibo. But most of the people who live in my diocese are poor, and they simply like to be with people who are suffering like them. In poverty you can also become spiritually anxious, looking for help. Clear teaching about God is attractive, but it also means that people turn to the occult, and a lot of these new movements are syncretistic – a mixture of Christianity and witchcraft. If someone is ill, they will go to any group that will make them well! In the older churches we give up too soon, and depend on scientific treatment. But scientific medicine is too expensive for most of our people, and it can't heal everything anyway! People are also looking for divination, they want to know what will happen next. They will see visions and dream dreams, and I do believe God has a hand in these things. Men make priests, but God makes prophets! In the end I think it is the Bible itself which is causing all these new movements.

Any group which studies the Bible properly will turn out with something!"

Thirdly, I asked the Bishop what his response was to these new movements.

"We are accepting their challenge, and are trying to learn from them in our own ministries. We are trying to preach the full Gospel, and to give opportunities to people to reach the full depth of their emotion. If it is the chance to cry that is taking people away from our church, we'll give them an opportunity to cry! We are adding extra meetings to our existing structure – the people have the time and they want to go to long prayer meetings. These things all start with prayer, and prayer makes a tremendous difference."

Other churches may be open to the blessings of Deeper Life, but there is a sense in which Deeper Life members have remained aloof from those same churches. When so many members have transferred their allegiance from Catholic, Anglican, Baptist, or Methodist, for example, it can be difficult for them to accept the integrity of the churches they have left behind them and which they have effectively rejected as inadequate. I found this separation particularly marked in the villages, and in student life: both areas where the smallness of the community should be a positive enabler to Christian unity.

When I visited the little Deeper Life Bible study fellowship in Oro-Ago, where I had previously taught, the group had just eight members. For Sunday worship five members of the group go to the large ECWA (Evangelical Churches of West Africa) church in the village, while one other goes to the smaller Baptist Church. Esther Adelike, who leads the group, and the young woman friend who shares her house, simply stay at home, use Deeper Life's "Search the Scriptures" and listen to a message cassette from Ilorin (Kwara State capital) or Lagos. I can sympathise with their desire to follow the Deeper Life programme when they have obviously gained so much from the ministry. But I wonder if they are not missing out on something that God wants to give them through corporate Sunday worship and wider fellowship at one of the churches in Oro-Ago. Reaching out for the best that God wants to give you is one thing – but it doesn't help your mission if people receive the impression that you are exclusive and regard different expressions of worship and fellowship as inferior. In every place I visited in Nigeria, when I met Christians who were not in Deeper Life, they warned me to be cautious and not to be too sympathetic. There is obviously quite a high level of distrust brought about by this separation, and by what are perceived as "sheep-stealing" tactics.

In Ilorin I met an ECWA pastor, Julius Akanbi, who is lecturer in Christian Religious Studies at the College of Education. He was sympathetic to Deeper Life, with a certain caution:

"Ordinary Christians perceive a 'holier than thou' attitude in Deeper Life. They don't understand them, while Deeper Life don't want their adherents to be 'polluted'. The strength of Deeper Life is that their missionary outreach is strong, and the members know how to study the Bible, and recognise the power of the word of God. But I think Deeper Life should give more room to Christian fellowship. To me, all who call on the name of Christ should be hand in hand. If you stay outside, you get a wrong impression. On the campus here, Deeper Life student members have their own Bible study, but they also join in the broader Fellowship of Christian Students. But we do need to extend the hand of fellowship more. It becomes a problem for them if they go to live somewhere where there isn't a Deeper Life Bible Church."

False prophets?

When I was in Imo State I went out to the little village of Nguru for their Sunday worship. The predominant affiliation in this part of Nigeria seemed to be with the Roman Catholic Church, who have endowed the area well with schools and clinics. The "Search the Scriptures" passage taken that day was about Jethro's visit to Moses (Exodus 18.1–27). We read about shared responsibility, authority and leadership:

> The work is too heavy for you; you cannot handle it alone
> . . . select capable men from all the people . . . and appoint
> them as officials . . . That will make your load lighter,
> because they will share it with you. (Exodus 18.18, 21,
> 22)

The "Search the Scriptures" leader commented, "We all have responsibility, if we don't do our job, the pastor will be doing everything and getting tired. We need to join hands and work together."

However, the main emphasis came across as one of obedience to the leadership, and this was followed by a sermon loosely based on Matthew 7.15: "Watch out for false prophets. They come to you in sheep's clothing, but inwardly they are ferocious wolves." The leader continued with such warnings as:

"We must be careful of evangelists, pastors, prophets, and others. Test the spirits in them, to see whether they are contrary to the word of God. If you dress anyhow, if you sisters don't cover your head, if you marry an unbeliever, if you forget your holiness: you won't go to heaven. You must be very careful. Many churches have deceived people. Many spiritual leaders have deceived people. There is condemnation for those people. They are thieves. No matter how many years they have spent in the Lord, they are stealing and destroying your soul. Their stomach is their God. If you don't pay their salary they run away. They can be bribed with cars and nice houses. When there is any danger they run away. When you are confused or sorrowing they run away. You should run away from them. Don't ever help them."

I found the Deeper Life in Nguru both legalistic and exclusive. Concerning legalism, Deeper Life's conviction is that you must repent of your sin, and accept Christ as Lord. But there is also teaching on lifestyle which can become legalistic while losing sight of a larger vision. Jesus was very critical of those who were too precise about a godly lifestyle at the expense of God's greater mission:

> Woe to you Pharisees, because you give God a tenth of your mint, rue and all other kinds of garden herbs, but you neglect justice and the love of God. You should have practised the latter without leaving the former undone. (Luke 11.42)

Then there was the exclusivism. There are "churches" in Nigeria which have doctrines and practices which are inconsistent with Scripture and Christian tradition. The mainline churches have a problem in distinguishing themselves from them, and protecting their own followers from being misguided. The simple answer is to reject all other groupings but your own as deviant to a greater or lesser extent. That is the simple answer, but it is far from being the correct answer! Jesus said, "He who is not with me is against me, and he who does not gather with me, scatters" (Luke 11.23). But he also told his disciples, "Whoever is not against you is for you" (Luke 9.50).

Our Christian faith is not always as clear-cut as we might like, and we have to struggle to "work out our salvation" (Philippians 2.12). Jesus said this to his disciples concerning his second coming:

> Then the King will say to those on his right, "Come, you who are blessed by my Father; take your inheritance, the kingdom prepared for you since the creation of the world. For I was hungry and you gave me something to eat, I was thirsty and you gave me something to drink, I was a stranger and you invited me in, I needed clothes and you clothed me, I was sick and you looked after me, I was in prison and you came to visit me."
>
> Then the righteous will answer him, "Lord, when did we see you hungry and feed you, or thirsty and give you something to drink? When did we see you a stranger and

invite you in, or needing clothes and clothe you? When did we see you sick or in prison and go to visit you?"

The King will reply, "I tell you the truth, whatever you did for one of the least of these brothers of mine, you did for me."

Then he will say to those on his left, "Depart from me, you who are cursed, into the eternal fire prepared for the devil and his angels. For I was hungry and you gave me nothing to eat, I was thirsty and you gave me nothing to drink, I was a stranger and you did not invite me in. I needed clothes and you did not clothe me. I was sick and in prison and you did not look after me."

They will also answer, "Lord, when did we see you hungry or thirsty or a stranger or needing clothes or sick or in prison, and did not help you?"

He will reply, "I tell you the truth, whatever you did not do for one of the least of these, you did not do for me."

Then they will go away to eternal punishment, but the righteous to eternal life. (Matthew 25.34–46)

Jesus concluded another parable with:

Not everyone who says to me, "Lord, Lord" will enter the kingdom of heaven, but only he who does the will of my Father who is in heaven. Many will say to me on that day, "Lord, Lord, did we not prophesy in your name, and in your name drive out demons and perform many miracles?" Then I will tell them plainly, "I never knew you. Away from me, you evildoers!" (Matthew 7.21–3)

It is clearly on a response to such readings that Deeper Life's emphasis on a holy and worthy lifestyle is based. But these texts should also warn us against any kind of exclusivism.

Kumuyi, as General Superintendent of Deeper Life, is struggling with a problem here. He has confessed that in his early days he was what he himself would now regard as legalistic and exclusive – although never really wanting those things, it was as much force of circumstance as his own immaturity. Things are much better now in Lagos, and that new openness has more or less got through to the state capitals. Once you get out to the towns and villages, though, the old habits are taking a longer time to disappear. This is not surprising when communication can be so difficult, and when virtually all of the pastors of these smaller Deeper Life Bible Churches are in full-time employment elsewhere and have no theological or Bible training at all.

Integration and separation

When I travelled to Imo State by car from Benin City I had the chance to meet a Deeper Life student group. To get to Imo from Benin involved crossing through the Niger delta, driving past thick forest and over rivers. At one point the road had quite seriously subsided because the water had washed the foundations away. In that area you find houses built on stilts in the mud, and people get about by boat or canoe rather than by road. As well as the usual goods I had come to expect to see for sale along the road, you could buy fresh fish, and large watersnails by the bagful.

Imo itself is not so wet, being farther inland, although still well-wooded. In Owerri, the state capital, I visited the campus of Alvan Ikoku College of Education, where a small Deeper Life Campus Fellowship of articulate and intelligent young people meets for Bible study and prayer. On Sundays, transport is arranged to take the students to the main church for worship. There is thus an effective system for integrating young people into the life of the whole church. (There is a similar arrangement for the school fellowships.) Normally the seven brothers and nine sisters would meet separately in their different hostels, but for my sake they had been gathered together into one group. One of the brothers told me that he used to be religious, but the lifestyle of the Christians he saw on the campus challenged him. One day, he asked a student friend – an unbeliever – who she thought might be the best people to worship with on the campus. She told him that if he wanted to "be real with God" then she had heard that Deeper Life were the most serious. He started to attend their meetings, listened and prayed, eventually confessed and was born again.

One sister said that since she had joined Deeper Life she had found the peace and joy of salvation. Also, that she was looking to God to help her academically, and in all her courses she had not got anything less than "credit". Another sister testified:

"One day when I was going to a lecture, I was challenged by the look of another girl, her dress, her lifestyle. She told me she was a Deeper Life member. So I joined her. Sometimes after discussing a Bible study, I didn't agree, so I was debating with myself. But when I went to the Deeper Life Bible Church, the pastor dealt with just those things I was concerned about right from the Bible. It was as if someone had told him those things that bothered me. This is a Bible church."

They were also sharing problems. One of the young men had a brother who had died three years previously. "Since then, he hasn't gone out of my mind. He left some children, and every day I think of them."

One of the sisters explained that she had had financial problems since she entered the college in 1986. Her brother had got sick, and couldn't keep up with the fees. "I have been on my own, but by the grace of God I have continued. Sometimes I don't have anything to eat, but a brother or sister will come and invite me to eat with them."

However I did not find the same type of co-operation in Owerri that I had found in Ilorin. The Co-ordinator for the Alvan Ikoku Fellowship told me that they met with other Christian groups when they had to, but they did not come together very often. Peter Okonkwo, the Co-ordinator for Imo State Deeper Life Campus Fellowships did not feel it necessary to meet with other groups, or with people in a similar role to his in other Christian organisations.

There is nothing wrong in setting up your own group – especially when it successfully integrates students into the life of the church so that they continue to be committed members as adults and transfer happily and effectively to the adult programmes. But it does not help if there is a sense of separation from united Christian work on the campus, or if members are presented with a choice of either "fellowshipping" with all Christians or only with Deeper Life. Impressions of exclusivity and superiority can go both ways, mistrust develops, and intolerance grows. Thus the whole work can turn into a negative experience, both in terms of an individual's spiritual development and of Christian witness. It is possible to programme co-operation if you want to.

Working in mission – sharing the struggle

I went on to visit Umuahia, to the east of the capital Owerri, and more or less in the centre of the state. The pastor is brother Israel Nwachukwu, a bright young man who started Deeper Life there when he arrived to work as an accountant in 1980. A Bible study of five people has now grown to a Sunday attendance of 450. He left accountancy to work full time for Deeper Life in 1986. He apologised that his church was not larger, but he had been seriously ill between February and August 1988. He had been "almost dying" – but he had regained full health by the end of October when I met him.

In Umuahia I met a young British family working in Nigeria as mission partners through CMS (Church Missionary Society). Martin and Sheena Greenfield – with their little daughter Hannah – work at Trinity Theological College, a joint venture of the Anglican, Methodist and Presbyterian churches. We talked a little about the work of mission, and the personal cost involved. Something which came across to me time and again about Deeper Life was their missionary commitment, whatever the cost. And here was a young couple, giving up a much more comfortable lifestyle in Britain, in the service of the same Lord. I was wondering what the relevance of my visit to Deeper Life might be to Christians in Britain, when Martin talked about his own feelings when he visits churches there:

"When we visit a church in Britain we want to find them doing the work of the Gospel: struggling, praying, trying. Some people working in mission here are really struggling – then when they visit Britain, they find a lot of Christians there not doing very much at all. When we visit a church we would really like to share with them in their work of mission there; to be with them and pray with them. Then they might join with us more, and pray with us in our mission here."

Working in mission means, it seems, being part of a struggle. Deeper Life have a clear identity, and through their workers' meetings, retreats, and crusades there is a real sense of struggling together for the sake of the Gospel. That unity makes them stronger. If there were an even wider sharing of the struggle – between denominations, and across the world – then it would undoubtedly be to God's glory. Furthermore, Christian mission might be more effective generally, and individuals might be better able simply to continue that struggle.

7

A faith to be experienced

I asked Kumuyi to clarify some of the teachings and practices of the Deeper Life Bible Church.

Salvation

"Basically, we preach about repentance and believing the Gospel," Kumuyi said. "By repentance we mean that you turn away from your old ways, from what the Bible defines as 'sin', turn to the Lord, and receive Jesus as your personal Saviour. You repent, but you cannot save yourself. Jesus paid the whole price on the cross of Calvary. You are saved by believing that Jesus died for you in order to redeem you. It's the same thing as being 'born again' – different terminology for just the same experience."

Sanctification and Baptism in the Holy Spirit

"Sanctification is basically 'being set apart' – the human part of sanctification is that you set yourself apart unto God. We are all Christians after we are born again, but in the Bible the Corinthian Christians were still babes in the Lord. Paul the apostle talked about their carnality, selfishness and a lot of other things. Jesus told his disciples who believed on him, 'Rejoice because your names are written in heaven,' which means that they were not total strangers to him. But two of his disciples came wanting to sit, one on the right side, the other on the left. We would say that though they were worshipping God, there was a lot of selfishness in their approach. But when you set yourself apart to the glory of God and leave everything to God, then he cleanses you from within of what you cannot free yourself from. Basically, this is a Wesleyan type of approach to the deeper experiences of the Christian life. That doesn't mean that after that time I cannot be tempted to be selfish, but at least I'm aware. I always want to tell the Lord that he should just make me want to seek for his glory, rather than for selfish ends."

I asked Pastor Kumuyi whether that meant that as we grow in faith, we sin less. He replied, "OK, but not that we are sinless. It's not 'sinless perfection'."

But when I was in the north of Nigeria, Kano State Overseer, Ransom Bello, did seem to be saying that after "sanctification", Christians are sinless. "Adam was sinless – but even he was tempted and fell," he told me. "It is my duty to remain holy. My cleansing is by both my action and God's action. We can be blameless – a pure heart – a holy heart – but no human being can be faultless. As we relate to people, we discover our faults! I forgot to take in my brother's washing when it rained, and he had even asked me to watch out for it. That was a fault – I'm only human. We can resist sin every day and be overcoming every day – it's enough. Nobody can be holier than Adam and Eve, and they fell. If there wasn't a need for obedience in the Christian life, there wouldn't be growth."

I asked S.O. Adejumo, Deeper Life State Overseer for Kwara, to explain what he understood by the work of the Spirit:

"When the children of Israel were in the wilderness, they grumbled. It is the same with Christians – they want to be satisfied, and selfishness creeps in. So the second work of grace (after salvation itself, which is the first work of grace) is sanctification. Its effect is to remove the selfish nature, and to start putting others first, loving God more, sacrificing for others and for God. You still need to grow in grace – your heart is tender, you are easily corrected, you are not faultless, but you have a heart of flesh, not of stone. Absolute perfection is only reached when we get to heaven – but on earth we can lead a victorious life, and live with a pure motive. The baptism in the Holy Spirit is the third work of grace. Normally the evidence for this is praying in a well-articulated language that you have not spoken before. It leads to a deeper prayer life, insight into the word of God, and effectiveness in witness; especially where you have been failing before, people you evangelise will melt by the Spirit's power."

As we were trying to clarify all this, we started laughing. Adejumo said, "Of course, one should be careful of being too logical! First, second, third, and all that. Every aspect of our life is by the grace of God. Is healing the fourth work of grace? Is provision the fifth? What are the sixth, seventh, and eighth? If I cut myself, the wound heals by itself, and that is God's grace at work. Salvation is all that is necessary – look at John 3.16. The thief on the cross got to heaven just by that act of faith (Luke 23.43). But for one's own good one should seek to grow in grace."

Kumuyi himself defined to me the baptism in the Holy Spirit in this way:

"We believe that Jesus said that we can receive the infilling of the baptism in the Holy Spirit. If we pray in faith, God will baptise us in the Holy Spirit. When he does, according to his promise, he will show us things to come. We will be more open to the Spirit of God and we are more open to the leadings of the Spirit. Then when we read our Scriptures, he throws more light on them, and we understand better. Then he said that the things he has spoken, he will bring to our remembrance. We say that it's easier for us, for the Spirit to help us recall the Scriptures at a time of need. Like when Jesus was tempted, he said, 'It is written . . .' Sometimes we

know the Scriptures, ordinarily, but at the time of need in
our lives, the more we are in the Spirit, the more he is able
to help us recall the Scriptures for our benefit. Also he helps
us in prayer. We all pray, but we are able to pray with more
faith and with the sense of a child of God, as we are baptised
in the Holy Spirit."

I saw one result of this sequence of teaching – particularly
on sanctification and sinlessness – in the prayer life of the
church. Confession as such does not figure very highly.
Repentance is taken very seriously – and there are always
opportunities to repent for sin committed. But their doctrine
takes at face value the Scripture:

> No-one who is born of God will continue to sin, because
> God's seed remains in him; he cannot go on sinning,
> because he has been born of God. (1 John 3.9)

Therefore, if you are "born again" (a true Christian) you will
not sin, so there is no need to confess. I found this theology
quite hard to handle. The Deeper Life leaders emphasised
to me that Christians still make mistakes and have faults,
although these lessen as you grow in the faith. But they
also maintained that Christians don't actually "sin", by
definition. I think that in saying this you could end up
calling one thing a "sin" before your conversion and the
same thing simply a "mistake" after conversion!

I mentioned to Pastor Kumuyi that some Christians talk
about the experience of being "slain in the Spirit". I didn't
see any evidence of this in Deeper Life.

"No. We have not seen much of that with us, and I have
not really done much study on it myself. I know that Paul the
apostle, on the way to Damascus, was overpowered by that
experience. In the Old Testament, the prophets had some
peculiar experiences, but I have been a little bit reserved
in developing doctrines out of experiences. I would have
reservations about thinking that the height of spirituality,
or the measure of the presence of God in a meeting, is
determined by being slain in the Spirit. I've heard of some

who will think much of that, and then they feel that whether
you are healed afterwards or not, or whether you really had a
measurable benefit or not, being slain in the Spirit itself has
its advantage. I'm not saying they are wrong, I'm only saying
that I've not seen that. It may be there in the Scripture, but
I've not seen it. I'm open to teaching, and 'education' on that
line."

The other side of the sanctification experience – what God
does in us – is what we can do for God. I asked Kumuyi to
expand his definition of "holiness" and "doing good works".
He explained:

"Love will not do anything evil to other people. When
you become a Christian you begin to do unto others what
you want them to do unto you. You apply that Christian
principle in your life and relationships. It is not that good
works save us, it is our faith in Christ that saves us. But as
a consequence of knowing Christ, we will not want to do evil
against our neighbours.

"And we grow in it, of course. Things that I might not
have been able to do for my fellow brother or sister five years
ago, as I know the Lord more, I will be able to do now. And
also things I may not be able to do for my neighbour now,
maybe in five years time, if I'm growing, I might be able to
do with relative ease."

Uniformity

Avoiding the potholes on a minor tarred road in Ilorin in
Kwara State, at the same time as overtaking a lorry, or
avoiding a taxi that has stopped to drop off or pick up
a passenger, I made my way to a meeting sponsored by
Deeper Life for ministers of other churches. A large room
had been booked on neutral territory. One of the ministers
present had travelled five hours from Lokoja just to be
there. The content of the teaching was good, and in this
role Deeper Life are probably most importantly offering
some kind of pastoral concern for these people who are

often free-lance, independent, giving a lot and maybe not receiving very much.

The fact that there were only independent Pentecostal ministers present at this meeting (the same group as were in the significant majority at the Deeper Life National Ministers' Conference I attended at IBTC in Lagos) demonstrates where Deeper Life is most at home and best received. So I can sympathise with those of other traditions and convictions who come less often. The teaching is well-studied and thorough, but you can get tired of being exhorted to "get your sanctification" and "get your baptism in the Holy Spirit as evidenced by speaking in tongues". In my own experience of faith, in my relationships with Christians and churches in different places, and in my reading of Scripture, I have seen variety rather than uniformity in the ways in which people come to God and stay with him.

Pastor Kumuyi is anxious for uniformity as a weapon against misunderstanding and false doctrine. But I don't see God creating uniformity. I see a new creation in every baby born – uniquely individual, with a potentially unique individual relationship with God. I think God is big enough for that!

The whole motivation for uniformity and effective teaching is a recognition of our frailty and fragility in faith. If someone drops out (or moves on) then we should see what our relationship with that person is – and test our own relationship with God – rather than simply declaring that "they can't have really been born again", as evidenced by the fact that they have abandoned true doctrine as we understand it.

I think people in Nigeria are looking for God. I believe that "salvation" comes only through trusting in Christ, which brings spiritual regeneration. But if some people testify to finding God in a different way from the way we understand, then we have to come up with a better answer than saying it is only due to bribery or "backsliding". Is the Holy Spirit so weak?

Miracles

I had the chance to discuss with the State Overseer for
Kwara, S.O. Adejumo, a couple of the issues where Deeper
Life members seem to feel themselves to be different from
other groups. I asked him about the doctrine I had heard
in Deeper Life all over Nigeria, that you can expect your
miracle from God if you have enough faith, and if there
is no unconfessed sin in your life. At the Ilorin Miracle
Revival Hour, Pastor Adejumo himself had been promising
and praying at the end:

"I believe God wants to change your life tonight. Ask God
what you want him to do for you. If you are sick, I command
every sickness out in Jesus' name. From your head to your
toe, from tonight you are healthy."

He explained to me:

"The preacher has to preach as if everybody will receive
their miracle. He doesn't want to puncture their faith. It
is a question of my obedience to raise their level of faith.
Of course, nobody can determine a miracle for anybody
except God himself – and he may not do it. But it is our
duty to raise the believers' level of faith. It is true that
many people will not receive their miracle, but if you have
all the faith, I believe you will either receive your miracle,
or know for sure from God that the miracle is not for you.
The Miracle Revival Hour is to raise the faith level. The
Sunday worship is to teach and stabilise the people, so
that they don't get discouraged by the hardships in their
lives."

One problem some Christians have with "miracles" in the
church (although it didn't seem to alarm Jesus or the early
apostles) is that miracles are also widely reported to be taking
place outside the Christian faith, as well as within it. Where
do these miracles come from, and if they take place outside
Christianity, what do they prove anyway? I asked Kumuyi
what his attitude was to miracles which reportedly occur in
the sects and the cults.

"To deny that such things take place at all in other than Christian gatherings would be to neglect and overlook a lot of information that is available," he admitted. "The Bible even calls those things miracles and wonders:

For false Christs and false prophets will appear and perform great signs and miracles to deceive even the elect – if that were possible. (Matthew 24.24)

Then Revelation 13 tells us of a Beast which looks miraculous to the world, but inspired writing accounts it as something that is coming from a satanic source. There are also references in Revelation 16.14 and 2 Thessalonians 2.9,10. So from the Bible perspective, it's true that those miracles can take place. But our own attitude is that those miracles alone are not enough for a Gospel minister. We have to see that the person working the miracles actually believes in the Lord, has a transparent type of life, and is not depending on another source. Even if somebody is using that type of satanic source to work miracles, people will still follow because they are ignorant. That is why we believe that church growth is not just getting a large number of people together. We need to know that a person is actually preaching the Gospel and staying with the word of God. It is not just that the miracles are taking place. And Jesus said that not all that say, 'Lord, Lord,' will get into the kingdom of heaven. Many will say in the last days, 'Have we not done this, even in his name?' and yet he will say he never knew them (Matthew 7.21–3). So those things are possible."

All the time I was in Imo State, Owerri Deeper Life Bible Church itself was running a "Heaven-sent Miracle Thunder" programme. Every night for a week, Monday to Saturday, the church was open for a special Miracle Revival programme, each evening session lasting from five thirty until around nine thirty. It was an opportunity for the Owerri Deeper Life members to strengthen their own faith, and also an evangelistic opportunity to reach out to friends and neighbours, to have something special to invite them to. The first hour or so consisted of choruses and prayer, then a twenty-minute explanation of the Gospel, with an opportunity for individuals to respond, either in terms of becoming born again, or in terms of recommitment. After more prayer and singing, together with identifying and welcoming "first-timers" and those who had just been born again, came a forty-five minute message to do with faith and miracles, followed by half an hour of "ministration and receiving of miracles". The closing fifteen to twenty minutes of the service consisted of a song, testimonies, and a closing prayer.

Until a long way into the services I attended, trucks and minibuses were arriving, bringing crowds of people to the church from all over Owerri – each night many of them turned out to be in the church for the first time. The enthusiasm of the members for inviting people, together with Deeper Life's reputation, was certainly drawing them in. The large white banner behind the lectern on the concrete dais announced in red writing, "With God all things are possible, Matthew 19.26", and in white on a blue splash, "EXPECT YOUR MIRACLE". The lectern itself was attractively decorated with a white and blue cloth with red, white, and pink rosettes sewn on to it. Pot plants were also spread along the front of the dais to create a comfortable atmosphere. The church is a concrete building with a metal roof, and a styled front reflecting the architecture of the Gbagada church. The original building was single-storey with three columns of benches. It is now being expanded on each side to double the ground floor capacity, and work is going ahead to build galleries on each side above the new extensions. Men and women were crowded in everywhere – but the central (original) area was reserved for non-members.

The messages were based on such verses as:

For God so loved the world that he gave his one and only Son, that whoever believes in him shall not perish but have eternal life. (John 3.16)

When evening came, many who were demon-possessed were brought to Jesus, and he drove out the spirits with a word and healed all the sick. (Matthew 8.16)

Those who wanted to turn to Christ for the first time were led in a simple prayer:

"Our Father in heaven, I thank you because you are the God of heaven. I know that I am a sinner, but I thank you because I have heard your word tonight, that Jesus Christ came to save me from sin. Father, I'm sorry for all my sins. I turn my back on all my sins, and I turn to follow Jesus Christ as my saviour. Jesus, come into my life. I receive you by faith, use your blood to wash away all my sins, change my life. I believe I am now saved. Thank you for saving me. In Jesus' name I pray. Amen."

Those who felt they needed a miracle were led in prayer thus:

"In your heart, believe God and expect your miracle. On the cross Jesus defeated every evil power and every sickness. We demand, every sickness and evil power, in the name of Jesus, release your captives. Amen. Wherever you are hiding, come out in Jesus' name. Amen. Paralysis: come out in Jesus' name. Amen. Blindness: come out in Jesus' name. Amen. Cancer: come out in Jesus' name. Amen. Dumbness: come out in Jesus' name. Amen. Deafness: come out in Jesus' name. Amen. You devil: come out in Jesus' name. AMEN!

"If you are barren, if you have had no child since you have been married, touch your stomach, and in nine months' time you will have a child. Be healed. Be free. Father, give them a child, in Jesus' name. Amen. If you have diabetes and have been taking insulin every day, raise your hand. I break the power of that sickness in Jesus' name. Amen. Go out of that body. The Holy Spirit is coming on you now. If your pregnancy is lasting more than nine months, let that evil bond be broken in Jesus' name, Amen. Let that evil bond be broken in Jesus' name, Amen. Let that evil bond be broken in Jesus' name, Amen. You are free in the name of Jesus Christ."

As a queue formed of people who wanted to give their testimonies, we were led in prayers of thanksgiving for all that we had received, "Thank God that you are a new creature. Your problems have all vanished away."

I have only been able to record in this book a small fraction of all the testimonies that I heard as I travelled. By the end of my journey, though, I had become tired of this kind of message. Yes, there were people who were healed. But there were also those who were not. I was sitting in the same row as a pregnant woman with a very weak and sick child on her lap, and the woman herself was barely strong enough to stand. There were also two men on the same row whom I noticed: one was blind, a patient and dignified-looking gentleman, the other a young, thin, lame man who could hardly stand unsupported. All three of these shuffled in at the start of the service, and all three shuffled out, with blank eyes, and discouraged faces, at the end. People whose lives are hard enough to start with were picked up for a moment, then dropped down to fall hard on the floor once more. There was no counselling, guidance, or encouragement for those who continued in need (probably the majority) except to come again tomorrow. I would want to treat people who are hurting with more respect and integrity. They were left to struggle on their own with their unanswered prayer.

But, for all that, the people keep coming. It is part of normal Nigerian flamboyancy to exaggerate. In Nigeria I have often been on the receiving end of outlandish promises which never materialised! (To be fair, this was less common in Deeper Life than more generally.) Perhaps the people take these declarations of miraculous intervention at that outlandish level and treat the whole thing a bit like bingo: "You can expect your miracle, and one day you will get it, but it really will be a miracle if you get it tonight." If that is the mentality that is operating, then I think there is a danger of the Gospel being treated in a similar manner, as something which may or may not be relevant. If you are promised salvation by faith, and healing as a consequence, then if you don't get your healing, why bother with salvation?

For the Nigerian, life can be seen as a lottery. If you do the right things you have a chance of winning the jackpot, but you are not disappointed if you win only a small prize, or even if you win nothing – at least you tried. "You tried" is a common compliment which is paid whether or not you have succeeded.

This works out in turning to God often, in different ways. But it does mean that in school, for instance, students will spend more energy praying for success than working for it; and if they gain success it is a sign of God's favour rather than their own effort, or that of their teachers. It is similar with promotion at work. Promotion is expected as a matter of right after only a few years, and when it does come it is like winning a lottery prize rather than as the result of conscientious work.

Perhaps this whole culture of giving up oneself to the forces of chance – a kind of fatalism, trusting in a god of chance who seems very capricious – is why there is little apparent disappointment at the non-occurrence of a miracle. You try – and you might get your miracle if God favours you. But if you don't get it, just try again. And of course, the danger here is that just as people turn to Deeper Life because other avenues have "failed", so there will be those whom Deeper Life fail, and so they move on to other systems. The "back door" in Deeper Life leads to other paths, other places, other gods, where a miracle may be available. Such is the danger of promising too much, of preaching with such assurance.

Becoming a member of Deeper Life

Akinwande is Co-ordinator for Agege District in Lagos. He explained that membership as such was quite simple:

"The General Superintendent always emphasises the need to be born again. You may be coming to the church, but if you're not born again you're not a member. The basis of membership is your own testimony of being born again."

Baptism

In Maiduguri (Borno State) I was able to witness a baptism service – the first they had held for a year. We were directed to the riverside, where there were several men and boys washing clothes. Pastor Adebayo and his assistants found a place where the bank was smooth, and the water deep enough. The Muslim doing his laundry at the same place did not seem to be disturbed by our presence – just mildly interested. The hundred or so baptism candidates had gathered under a nearby mango tree. They were singing choruses, and giving their testimonies to each other. Then they filed down to the waterside.

Pastor Adebayo gave them a short exhortation, reminding them that water baptism is not a sin-remover – "it is the blood of Jesus that cleanses us from sin"; it is belief which matters, not baptism, but baptism is both public and scriptural. He reminded the people that after his own baptism, Jesus was found in the wilderness – not in a beer parlour or harlot's house.

As I understand them, Deeper Life teach that the proper method of baptism is for adults, after conversion, by immersion in a river. If you have been born again and baptised before joining Deeper Life, then you do not need to be baptised again. If you were baptised as an infant, or as an adult but before true conversion to Christ, then you still need to be baptised "in the proper way".

After a short time of prayer the candidates formed two lines – sisters and brothers – and started singing choruses. Pastor Adebayo and his two assistants waded out into the river, to be able to baptise three at a time. Three more brothers positioned themselves in the river to help the candidates get back to the bank, because the current was quite strong. I had got used in Deeper Life to people praying and worshipping in a very self-controlled manner, but this experience seemed to affect people very deeply. I regret I did not have time to stay to witness everybody's baptism, but of those that I did see, a fair number coming out of the water looked overwhelmed. The brothers assisting against the current actually had to carry some people out of the water after their immersion.

But I had to leave as I was already late and they were expecting me in Kano. We walked away from the ceremony, up the river bank and along towards the main road. The singing died away in the distance, and by the time we got to the mango tree, all I could hear was the clapping. Then the crickets and cicadas, and the motor noises from the road, drowned out the distant sounds of celebration. We reached our car and climbed in. I felt as though I had walked through twenty centuries.

I asked Pastor Kumuyi at what point in Deeper Life's history people started asking for water baptism.

"We have been doing water baptism since we started, but what we would do then is to take them to other ministers, like the Four Square Gospel Church here in Lagos, because they agreed that they wouldn't tie them down to the Four Square. Some of them stayed in the Four Square church, some of them went to other churches. But now we are a church, we conduct the water baptism ourselves. Once we see that their life corresponds to their testimony, that they are actually born again, then we allow them to be baptised in water. In Lagos, we do that generally about once a month, and we do it by immersion."

Akinwande is Co-ordinator in Lagos for Agege District. He explained:

"Without being born again no one is qualified to be baptised. Individuals will give their testimony, then they will go for eight evenings of baptism training in their Zones. The training exposes them to the Bible, so that we don't just take anything for granted. The Spirit of God should testify to their conversion. Then they come together to be interviewed at the central church. They give their testimonies, then, if we are sure, by the grace of God there is nothing hindering them from being baptised. Very, very few drop out of baptism training, and even if they do they will be given an opportunity to come back."

Thus Deeper Life is not a sect. It is possible at any stage to drop out, but not many do. They want to stay, and the pastoring and teaching is such that they are enabled to stay.

"Confirmation?"

At one Sunday worship service at Gbagada, after the "Search the Scripture" session on following up new Christians, came the regular opportunity to ask questions of the pastor. Acts 14.21–2 had been referred to in the study:

> They preached the good news in that city and won a large number of disciples. Then they returned to Lystra, Iconium and Antioch, strengthening [KJV: "confirming"] the disciples and encouraging them to remain true to the faith. "We must go through many hardships to enter the kingdom of God," they said.

One of the people who raised their hands was a young man who was asked by the ushers to make his way to a microphone. He came forward and, rather nervously, asked his question of Pastor Kumuyi:

"What does it mean in Acts 14 when it says that Paul and Barnabas confirmed the disciples? Was that what they did after baptism, like in the Anglican and some other churches here in Nigeria?"

"Which church are you a member of?" Kumuyi asked the young man.

"The Deeper Life Bible Church."

"Since when?"

"1985."

"Have you been baptised?"

"Yes – in August 1987."

"Have you started confirmation classes yet?" Kumuyi asked, to laughter from the congregation.

"No."

"Now we must be concerned about what the Bible says. There are churches that practise infant baptism, but those infants are only babies and don't know how to repent and be born again. You're a 'member' of the church, but you may not be born again. Look at Matthew 15.1–3:

> Then some Pharisees and teachers of the law came to Jesus from Jerusalem and asked, 'Why do your disciples break the tradition of the elders? They don't wash their hands before they eat!' Jesus replied, 'And why do you break the command of God for the sake of your tradition?'

There are some people in those churches who are more worried about tradition than the command of God. There are people who are 'confirmed', who drink alcohol, smoke tobacco, get involved with adultery, polygamy, or secret societies. They are only 'nominal Christians'. But if you are a disciple, it means that a conversion experience has taken place – you forsake your sins and embrace Christ:

> Anyone who does not carry his cross and follow me cannot be my disciple. (Luke 14.27)

Then it is important to continue:

> To the Jews who had believed him, Jesus said. 'If you hold to my teaching [KJV: "continue in my word"], you are really my disciples.' (John 8.31)

When Luke writes about Paul and Barnabas 'confirming' the disciples in Acts 14, did he use a ritual, or a ceremony? No. They were exhorting them to 'continue'. You can't continue something you haven't started! The 'confirmation' is what we are doing for you here – like when you ask a question. All that we are doing on Sunday, Monday, and Thursday is confirmation.

"This is confirmation:

to prepare God's people for works of service, so that the
body of Christ may be built up until we all reach unity
in the faith and in the knowledge of the Son of God and
become mature, attaining to the whole measure of the
fullness of Christ. Then we will no longer be infants,
tossed back and forth by the waves, and blown here and
there by every wind of teaching and by the cunning and
craftiness of men in their deceitful scheming (Ephesians
4.12–14).

It is confirmation when you have been taught and are no
more a child. The New Testament does not have a religious
programme for those who are not converted."

But it seems to me that dissatisfaction with the local
expression of a Christian practice does not invalidate it.
There may be many who call themselves Christians who
have been confirmed yet who appear to engage in an
un-Christian lifestyle. But who is going to cast the first
stone? There are many fine Christians who were baptised as
infants and were subsequently confirmed, and who grew as
Christian adults. There are also those who have been "born
again" as adults, received adult baptism by immersion –
and then "backslidden". You cannot prove the inadequacy
of a particular church's practice by pointing the finger at its
failures.

Babies and Children

The cases for and against infant baptism have been well
argued. Suffice it to say that if we look at the Bible, there are
cases of households being baptised (Acts 16.15, 1 Corinthians
1.16). Most Christians now acknowledge that what we need
in society are more Christian *families*, and we therefore need
to do something with the babies!

Nevertheless, Deeper Life's evangelistic vision is of adults,
as individuals, repenting of their sins and turning to Christ.
Children, as such are therefore "lost" until "found". While

I am prepared to accept that there are many Christians who find, in all conscience, that they cannot baptise infants, I found it an omission in Deeper Life that there was no kind of dedication or even thanksgiving ceremony for newborn infants beyond the participation of the House Caring Fellowship in the normal naming ceremony.

This is not to say that Deeper Life are not increasingly concerned about their pregnant women, new babies, and children. An important development for the women in Deeper Life in 1983 was the starting of the Faith Maternity Home, just over the road from the Gbagada church building. Founded to provide a free maternity service for the Deeper Life members who need it, it is a valuable ministry when so many of the people are poor and medical help is so expensive. It is currently staffed full time by Comfort Fawole, a qualified resident midwife. Other Deeper Life members who are qualified midwives help out in their spare time. They have ante-natal clinics each week, as well as a one-bed examination room, a two-bed delivery room, and a six-bed post-natal ward. Any problems are referred to the nearby Gbagada General Hospital, while the Faith Maternity Home itself handled just over 300 deliveries in 1987. They keep busy! The day I visited I met two babies: one six hours old, the other had been in the world just two days.

The children's Deeper Life Bible Church started with about 150 children in 1983 after a four-day programme of rallies around Lagos to publicise its formation. The leader at that time was Ngozi Ejiogu. Currently the Children's Co-ordinator is Grace Adebayo.

"The children's work of the church means a lot," she told me. "The foundation needs to be strong, because the children are the leaders of tomorrow. Once they are converted and brought up in the way of the Lord, their lives will affect their families and the whole nation. We need to sacrifice whatever we have for the children. Some children come to us from homes where their parents are not converted, then they face persecution and are stopped from coming to church. But as children they still need to be obedient, and must be good children. Some parents have now been converted through the conviction of the children. Some children are involved with occultic groups – many have been delivered and given their lives to Christ. Many of our children are really becoming evangelists. Last Easter we had a children's evangelistic programme, and many adults were converted through the witness of the children. The power of God was really manifested there."

At the Children's Church on the Sunday I visited them in October 1988, there were over 13,000 children aged between three and fifteen. In October 1987 a Monday Bible study for the children was started. After one year, around 1,700 children regularly attend. The Thursday Miracle Revival Hour for children was started in April 1988, and after just six months had reached a regular attendance of about 1,500.

The Lord's Supper

I asked Pastor Kumuyi what was the role of the Lord's Supper in Deeper Life worship, as in all the time I was with them, I saw no evidence of this ordinance.

"In some of the states they have planted the local fruit of the vine. When it is fresh they can easily use it. In Lagos we have been having difficulty. That's what has been delaying us, because of the large number."

"So have you celebrated the Lord's Supper here?"

"No, only among the workers before, nationally."

"So it will be quite a rare event?"

"Once we start the process, not every Sunday of course, but it will be regular."

"Do you have any other 'ordinances' apart from Baptism and the Lord's Supper in the church?"

"No."

Death

I asked Akinwande in Lagos what happens when someone dies:

"When a member of the church dies, we take the corpse to the burial ground and appointed leaders will conduct the funeral service. They may be appointed by the GS, or this may be done in the Zones."

Philip Olasupo Oluwi (Mushin Co-ordinator) added:

"In the case of bereavement we rally round. If need be, church members will buy a coffin, and even provide a vehicle to take the corpse to the family's home town. Deeper Life members will accompany the bereaved and the corpse, while we also send a letter through the relevant State Overseer to Deeper Life members in that locality so that they can rally round too."

While I was in Lagos, in Surulere District the husband of a Deeper Life member went one Wednesday to the bank where he worked. When he left the bank to come home, he was carrying a briefcase and hailed a taxi. Some armed robbers came up, shot him dead, grabbed the bag, and made off into the crowd. They obviously thought he was carrying a bag full of money, while it only contained a few papers. The Deeper Life sisters immediately gathered round to comfort the wife and protect her from her family – idol-worshippers who were trying to torture her into the traditional mourning by shaving her head and making her sleep on the floor. The District Co-ordinator was anxious that more Deeper Life members should go to help her straight away, and travel with her back to the state where her family live. He was also going to ask the GS to write to the Deeper Life State Overseer there, and her local Deeper Life pastor, to ensure that the brethren there continued to protect her and look after her.

This level of practical support is one of the reasons why there are so few full-time paid pastoral staff in Deeper Life.

"We have to help our people," Kumuyi explained. "Not with elaborate things, but when there is a death, for example, we help with the coffin and with transportation. Many people in Lagos are from other states, and if we lose anybody their relatives may want the person to be buried in their state – so sometimes we take on that responsibility. At the Faith Maternity Home, we don't take money from any of the people who come in there. Sometimes when our members have some basic needs we have to help. So we spend money on those areas, taking care of the people. Too many people on the full-time staff here would really drain us dry of the money we need to help the people!"

Caring

It seems that it is in the caring that much of the life and strength of the Deeper Life church occurs – practical, everyday caring – together with Bible study and evangelism. The miracles and healings are obviously encouraging signs of God's powerful involvement in the life of the church – but the caring continues for every member, every day.

Akinwande wanted to make a point of this caring aspect of the church which all the members participate in and experience:

"We emphasise both the spiritual life, and also catering for members' needs. The church cares for the needy. If a family needs financial aid, the House Caring Fellowship leader will see what to do. If the House Caring Fellowship cannot help, they ask the Area. If the Area cannot help, they ask the Zone! By the grace of God the church has helped many families with practical caring and love. One man was not OK financially, so his House Caring Fellowship paid his house rent for him. One needy family was given foodstuffs by the House Caring Fellowship. I know a brother who needed some material to make himself some clothes. Somebody wrapped some cloth, wrote the brother's name on it, and left it at the church. So the brother received the cloth and he didn't know who it came from. I have seen many things like that. If you have a problem, another member of your House Caring Fellowship will come to pray with you. Many problems have been solved in this way."

Philip Olasupo Oluwi added:

"If a wife has an unbelieving husband, we send a delegation to plead with the husband to allow his wife to continue coming to the church. It is like an extended family – a spiritual family – the whole of Deeper Life – in the membership of Deeper Life. Of course, if our neighbour is sick, we help – but the love and caring is not as deep as for a fellow-member. When a member is sick, it is the House Caring Fellowship's responsibility to take care of them: to visit, even sleep in their house, especially if they can't take care of themselves. The House Caring Fellowship will cook for them, and buy what they need.

"Recently a fire burnt a member's home. We got them cooking utensils, clothing, food, and resettled them immediately. We provide food or money for our members who are unemployed. There is a couple I know who had a house on a government housing estate. He was out of work so they lost the house because they couldn't keep up the payments. We accommodated him and his family with another member."

As I travelled and spoke to people, I found many – particularly the poor – who had received both spiritually and materially through Deeper Life.

On the Sunday evening I was in Owerri I asked if I could sit in on one of the House Caring Fellowships for sisters, and was told that this would be possible. I was warned by one of the brothers that the sisters would be late because of their family duties of cooking food and looking after the children. I wondered to myself why, if that was a problem for the sisters, they were asked to meet at an inconvenient time, or why the brothers didn't lend a hand. I got along to Ikenegbu in Owerri where a group of women were, in fact, already gathered on a verandah and on the ground outside in the shade of the house.

Charity Nwakonkwo led us in a simple but effective time of testimony, Bible study and prayer. The effect of the Heaven-sent Miracle Thunder programme that week was evident in that, of the sixteen women present, six were newcomers. If that pattern was repeated through the church, and the people stayed, significant growth will have taken place! The meeting was in a mixture of Igbo and, for my benefit, English. One of the testimonies in Igbo was to the effect that three weeks previously one of the sisters had had her house broken into, and had N60 stolen. She came to her House Caring Fellowship for prayer. She was reporting that due to the programme in church that week, a girl had come and confessed that she was the thief, returned the money, and had joined Deeper Life.

But the great strength of the House Caring Fellowship system is that it is a place where people can bring their needs. They share in the expectation of God's intervention, but there is also obviously great power in the act of sharing itself. Let me list just some of the prayer requests that night:

I have been married for two years, but have no children yet; and I want God to protect my family.

I am looking for a job, and I want salvation.

I want the Lord to heal my skin problem.

I have been married for three and a half years, but have no children.

I want God to give me a job.

I want God to give me the power to do his work.

I need money to start work in the market next year.

I have a fever.

I want my husband to be saved, and I need wisdom in all that I do.

My husband is overdue for promotion.

I am pleading that God almighty should have mercy, and provide me with a life partner.

If we are engaged in a struggle, we do well to share it with each other, and to share it with God. The faith that people experience in Deeper Life certainly has its powerful, spiritual dimension, but they also receive practical love and participate in mutual concern.

8

"God blessed my beans"

From south-west to north-east

I hope I have managed to convey to the non-Nigerian reader the wide variety of cultures and climates that can be encountered in this richly diverse country. I spent a lot of my time in Lagos, at Deeper Life's central church. But I knew I had to get out and go somewhere to see Deeper Life in a completely different setting. So I left Lagos early one Tuesday morning that October to travel to Borno State and its capital, Maiduguri, in the far north-east of Nigeria. It is virtually the farthest you can go from Lagos, and still be in Nigeria. Deeper Life formed their first fellowship there as far back as 1978. Unfortunately the airline pilot did not show up at the airport, so the journey did not turn out to be as easy as I had hoped. We managed to get on another flight as far as Jos (about half-way), and from there we would continue our journey by road.

As soon as I got out of the plane at Jos the difference in atmosphere and climate was striking. Jos is on a high plateau, and thus cooler than other parts of Nigeria. I could feel the cool breeze, but the heat was so dry compared with the humidity of Lagos that the breeze was hardly refreshing. As you travel north in Nigeria, the environment becomes arid. (If you continued north through the neighbouring country of Niger you would reach the Sahara Desert). So as we drove from Jos up to Maiduguri, cacti began to form a significant part of the landscape. If planted close together, they can make an efficient fence. If growing singly, they are a convenient tethering post for a goat. Outside the cities on the way, most people were living in enclosed mud-built compounds with thatched roofs. After we descended from the plateau, the hilly landscape flattened out as we travelled, and trees became smaller, fewer and farther between. As the trees become rarer, so collecting firewood becomes a task (or even a business), and deforestation becomes a problem. We often passed children in twos and threes carrying home bundles of firewood for the evening, which they would have collected after school, or after a day's work on the farm. Also by the roadside would be piles of wood for sale for the more monied members of the community. And as each year the trees become rarer, the fertile soil which the tree roots used to hold together is washed away by the rain. The government has a tree-planting programme, but it is difficult to keep up with the local energy needs of the people.

And it was hot and dry! Some slight relief came through having the car windows open – but it was like having an electric fan heater full on in your face! When we were driving behind a lorry its exhaust fumes stung my eyes and nose.

Our driver from Jos to Maiduguri was a Muslim, so we had to stop when it was time for him to pray. Prayer is one of the five pillars of Islam, and it is necessary for a Muslim to pray at set times five times a day. So at three forty-five and six thirty he parked the car and found a suitable space to pray for a few moments. Some non-Muslims may complain at the delay – I thought stopping for a break from time to time was not such a bad idea, and might actually help the driver to drive us more safely! I was travelling with Deeper Life brother Richard Adebayo, who is State Overseer for Borno, and Pastor of the Deeper Life Bible Church in Maiduguri. As we waited the first time, he told me, "You have to be sympathetic! I was once a Muslim, they are

my brothers! And we have something to learn from these
Muslims. They pray five times a day, and give generously
to those in need."

Seven and a half hours after leaving Jos we entered
Maiduguri by its smart wide dual carriageway. Off to the
right the Deeper Life Bible Church was signposted down a
sandy street. A welcome sight after a long day!

Maiduguri – the major city of the Kanuri people – is
flat, clean and spacious, with uncongested streets. Large
deciduous trees have been planted to make the city attractive
– and to provide shade. Most buildings are just one or two
storeys high. Every few hundred yards there are mats on
the ground, some of which are for sleeping on. Others
act as Muslim praying grounds, and are well used. The
concrete buildings with corrugated iron roofs are painted
in pastel colours, and most of the paintwork on the public
buildings was well maintained, giving a clean atmosphere in
the bright, clear light. The dominant religion is proclaimed
by the first building you see on entering the city after the
magnificent Maiduguri Arch – the El Kanemi College of
Islamic Theology. Just a little farther into the city you pass
the Government Arabic Teachers College.

In the market the stalls were constructed from thick
branches supporting thatched roofs, and as many men were
selling as women. In the south it is more common to find
only women selling in the markets. In the more rural areas
of the north, it will only be the men. Not all the children
are in school, and those that are not do not have to work
all the time – there is always time to play; throwing sticks
at trees to knock down firewood can be a good game too!
And movement is easier in a city where you don't really
need storm drains.

Walking through Maiduguri, there seemed to be lots of
fruit and vegetables for sale, but they do have problems
with drought, desertification and deforestation. One report
I read claimed that fifty-five per cent of Borno State could
be classified as "arid". It certainly was a hot, dry, dusty
atmosphere that completely dried out my nose and throat,

although Maiduguri does feel green, with grass still growing in the shady places. Hot gusts of wind blew sand and Harmattan dust into the city from the Sahara. In November and December it will get much dustier, and colder at night. The earth is hard-baked clay with a dusting of sand on top – small channels are sometimes cut through the sand by columns of soldier ants. Some men trading chickens by the roadside were selling them alive so that you could be sure the one you bought was fresh.

Workers' prayer meeting

The "workers'" prayer meeting is held in Maiduguri Deeper Life Bible Church on Wednesdays at 6 p.m. I arrived at the simple oblong building about ten minutes early, and a dozen or so brothers and sisters were there already. Most of them were praying individually, one of the women was feeding her baby, while another sister was humming a chorus. The plain wooden benches are set out on the swept concrete floor. I was grateful that fans hung from the unpainted asbestos ceiling, while the red metal shutters over the window spaces in the blue walls had been opened to let in the evening breeze. On a simple dais only fifty centimetres above floor level is a wooden lectern and microphone, but in each of the two front corners, tubs of artificial flowers brighten the atmosphere. Painted in red on the wall behind the lectern are the words, "With God all things are possible."

By six o'clock it was already dusk outside, so the light coming through the windows was fading. The buildings next door to the church on each side are very close, but through the left-hand window at the front you can catch sight of long stalks of millet waving over the breeze-block wall. The church was filling slowly, some people praying, others reading their Bibles. By the time it was dark, at six twenty, nearly a hundred workers were present – almost all of them in their twenties and thirties, together with a few babies and children. We sang choruses until seven o'clock, when the

pastor gave a relaxed exposition of Isaiah 45 for half an hour.
He particularly drew out the sentence:

> They will come over to you
>   and will be yours . . .
> They will bow down before you
>   and plead with you, saying,
> "Surely God is with you, and there is no other;
>   there is no other god." (Isaiah 45.14)

"We thank God that this is already happening to us here.
The people know that God is with us. God is with you. If you
have a headache or a stomach pain, you may feel it, but you
can drive it out, because God is with you."

From seven thirty to eight we then prayed together about
different things that came out of the passage. One brother
said we could look at verses 1–3 and substitute our own name
for that of Cyrus. The pastor amplified the idea by saying:

"This land is for Christ – everyone will hear, in the name
of Jesus. We need to break the fear of the people. They're
frightened that the Imam [Muslim teacher] will disapprove,
that they'll be thrown out of their village. We want to ask the
Lord to remove the cotton wool from their ears. We must
pray that the power of God will move. We must pray for
our Muslim friends, that they will know Christ. We must
exhort the Lord to pour down salvation, righteousness and
justice on this nation."

Another brother quoted verse 4 ("I call you by name") and
verse 5 ("I will strengthen you") to say, "God understands
our identity. God has strengthened us and equipped us. Let
the people see us and desire our God."

"We need to reach out to people," the pastor added. "God
knows their names, and we need his strength to reach out to
others."

A third brother read verse 19:

> I have not spoken in secret,
>   from somewhere in a land of darkness;
> I have not said to Jacob's descendants,

> "Seek me in vain,"
>> I, the LORD, speak the truth;
>>> I declare what is right.

and said, "God will give us his power and his Spirit, so that people will know we are not serving him in vain."

The pastor applied this: "Remember, God made the earth to praise him. We want a new anointing from above. We need spiritual food."

So, as the people contributed their ideas for prayer and praise, the pastor helped to keep the ideas together, and the people prayed aloud, talking to God over what they had thought as they listened to the exposition and tried to apply it. By the Spirit of God, the pastor and the people, the word of God in the Bible, and the Lord himself were interacting in this meeting. Their evangelistic concern came across strongly, as did their vulnerability in the predominantly Muslim north of Nigeria.

The needs of the poor

For the last half hour of the meeting – from eight to eight thirty – Pastor Adebayo led us in a time of prayer for Christian believers throughout the world, for the leaders and evangelists of Deeper Life, the pastors of other denominations, and for the Miracle Revival Hour next Friday evening. We then went on to pray for specific requests from some of the workers. One brother was being attacked by people involved with evil spirits, one sister's husband was threatening to throw her out because of her faith, one brother's vehicle was giving trouble and he couldn't afford to get it repaired, another brother had got a place at university, but didn't have enough money to go. These were just the type of prayer requests that became so familiar to me whilst I was with Deeper Life. People were conscious of evil – they knew when they were being attacked, and one of the great strengths the people perceived in Deeper Life was that they could deal with those forces effectively. Similarly it was often sadly true that an individual's conversion could bring conflict in a family – and this was just as likely to be the case whatever the religion of the other partner, whether Islam, nominal Christianity, or a local traditional religion. It seems the partner feels threatened by such a strong faith. A husband, in particular, will feel his authority and his expectation of marriage threatened when something seems to have a greater claim on his wife than he does. Most husbands find this very difficult to cope with.

Likewise, to pray for a troublesome vehicle is no trivial matter. A vehicle is hard to come by in Nigeria because things are so very expensive now, and the price of spare parts, if they are available at all, is astronomical. A lot of people – traders and drivers most obviously – will depend on their vehicles, so if one starts to go wrong it really is very bad news indeed for the owner. It could mean the end of their livelihood. Similarly, education is much prized and highly sought after. To gain admission to a university does not come easily at all – but then to be frustrated at the last moment because you cannot raise the money to pay the fees is distressing. We might not pray for these things in the UK – but it would be extraordinary and cruel not to pray for them in a church in Nigeria today. These are the real needs of the people, and Deeper Life are bringing them before God. I wonder if there are equivalent deep needs elsewhere that people are having to carry on their own.

Requests like this also proved again to me that Deeper Life are not being narrowly "triumphalistic" in their church life. They do not pretend to claim that you have no problems when you become a Christian, because every meeting has its long list of prayer requests from the brothers and sisters. They are not preaching a "prosperity gospel" when they accept that so many of their people are, and will be, poor. But that doesn't mean you don't pray about it, or that you don't hope, and even expect, God to do something about it, as a father loves his children. So the meeting concluded with the pastor encouraging us to "Pray for yourself. What do you want God to do for you?"

At the end of the meeting, a young mother brought forward her daughter who she was carrying on her back. The child was very sick with measles and we prayed for her. There was no instantaneous healing – we prayed for her again at the meeting the next Friday. But we prayed and we hoped – could we have done less?

The meeting closed with a reminder to come on time to the Miracle Revival Hour on Friday, and especially to look out for and welcome newcomers. We spent a few moments in silent prayer together, and then departed.

Isa Mohammed

After the meeting I met a young Fulani kola-nut seller from Bulabuline called Isa Mohammed, who had come into contact with Deeper Life just three weeks before. He was someone on the edge of society, with practically nothing to call his own. Another man was able to interpret for us as he hesitantly told me his story. As a simple street trader, the insecurity of his position in the community had made him insecure as a person, but he was beginning to find a new confidence. We were able to exchange smiles by the end of our conversation! One of the Maiduguri House Caring Fellowships was meeting, and Pastor Adebayo was speaking to them. Isa overheard what was being said. He heard that if he followed Christ, God would protect him and take care of his problems – now and in eternity. He was convinced by what he heard. The House Caring Fellowship members asked him whether he agreed with what the pastor had been saying, and he said he did. They prayed for his sickness – he was suffering from VD – and he had not had any of the symptoms since. He had tried many traditional medicines, and been to different hospitals, but for the two months before Deeper Life prayed for him he had been in pain.

"Now he has totally believed in Christ," the interpreter told me, "and he is going to continue. He will come to our services, and has joined the House Caring Fellowship. He says he doesn't mind what his family and friends may say, because he has seen the truth. None of them were able to help him when he wasn't well, but God helped him. His problem now is that everything is in English in Deeper Life. His mother tongue is Fulani, but in the church we do provide translation into Hausa, which he can speak a little bit."

Miracle Revival Hour

The Deeper Life Bible Church in Maiduguri fills twice on a Sunday, with 750 adults attending Sunday worship. Three hundred come to the Tuesday Bible study, while 340 regularly attend the Friday Miracle Revival Hour. There are 103 House Caring Fellowships. And the numbers are increasing. We visited the site for the new Deeper Life Bible Church. It is a little over an acre, in an undeveloped part of the city, but a good location which will become quite central fairly soon, with the current pace of building there. A number of Christian groups have been able to get land there (the Deeper Life Bible Church will be next to the Bible Society). They have a rectangular plot, a short distance from the main road into the city centre from the west. Previously this land was being farmed. We drove along the dried earth and sand path to the site near the railway line, walked past a self-governing herd of cattle, and through a millet field, the stalks three metres tall, waving grain over our heads. Fertile land, but still dry: the green leaves of the millet which had fallen to the ground, and the small green weeds and grass underfoot, crunched with brittle dryness as we walked through.

They are assured of a 5,000 capacity building here. If they can get a neighbouring plot, they could get up to 10,000. That is not an unreasonable vision, when they were able to get a 1,300 attendance at a crusade in the smaller settlement of Biu, two hours to the south of Maiduguri. And the people keep coming.

At the Miracle Revival Hour that evening there was a large bundle of prayer requests already handed in – people are bringing their needs to God in this place. Some of the requests were read out and specifically prayed for by everybody at the service – problems with sickness, demonic oppression, a woman with an alcoholic husband – then the whole bundle was lifted high for all to see with the words, "God knows the contents of every request here: joblessness, barrenness, troubles here and there. Please pray for all these needs."

And the people prayed.

One of the testimonies, after we finished praying, was from fifteen-year-old Onome Osiboku. She was wearing a simple yellow and blue patterned buba (blouse) and wrapper (skirt), and a white head-tie. She explained that her brother had been suffering from a stomach ulcer for the past three months. But the preceding Friday at the Miracle Revival Hour, the pastor had told those who have sick people at home to lay their hands on their own body in place of the sick. Then when they get home, to lay their hands on the sick at home, and that they would recover:

"I went home and laid my hand on my brother's stomach. My other brother was laughing at me. I said, 'Don't laugh at me. You watch and see what will happen!' Since I prayed, that brother has had no pain in his stomach at all. He used to wake up every night crying with pain, now he isn't crying any more."

The hour-long sermon from the pastor started with a reading from Matthew 8.24-6:

Without warning, a furious storm came up on the lake, so that the waves swept over the boat. But Jesus was sleeping. The disciples went and woke him, saying, "Lord, save us! We're going to drown!"

He replied, "You of little faith, why are you so afraid?" Then he got up and rebuked the winds and the waves, and it was completely calm.

The pastor then asked, and answered, these questions:

How will I secure a safe place in this troubled world?

When the disciples needed help, they didn't ask the sea, or the boat, they asked Jesus. "Herbalists can't solve your problem – there is no security in any wrist band or arm band. Christ calmed the sea, and he is going to calm your problem tonight."

What do I do to have a permanent place?

"If you stay away from sin, you have a permanent place. Forget the wizards and witches – if you have a permanent place, they have no power over you."

"How do I get out from my present predicament?

Have faith in Christ, that he is able, and tell him about it."

The last quarter of an hour of the service was a time when we could pray for our own needs in the presence of God. The pastor led the prayers for different types of needs, so there was a chance to pray for others, as well as for ourselves. The prayer was active – and loud sometimes – but everyone seemed self-controlled. (There were no involuntary sounds or movements that I could see!) The purpose of the meeting was to put people in touch with God, and I think it worked.

From city to town . . .

One afternoon we drove 190 kilometres south from Maiduguri to Biu, a journey of two hours. Biu, the main town of the mainly Muslim Bura people, is greener than Maiduguri because it is on a plateau and so has a milder climate. The Deeper Life pastor there is Stephen Wazo, who is originally from neighbouring Kaduna State. This small fellowship started with twelve adults in 1984. The membership in 1988 had reached around fifty, while at the Miracle Revival Hour I attended there, I counted 118 adults. The church has six House Caring Fellowships.

Pastor Wazo is the Deeper Life District Pastor for the larger Biu local government area, so he has oversight of smaller Deeper Life Fellowships meeting in nearby villages. He told me, "We have now opened six locations. We go somewhere, someone is healed, and a fellowship starts. In Biu here there has been a real spiritual battle to get land, but we were able to get this plot eight months ago. Up till then we were meeting in a shop."

The new building at Biu is far from finished, with breeze-block walls about a metre high, then an iron roof over half that area supported by wooden poles. It is an adequate place for worship. Unfortunately there was a power cut that night, so we worshipped by candle-light.

This Thursday Miracle Revival Hour at Biu included the now familiar prayer requests: an unemployed brother, a sister not menstruating, a brother troubled by bad dreams from the Devil, a sister starting labour pains.

A brother gave testimony that on the preceding Friday he had travelled to Maiduguri with a key from work. He came back on Sunday, and discovered on Monday morning that he had lost the key. He thought he must have dropped it in the taxi he travelled in on Sunday night, but he couldn't remember the taxi number. His colleagues at work said, "It's the governor for you – you're on your way to gaol!" He prayed and went out in search of the taxi. He looked all day on the Monday until it was dark, with no success.

"I decided to go back to my house to get ready for prison on Tuesday. But near my home I had to jump out of the way of a taxi that came to park by me – it was the same driver! I told him I was looking for a key. He asked me, 'Do you mean this one?'"

. . . and the village of Kunkumi

The political and economic centre for the Hausa is Kano City, the capital of Kano State. Kano is as flat as Maiduguri, with surrounding villages in the same mud-built pattern of compounds, but with iron roofs more common than thatch. The city of Kano itself is much more densely populated than Maiduguri. The buildings are packed tightly, and two-, three-, or four-storey houses are common. The skyline is dominated by a few skyscrapers, a telecommunications tower – and the minarets.

Some of the streets in Kano seem to be more crowded with traders than buyers, but there is space for the Muslim praying grounds: maybe just a mat, or seventy-five centimetre walls forming a three- or four-metre-sided square. Islam stresses the equality of believers before God, but in some people I saw the same attitude as in the predominantly Christian parts of Nigeria: the respect for elders which at its best is obviously a fine quality, but which can be ingratiating and unthinking too. The other side of this is the dismissive attitude to "inferiors" – the husband who walked through the door, letting it shut in the face of his wife rather than holding it open for her. There is tremendous strength in the quality of respect for elders which I believe is godly and which we in the West need to restore to our society. But the church has to work to develop this Nigerian instinct into a consistently positive attitude to elders, alongside compassion for the poor, less able, and weak.

One Monday we travelled 120 kilometres from Kano City to Kunkumi – just over the border into Kaduna State on the Zaria road. Although as far north as Maiduguri, Kano State is not as sandy and arid as Borno, and the vegetation is almost savannah. There were fairly frequent trees and bushes, and a fair amount of undergrowth, even though the dry season had already started. Noticeable to me from time to time were pools and ponds where people came to wash and fetch water.

Kunkumi is one of the villages of the Maguzawa people, distinct from the Hausa, but who use Hausa as their *lingua franca*. Alongside the main road are spacious single-storey concrete houses and shops with verandahs. Turning off the tarmac in between two of these we could drive only about a hundred metres before the track between the mud-built compounds was too narrow for a car to pass through. We left the car in front of a large pile of dried maize which was ready for grinding into flour.

Deeper Life's ministry in Kunkumi started in 1981, and had really been in terms of renewing the faith of nominal Christians. Deeper Life are offering an experience of God and an opportunity for discipleship. The regular membership of the Deeper Life Bible Church there has now reached forty adults. Because there is no electricity yet in the village, and because the majority of the small population are subsistence farmers, the weekday services are held at 3.30 p.m. rather than later in the evening.

They have three House Caring Fellowships, which meet in three compounds. I went to visit the Bature compound. From outside, all you can see is a plot of land maybe twelve metres square, surrounded by three-metre-high mud walls. We were welcomed through the corrugated iron door into the kitchen, where a pot was cooking on a small wood fire; then through the kitchen (hot and smoky!) into the centre of the compound where maize, peppers, and okra were spread out on the ground and on the metal roofs to dry. Two children were sitting in the middle of the compound eating some food. They got up and ran into their room as we entered. It was a colourful and cheerful scene with the yellow, red, and green vegetables on the ground, and decorating the roofs against a bright blue sky and rich red-brown walls.

Brother Bature was happily telling us that this was a Christian compound, and we were most welcome! Most of the conversations I had in Kunkumi were only possible because Pastor Inuwa from Tudun Wada, who used to live in the village, could interpret for me. Pastor Inuwa had been a member of the Deeper Life Bible Church in this village for some years, but then was called to Kano with three others, trained, and sent to plant a Deeper Life Bible Church in the nearby village of Sabon Abuja. The current pastor of Kunkumi – Alhamdu Nassara – was not around on the day I visited. I wondered whether they were not weakening Kunkumi by sending out people from the church to pastor neighbouring villages, when the sending church was still so comparatively small. The State Overseer told me later, "The Kunkumi church is strong – they understand a lot. We can't wait for them to grow more, while other areas are lacking a witness. The people from Kunkumi can reach people who speak Hausa – and someone who has been in a church for five years is ready to be sent out if they have really been following the Lord during that time."

In the left-hand corner, next to the kitchen building, was a well. Down the left-hand side of the square was a three-roomed building with a verandah. Opposite the kitchen was a similar building. Diagonally opposite the well was a roofed-over pen for a few goats and chickens, while a simpler one- or two-roomed building was to the right of the kitchen.

I should mention – to forestall any misconceptions – that the mud floors of the compound outside, and of the rooms inside, were immaculately clean, while the rooms themselves were cool and comfortable. There was a tangible sense of contentment in all the homes I visited, despite the obvious hardship of the lifestyle. In this one compound live two men, three women, and eight children.

Ibrahim Bature told me how he loved hearing the true word of God, and how it built him up:

"It's the church where I can get life. Most of the time, if the family has a problem, or sickness, God will heal us and deliver us. Our four-year-old, Nuhu, had a badly swollen boil on his body just recently. We prayed, and the boil just went away. God has blessed our farm this year. Maize, guinea corn, millet, rice, beans, okra, peppers – they have all done well. We've had enough left over to sell some. We just thank God for the way he has been blessing us. We have no problems to pray about just now!"

In another compound I met Laatu Andrew, who has a radiant smile and a real sense of peace about her:

"I always wanted to be a member of God – to be free in the Word of God, to praise him and serve him. I saw the Deeper Life people, and they impressed me. I joined Deeper

Life to have peace of mind, and I enjoy my life now, I'm free to praise God."

I asked Laatu what in particular God had done for her. She told me that some time ago her husband had left her with her two girls, Patricia, aged eleven, and Florence, who was three. She is a primary school teacher but supplements her small income by growing food for herself and the children. Now God is providing her with things for her children to eat – she is not worried about anything: "My husband is in Zaria. He does not help us. But I grow maize and beans. I got plenty of beans this year – God blessed my beans – and now we have enough to eat."

My last visit in Kunkumi was to a larger compound where Matta Ibrahim lived with her three children, two boys, aged twelve and seven, and a girl of nine. Her husband had travelled away on the day I visited, while his second wife (see Chapter 10 for some discussion on polygamy) came to live in the compound at weekends. By now it was too dark to sit inside without artificial light. Sister Matta welcomed us and brought out two rugs for us to sit on outside. Food was cooking on a wood fire in one corner of the compound, the flames providing the light. The only sounds around us were the cicadas, children playing, and adults talking and telling stories in neighbouring compounds. The whole village was in conversation, relaxing after a day's work. The fresh wood smoke in the open air didn't sting the eyes or smell unpleasant. When we started talking the sky was quite light, but by the time we had finished it was dark, the fire only embers, and we were sitting in moonlight. My translator sat next to me while Matta sat on an upturned bowl. The three children grouped around her, watching me, chewing roasted maize.

Matta was born in a nearby village, and had been brought up an Anglican, but started attending Deeper Life six years ago when she moved to Kunkumi to get married. However, her new husband didn't like the Deeper Life Bible Church. One time, she remembered, the sermon topic in church was the Holy Spirit, and she prayed to receive the Holy Spirit.

That evening she came back home, and when she began to pray in her room, her husband started beating her.

She told me that because of what she learnt in the church she believed in Christ. Her husband neglected her, and tried to stop her going there. One day she came back from the Bible study and found he had packed up all her property and left it outside. She told her husband, "I'm enjoying the church. Most of the things I was doing before I don't do now because of the light of Christ in me. I see nothing wrong with that church – unless it's the word of God that's wrong."

Her parents supported her husband, and the Anglican elders visited and told her not to go to Deeper Life, so for a while she did go to the Anglican church again, but also attended Deeper Life sometimes. Her parents warned her that if there was a problem between her and her husband, she should not turn to them. But she wanted to remain in Deeper Life, she didn't want to change back because she felt she didn't grow spiritually when she was attending the Anglican church.

"They really want me to go to the Anglican church, but I believe Deeper Life teach the word of God. The Lord has done many things for us. He has been protecting the children. When they are sick, if I pray, God just heals them."

Emmanuel Ajayi, Deeper Life's Protocol Officer, who was my companion throughout my trip, told me just before I was about to return to Britain, "Kunkumi was the most memorable place. The faith and witness of those people! What I was praying for in my former church, I saw in Deeper Life."

Evangelism amidst poverty

After we had visited Kunkumi, I was discussing the Deeper Life Bible Church's outreach with brother Ransom Bello, the Kano State Overseer. He was explaining that there is more to mission than evangelism, although that is primary. In Kano Deeper Life have repaired and maintain the road around the church, and through CAN (the Christian Association of Nigeria) were involved in relief work for those affected by the flooding in Kano State earlier in 1988. It is already part of their vision to start a primary school in Kano, and in a place like Kunkumi they would like to provide medical services, particularly nutritional education. Even though they can't afford to pay the Kunkumi pastor a wage, their vision of the breadth of mission is not lacking.

The State Overseer for Kwara (still in the north, but not the far north), Pastor Adejumo, had a similar vision when I spoke to him about the injustice in society where so many people are so very poor.

"We can speak to our members about injustice. We can pray for the government. We encourage sharing within the fellowship – e.g. helping with medical expenses, clothing, school fees for our poorer members – ideally within a House Caring Fellowship, but if that's not possible, people can come to the central fund here.

"We've improved the public road to our place – we want to get our own building finished first! We'd like to build nursery and primary schools in time. Kwara is linked with the Gambia – and we're thinking about a school or hospital there."

"As a church we can change people," said Ransom Bello. "People make up society – if we can change people, society will change. For example, we have an outreach to the prison, and many are converted. One boy was sentenced to seventeen years; he was converted through our visiting him and praying with him. He earned his release through good behaviour after only three and a half years.

"We stand for the truth. We work faithfully and trust-worthily. We teach forcefully against bribery and corruption. Our members who are in responsible posts are ensuring honest standards. It may look gradual, but it works. Outward compliance looks well, but to remain stable it has to be from the inside. Our membership in Kano City is 4,500 – so in many offices and places we are a presence for justice and order."

I asked Pastor Kumuyi whether he saw the church having a social responsibility towards the poor as well as an evangelistic mission:

"Honestly, I would think that we need to address such a question more than we have ever done. I have read a little about what is happening in South America, concerning what the Evangelicals would call a Social Gospel. But even the Evangelicals are now realising that it's both personal and social. They have realised it's not just the individual approach of getting saved and preparing to meet the Lord. I think there is a shift now, a shift to concern about injustice. I would say that we have not really thought of that, as a church. What we should be doing is that we should co-operate with the community. For example, if we need to develop the road in our community here, we will do that together. If the hospital there is having a programme for the invalids, we can contribute financially. We are also supposed to get involved with homes for the handicapped and the prisons. We would try to see what to do. But I know from what I have been reading that we can do more. I wouldn't talk in terms of 'organising the poor to seek justice'. I've never thought it's right for the church to be confrontational to the government.

"I'm open. You see, we count all this as good works. Not just good works now from the point of view of the individual Christian, but from the point of view of the church community. As a church of this size we need to ask ourselves what we can do, intelligently and legitimately, to help solve a particular problem in society. I would say that is part of good works, as an expression of our faith in Christ. I think we should get into more of that, depending too on how enlightened we are. We may need to know what other churches are doing in other places. We may not be able to transplant completely what they are doing but we would be able to adapt and see that this is a calling. When it comes to sinking wells and building roads in the rural areas, for example, that is something we should be thinking about, but honestly we have not been addressing those issues."

Poverty and prosperity

One Saturday evening in Lagos, at the Gbagada church, I heard Kumuyi address the "workers" (leaders, ushers, choir, etc.) on "The reasons for our poverty". We had been there since four o'clock, preparing the "Search the Scriptures" passage for the groups at the start of the Sunday morning service, followed by meetings in Area groups to go over the House Caring Fellowship notes for the next day. At seven o'clock Kumuyi stood up to preach for half an hour:

"There are promises for all mankind – and there are special promises for those who serve. There is no reason why we should be spiritually stagnant or poor. In the Old Testament, God in heaven provided for his own people. God will prosper and bless his own people. Were Moses, Elijah, Peter, James or Paul invalids? Did they depend on non-believers for their bread? Look at this promise of God:

> Worship the LORD your God, and his blessing will be on your food and water. I will take away sickness from among you, and none will miscarry or be barren in your land. I will give you a full life span. (Exodus 23.25–6)

God is not going to tease us. In some churches, if they see a promise not fulfilled in their ministers' own lives, they are silent on that. They don't want to read the Bible about the promise, or preach about it. You may ask, 'What is the reason for my barrenness, or poverty, or sickness?' A doctor will *examine* you if you ask such a question. Why can't we Christians be sincere? Why do we cover up?

"God still cares. Jesus can still provide, like when he fed the five thousand. If we make an excuse, we're no better than those who make excuses for living in sin.

> May those who delight in my vindication
>   shout for joy and gladness;
> may they always say, 'The LORD be exalted,

> who delights in the well-being [KJV: prosperity] of
> his servant.'
>
> > (Psalm 35.27)

And everyone who has left houses or brothers or sisters
or father or mother or children or fields for my sake will
receive a hundred times as much and will inherit eternal
life. (Matthew 19.29)

Jesus meant what he said, and said what he meant. Don't
add to it or take away from it. You will receive a hundred
times as much.

"You need to say, 'I don't know why I didn't get it before,
but now I claim it.' Don't regret, cry, look back at being poor:
wake up and claim it. Are you saying, 'I've not got the houses,
brothers, sisters, but I've got the persecution' – why are you
claiming persecution but not the other? Jesus was the truth,
and he never said anything false. This is not the Devil – you
just don't know the promises of God. Now we're going to
claim the promises of God, and in a few years' time we'll be
able to say like David:

> I was young and now I am old,
>   yet I have never seen the righteous forsaken
>   or their children begging bread. (Psalm 37.25)

"People say, 'Your reward is in heaven, over here we're
supposed to be hungry and suffering.' Job said of people
like that, 'You're miserable counsellors!' Didn't Jesus tell
you, 'Therefore I tell you, whatever you ask for in prayer,
believe that you have received it, and it will be yours.' (Mark
11.24)? I believe tonight will be a turning point. Look at
when Jesus got the coin from inside the fish (Matthew
17.24–7). Jesus also said, 'I tell you the truth, anyone
who has faith in me will do what I have been doing. He
will do even greater things than these, because I am going
to the Father' (John 14.12). Do you think Peter threw the
fish back, or did he take it back to his wife?! That's the

hundredfold! Are you just throwing away the blessing of God?

"Just like God provided for the Israelites in the wilderness, can't he do the same today? Should the believers be begging? That's an insult to God! I'm waiting for the day when nobody in this church will be begging, but will have plenty to lend to the unbelievers . . ."

So the pastor concluded his sermon, and invited people to stand and pray, and pray they did. Men and women were on their feet, pleading with God to provide for them, making their claims in faith. Afterwards, Kumuyi apologised to me that the people made so much noise when they prayed! He hoped I wasn't disturbed by it. There certainly was uproar – but it was to do with frustration and fear being released, rather than emotion being whipped up. The people were in control of themselves as they poured out their hearts to God. The message was obviously one that deeply affected them – one that they needed to hear – and raised matters in their lives that they needed to bring before God. Why should I be offended when people *pray*?

But as they prayed, I couldn't help wondering, what type of "prosperity" is it that God provides? For what purpose? And isn't it merely offensive to say that Moses and Paul were not invalids?

But then (in my perplexity!) what else, in all honesty, can God's promises of provision mean? What right have I, who am wealthy, to smile when the poor plead to God for bread? So then the question becomes: are there ways in which we work against God by being satisfied with injustice in society (locally, nationally, and globally)?

As an observer, did I see in the people there two groups: one, the grateful, prosperous urban professionals; and two, the desperate urban poor? Was there complacency in the first group? Are the second group being misguided and misdirected? If God makes demands of the poor believer for faith, persistence, hope, and contentment, what demands does he make of the rich?

It is as dangerous to take one sermon out of the context of the life of a church as it is to take a verse out of its context in the Bible. This was a sermon addressed to the poor; they should serve God and have faith that he will provide for them. There is another sermon to be addressed to the rich, concerning what we do with that prosperity which God has already given us.

After five minutes Pastor Kumuyi asked, over the hubbub of prayer, "Has God changed?"

"NO!" came the reply, and further prayer. After a few more minutes, the pastor reminded the people:

"Doubt will keep you out of the Kingdom. Doubt will keep you away from the promises of God." And then, in prayer, "God, we are not going to stay blind to your promises any more. I claim authority from you for these workers over sickness, barrenness, impotence, or if they are tormented by the Devil. As many of us that are owing, you will give them prosperity – our children who we can't keep in school because we can't afford their school fees; people who are terrified by demon enemies; people who are in trouble or in arguments because there is not enough in the family. We're not doubters, we're believers, and we pray we'll begin to see the change. We're more than conquerors!"

And the people applauded.

"Don't worry," Kumuyi continued. "Forget last month. If anyone is sick in your Zone, the Lord has anointed you: lay your hand on them and they will be healed. Get your children ready for school. Get your home ready for the new baby. Go now, in the joy of the Lord, and be a blessing to the people."

After the meeting, I asked Kumuyi whether he was preaching a God who can be manipulated to fulfil our own desires.

"I think most people in Nigeria would feel that we in Deeper Life are negative to 'prosperity'! If we were to be accused of preaching the prosperity gospel, all the other churches would defend us and insist that they think we are negative. If you see the lifestyle of the people who preach prosperity gospel, they 'live high'; and they don't only talk about God providing for you, they also use gimmicks to get money out of people. Since you have been around you will see that we are not like that.

"But on the other hand you want to encourage people, because they are poor, they are sick, and they have problems. They come to the church because they believe that God is love and God will cater for them. The father will cater for his' children. If the father has made promises to the child, that child will have the right to ask the father, 'Would you please fulfil it?' That child will not see himself as manipulating the father, because he's asking his father to fulfil his promise. The only difference here is that God has made the general promises in the Bible, and he's not spoken to me directly. Therefore what we teach them is that our first attitude of approach is to look at that promise and pray on the basis of those promises. There has to be a basis for our prayer and for our believing in God.

"Now if you pray, God may say, 'No,' like he told Moses when he wanted to go to the land of Canaan. Moses said, 'Lord, please,' and God said, 'Don't speak about the matter any more.' This was a 'No' from God. Then in the case of Paul, when a messenger of the Devil was buffeting him, he prayed about it and he was persistent until God said, 'No, my grace is sufficient for you.' So we should have the attitude of examining the promises of God, standing on those promises of the Lord, and praying unto the Lord. If God says no, then we have come to the area of submitting to the will of God. We do not pry into or try to investigate the secret of God's sovereignty, but we joyfully accept the will of God when he tells us that his grace is sufficient for us in our situation. We do not measure our relationship with the Lord in terms of whether we are being healed, or getting prospered, or getting a job; we just know that we can ask him to meet our needs. If he meets them, we are happy."

So Deeper Life tend to assume that the answer from God should be "Yes" unless he clearly says "No". However, it seems to me that it is often up to us as Christians to say

"No" to ourselves. When Jesus was tempted to turn stones to bread in the desert he said "No." He stayed in the desert, and soon said "Yes", to the cross. But just as we should not assume God's "Yes", no more should we assume his "No". In too many churches in Britain, we assume the answer is always "No".

In the mission of the church in areas of deprivation, Deeper Life have held to evangelism as the first priority, but they also understand that "development" work in a wider sense should be part of the witness of the church, and indeed that perhaps the witness is weakened without it. Seeking justice in society can come by our own efforts under God's direction, but also by supernatural intervention in righting the wrongs that people are suffering.

9

Deeper family life

Pregnancy and childbirth

Off the busy Ozigbo Street in Benin City a track has been
cleared out of the forest, with houses to left and right. I
suppose the vegetation absorbs the noise, but very quickly
all I could hear in the background were cocks crowing,
women talking, and wood being chopped. We climbed the
outside steps to a flat where Joshua and Elizabeth Ogbole
live. It was a pleasant room with light green walls and a blue
and red check lino floor. As we sat down, Elizabeth proudly
wheeled in a cot with a child asleep in it. Hanging on the cot
was a card, proclaiming, "He reigns, Jesus is Lord".

Joshua and Elizabeth are from Bendel State, and were
married in 1984. Joshua is a local government officer in
Warri, while Elizabeth teaches in a nearby primary school.
When they moved to Benin City, a friend invited them to the
Deeper Life Bible Church. That evening the message was on
cassette, a sermon by the General Superintendent.

"We discovered some truth that night," Joshua explained,
"as distinct from what we had been exposed to before. We
had worshipped in different churches. We were both born
into the Anglican tradition, and had both been baptised.
When I was old enough, I was confirmed. Elizabeth joined

the Church of God Mission, which I later also joined. When I was at university, I worshipped in a non-denominational church, and while I was doing my NYSC [National Youth Service Corps – a compulsory year's public service after graduation] the closest church to me was ECWA, so I joined them. But at Deeper Life we saw some differences. There was authoritative preaching, and every statement was backed up by the Bible – so we gradually became members and are now both House Caring Fellowship leaders."

"But before then we had our problems," Elizabeth continued. "Three months after our wedding, my periods stopped, so we thought I was pregnant. But it continued for a long time, and I had none of the symptoms. We consulted three gynaecologists, who thought it was a hormonal problem and prescribed some drugs. Those didn't work, so they prescribed a more powerful drug. I was also encouraged to drink a lot of *ogbolo* (a soup made from doca nut, which is very rich in vitamin E). But nothing happened, I got tired and depressed."

"One day," Joshua told me, "I came back from work, and found a note from my wife. She wrote that she was feeling so weak from the drugs that she felt she was dying, all for the sake of getting a child. We decided to get rid of all the drugs. Then in May 1986, at the Friday Miracle Revival Hour, our pastor preached on Matthew 15.13, where Jesus said: 'Every plant that my heavenly Father has not planted will be pulled up by the roots.' Then when it came to the time to pray, the pastor mentioned that a woman had some problems – and he was describing my wife's symptoms. Elizabeth and I were sitting in different places, and we both raised our hands. The pastor prayed and immediately an 'internal heat' which my wife had been feeling for a long time in her lower abdomen stopped."

In Lagos I met Dr (Mrs) Joyce C. Ezeibe of the Jedonec Hospital. She explained to me that internal heat (feeling very hot inside) is one of the symptoms of high blood pressure. Joyce is a member of Deeper Life as well as a medical doctor. I asked her what she felt about miraculous healing.

"I don't find it difficult to believe these testimonies," she said. "Only when you send someone away, saying there's no hope, you feel embarrassed when they come back and everything is all right!"

I was also able to talk with Dr (Mrs) Toyin Taiwo, who works in a private hospital in Ilasamaja, Lagos. I asked her the same question:

"There's a lot of witchcraft here – terrible evil things. Before I became a Christian, I hardly believed it, but since I've got closer to the Lord I can see that it's rife. When I'm treating people, it might seem like they have ordinary complaints, but if I feel genuinely led by the Spirit, I might question the patient about their spiritual life. The problem may have been caused by a familiar spirit. These sometimes inhabit a person during the day, but a fish at night when the spirit leaves the body. Or it may be an *ogbanje* spirit, killing a woman's children each time she delivers.

"Internal heat is a common complaint in Nigeria, but if you check temperature, blood pressure, and so on, everything is often normal. They feel hot inside, sometimes in bursts, sometimes permanently. I've tried anti-malarials, tranquillisers, and many other things. Now I think it's one of the ways in which spiritual oppression is manifested. They feel as if they are on fire, but their skin is quite cool and normal to the touch.

"I would never attempt to explain the supernatural by natural means. Even unbelieving doctors will advise spiritual help if they can't understand what's going on. Men tend to go into the cults or secrets societies if they are looking for power. Women seem more born into the spirit world, mother to daughter. Women seem to be in contact with the spirits more naturally than men. Pregnancies get tampered with a lot – the spirits seem to find women more vulnerable when they are pregnant. In my own case, in 1985 I had my first baby by Caesarean section. I hadn't expected an operation, but I was in labour for such a long time. After the operation I went to the doctors and they wanted to check why I had a problem. I looked at the X-ray with them, and I saw that I had a very narrow pelvis. I agreed, as a doctor, that I could not have had the baby naturally.

"When I joined Deeper Life, and I was pregnant again, I knew I just wanted a normal delivery as my miracle. I tried to work out how God would do it – would he make my pelvis bigger? Then I went on trying to work out how he made the blind eyes see, and the deaf ears hear. But the Spirit said, 'Don't try to work it out.'

"One night, I had a dream. It was like something fell out of my body. Someone picked it up and showed it to me. It looked a bit like a small corkscrew. They said, 'This is what stopped your first pregnancy.' When it came to full term, the baby was born naturally in three hours – and it was bigger than the first. The first one couldn't get through my pelvis, but the second one did. If something is a miracle, you can't explain it naturally. The supernatural and the natural are like two parallel lines."

Through the ministry of Deeper Life in Benin, Elizabeth's internal heat had been dealt with at that meeting, whether it was high blood pressure or some form of spiritual oppression. The next morning Joshua had to travel down to Warri.

"When I got back," he explained, "my wife told me that she had started a period – after fifteen months! We consider that a real miracle. We know God did it. That evening the General Superintendent was in Benin for an IFL programme. He prayed for us, and two months later Elizabeth conceived. At the seventh month (early 1987) she began to feel very ill. We had been anxious about a number of things. Then one day while I was at work in Warri I had a telephone call from Benin to say that the doctor was going to do an operation on my wife to remove the baby because of high blood pressure. I rushed straight to our church, where I met the pastor and we prayed together. In prayer we agreed that no operation was necessary. At five the next morning, while the doctor was preparing for the operation, the dead foetus was expelled naturally, so there was no operation. We lost the baby. But we didn't lose hope in God."

"Today we have a little baby," Elizabeth continued. "I conceived again at the end of 1987, and throughout the pregnancy we believed and trusted God. The due date was July 15th, this year. The doctor had told us – at the eighth month – that the baby was lying across. We went to Deeper Life Bible Church for prayer, believing that even at the eleventh hour God would turn the baby around, and the baby turned. Then on July 10th I started my maternity leave. We waited, but the baby did not come. At that time we were preparing for the Deeper Life Miracle Crusade in Benin on July 22nd and 23rd, when brother Kumuyi would be ministering. We were going round the town – me with my big tummy – inviting people to come to the crusade."

A week after the baby was due, Elizabeth went for a check-up. The chief gynaecologist said that the baby had turned again and was head up – so a Caesarean would be necessary. But Elizabeth just went home, made up the cot, and said, "There'll be no operation. Nothing abnormal is going to happen."

Joshua picked up the story again:

"On July 22nd I got home from work. I found my wife with the others working at the crusade ground – still with her big tummy – and we separated to do our different jobs for the evening. During the ministration the first group of people the General Superintendent prayed for were women whose pregnancies were overdue. As he was praying Elizabeth had a birth pang, and she ran home. I got home after the crusade and the pastor's wife from Warri met me at our door to tell me that my wife was in labour. Two Deeper Life sisters who are nurses live near here. We called them, and they said the labour would take a few hours. My wife refused to go to hospital – she said she wanted God's intervention. At 10.55 on the morning of July 23rd the baby boy was delivered naturally at home to the glory of God. We have named him Jesuremen ('Jesus gave to me') Onosereba ('The one that God helped')."

Elizabeth added: "When my family heard, they were very thrilled. Now they believe that God can do great things."

By the time we had finished talking, baby Jesuremen Onosereba had woken up, and was happy to inspect me from the safety of his mother's arm. We made our farewells, climbing down the steps to the children playing around our car parked below. A couple of the younger children didn't really understand about cars, so we had to lift them out of the way before we could move. Children are a precious commodity.

A sceptic might put this type of "miracle" down to technique or coincidence. It would seem fairly safe to pray for overdue pregnancies because you can be fairly certain that a child will be born within a few days of your prayer! But in many cases in Nigeria, parents in such situations will attribute a delayed delivery to evil spirits which need to be exorcised, particularly when there have been previous complications. Sometimes they may be right. I heard of many cases where a pregnancy was overdue not only by days or weeks, but even by months. You can be on shaky ground if you try to argue with someone else about their perception of reality. They may be wrong, and you may be right. Or it could be the other way round! What is certain is that the Devil is seeking to destroy families. In Nigeria it seems common for evil spirits to attack pregnancies. In the UK we are seeing broken families and child abuse. I don't suppose "demons" are responsible every time – but perhaps we are seeing in the UK different manifestations of evil, but manifestations of evil none the less, which therefore need to be dealt with at the spiritual level.

Dr Joyce Ezeibe had also mentioned problems with pregnancies:

"We believe God is able to do many things. There are still powers of darkness which can tie up a pregnancy. I have had pregnant women coming to me saying it has been two or three years since they have become pregnant. Now their tummy might be big, but all I can feel is a mass, and on palpation, there seems to be nothing there. Not long after, a baby gets delivered."

I heard of a Deeper Life woman member in Surulere District of the Gbagada Deeper Life Bible Church in Lagos who had been pregnant for four years – and believed she had not gone into labour because of an evil charm on her. She had had a positive pregnancy test from one doctor, while another doctor said it was just a fibrous growth. Her Zonal leader told me she had sent a handkerchief to Pastor Kumuyi, who had prayed over it and sent it back to her. Another Zonal leader mentioned that he had had a similar case in his Zone recently, and a child had been born soon after prayer.

In Kano, in the north of Nigeria, I met Dr Akin Dare of the Castle Clinic and Maternity Home, who commented:

"Before I became a Christian I thought this type of thing was just a mistake, that these women had made a mistake concerning their dates. Because of the climate here in Africa a woman can stop menstruation, or have an irregular menses, or even a loss of menses, and then become pregnant without apparently menstruating. So the women will feel the pregnancy is post-date. A foetus above forty-two weeks is unlikely to survive, because nutrition to the baby becomes compromised. The environment here in Africa is superstitious, but there are strange things that do happen. I had a patient whose menses ceased for four months. She came and had a positive pregnancy test – it was the first month. When she came for a check-up in the fifth month I couldn't palpate the uterus, and she gave a negative pregnancy test. I booked her into the theatre to evacuate her. She pleaded with me not to do the operation, and I had to agree, because I can't operate without the patient's permission. Two weeks later her junior sister and an elderly woman admitted that they had 'sucked off' (spiritually tampered with) the pregnancy. The church prayed. When she came to the clinic, I felt her uterus again – she was definitely pregnant, and I was able to pick up the foetal heart beat. If a demon is trying to oppress a woman, it will concentrate on childbearing, causing infertility, a delayed delivery, or a deformed baby."

I found much of what I heard about pregnancies to be very strange, and I confessed my scepticism to the Deeper Life brothers and sisters. There is so much social pressure on Nigerian women to bear children that I felt there must be a temptation to them to consider themselves pregnant as soon as they miss a period, or even to claim that they are still pregnant after a miscarriage. The expectation in marriage is to get pregnant immediately – any delay must be due to demonic interference.

Nevertheless, my Western approach to pregnancy need not be the best approach. Why do couples the world over experience problems and pain in conceiving and bearing children? In the West, are we merely describing symptoms, when Africans are getting closer to causes? These Africans saw God at work in their lives in this area, and consequently their faith in other areas grew. We in the UK can diminish the work of God by taking a superior – and superficial – attitude to such matters. Surely we need to turn to the power of Jesus Christ, the "second Adam" (1 Corinthians 15.45), to begin to relieve the effects of the fall in Genesis 3.16:

> I will greatly increase your pains in childbearing;
> with pain you will give birth to children.

Children

I travelled down to Sapele – a town fifty kilometres south of Benin – and learnt more about spirit interference with children. It was a Monday, and in fact a public holiday in Nigeria to celebrate Id-El-Moulud, commemorating the birth of Mohammed. Accompanying me were both the Deeper Life Bendel State Overseer, Francis A. Ighalo, and the pastor for Sapele, Emmanuel Obe. When we stopped for fuel, the garage was on a slight incline. The minibus next to us had to be held in position by some children because its brakes weren't strong enough to hold it still while they were filling its tank with petrol. That task done, the children continued their job of selling plums and kola nuts, while some men were trying to persuade us to buy ice creams, or leather belts.

Once on our way there were stalls from time to time the whole length of the road, which leads on to the major oil terminal at Warri. There were yams, pineapples, bananas, and firewood in abundance – if you had the money. The forest grew thickly on either side – trees ten or fifteen metres high, with thick undergrowth, and netted together with creepers. Then occasional patches of more open ground, with grass and bushes only growing up to a metre or so, but with palm trees and banana fronds pushing up four to five metres through the web of creepers. We passed two women taking home a tree for firewood, one carrying the main trunk, the other carrying three smaller pieces. There was a man with two animals he had successfully hunted – "bush meat" is much sought after in the cities! In one township we drove through, there had been an accident where a large articulated truck had run off the road, ploughing into the end of one building, narrowly missing the front of another. The cab was mangled under a collapsed iron roof and crumbled mud walls. It seemed as though the truck had been abandoned for some time, while the residents had to continue to live in the two houses – one of which was half demolished, the other's front completely obstructed by the container load. That wasn't the only abandoned vehicle I saw.

As we continued down to the delta the palm forest thickened even more, and the humidity increased. So we arrived at Sapele – one of the main towns of the Urhobo people. Because of the profuse palm forests in this area, Sapele's main industry is in palm oil and palm wine. Francis explained to me that apart from Christianity, the Jehovah's Witnesses and the "white garment" churches were strong, together with various secret societies. But underlying most people's spirituality was a reverence for the water spirits and river spirits. Deeper Life members did not dispute the existence of these spirits – it was a question of Christ being Lord and Saviour, and the believer having power and authority over the water spirits by the Holy Spirit. They also explained that a number of women, especially, will leave their bodies to inhabit fish at night.

Among the people I talked to, the activity of the spirit world in family life, particularly affecting children, became clear. I visited Esther Bokna and one of her six children, her fourteen-year-old daughter, Omowumi, in their upstairs flat in Sapele. Outside, children were playing with the sandy earth, making castles, and digging out lakes and rivers to float tin cans in. Esther sat in an armchair, while Omowumi in her plain red dress sat on one of the arms, leaning affectionately against her mother. Esther was wearing a simple check wrapper, with a green blouse, and a yellow and blue head tie. We sat around a formica-topped coffee table as they told me their story, with the help of an interpreter.

They used to attend the "white garment" Cherubim and Seraphim church, when Omowumi became very sick. The illness continued and she started losing weight. It got to the point where she was too weak to walk at all, and even seemed to be mentally disturbed, often talking incoherently. Omowumi should have been in Form II at secondary school by then, but she was only in Form I because she was so sick she couldn't get to school at all. The mother took her daughter to the Cherubim and Seraphim and they suggested various remedies which included a seven-day fast; a fourteen-day fast; abstaining from oil, salt, and pepper; and bathing in the river every day for twenty-one days. They tried all these things, but the illness continued. Then in May 1988 someone from Deeper Life visited Esther and invited her to come to their church. She was looking for a solution for her sick child, when she heard of the Miracle Crusade that was about to take place in Benin City (July 1988). Esther took her daughter to the crusade. At the end of the meeting, Pastor Kumuyi prayed, "Those of you who have not received anything now, your miracle will follow you home."

Esther trusted what the General Superintendent had said, and came back home with the child still sick. They travelled back to Sapele from Benin on a lorry, and when it was time to get off, Omowumi fell from the lorry, but was strong enough to pick herself up off the ground. Esther felt that what "the man of God" had said had already taken place – Omowumi was obviously stronger than she had been before.

That night Omowumi dreamt that a big snake came out of her stomach. As the snake was going, she shouted the name of Jesus, and a large iron fork appeared and held the snake to the ground. Then fire came down and burnt the snake. When she woke up the next morning, the sickness had vanished. She jumped out of bed and ran to tell her mother, "I've been healed, I've been healed!"

Esther told me, "After the miracle, I surrendered myself totally to the Lord Jesus Christ. I have joined Deeper Life, and am a member of a House Caring Fellowship near here."

"I've joined the church, too," Omowumi added, "and I'm leading a junior House Caring Fellowship."

I asked Omowumi how she had felt when she was sick, and what she thought when her mother took her to the Deeper Life crusade.

"When I was sick I felt weak and tired all the time. I couldn't walk – I would feel dizzy. I couldn't eat much, because I couldn't keep my food down. The crusade was very nice. When Pastor Kumuyi asked for those who wanted to give their lives to Jesus Christ, I said I was willing. That was before I was healed – but I thought I would be healed. In the lorry coming home I was so happy. I was weak and tired and coughing – but I believed I was healed. Then when I had that dream I was amazed – I've never had a dream like that before. God must have sent the fire to destroy the snake."

"She's had no problems since then," Esther confirmed. "She's regaining weight well now, and is very prayerful. If she prays for anybody, she orders the Devil out. We have felt the impact in our family!"

The testimonies of Joshua and Elizabeth Ogbole, and Esther and Omowumi Bokna, are just two out of many that I heard as a result of the Benin Deeper Life Crusade in July 1988. Before the crusade, attendance at Deeper Life Sunday worship in Sapele averaged just 700. After the crusade, attendance had reached a steady 770 by October. The Sapele Deeper Life Bible Church where Esther and Omowumi worship is a wooden structure – but they have bought a larger plot of land, and were hoping to complete a permanent bigger building by the end of 1989. In Benin City itself (Joshua and Elizabeth's home), extensive building work is also taking place on the current structure. Attendance at Sunday worship was a little over 3,600 in the July, and reached to over 3,900 in August (a similar ten per cent increase), but by October the attendance had dropped back to averaging 3,600 again. This may have something to do with the heavy rain they had that season.

In the early evening of October 4th, 1988, we drove out to Somolu in Lagos. The area is crowded with small streets, all available space packed with one- and two-storey concrete buildings. Some of the houses are built in such a way that the front room is turned into a shop. The mud pavement is separated from the mud road by a concrete storm-drain. In front of those buildings that are not shops, street traders sit shoulder to shoulder with their wares in front of them on a piece of cloth or plastic. Other traders – particularly children – walk with arms full of loaves of bread or packets of biscuits, ready to dash towards anyone who shows any interest in buying. There seemed to be more sellers than buyers – an economy where simply by a glance or a wave of the hand the monied few can be crowded around with sellers undercutting each other. Such is the value of a few pence.

We parked in front of a single-storey building, and walked down the narrow passage that separated it from the grander two-storey house next door. A doorway on the right opened straight into a small room, with the window in the wall opposite the door. On our left was a double bed with a young man asleep on it. To the left of the window, on the opposite wall to the bed, was a small wardrobe. To the right of the door some small armchairs fitted against the wall and round the corner. Accommodation for a family.

Sade Odesola – a sixteen-year-old secondary school student – and her mother came in after us and sat on the bed, while my interpreter and I sat in two of the chairs. The two of them had become members of Deeper Life in 1986, and they are both members of a House Caring Fellowship which they attend regularly.

They told me how, during the long vacation two months previously, the mother had sent Sade out one Tuesday morning at about eleven o'clock to sell some nylon bags in the market. As soon as a child is old enough to do any task which may help the family – housework, farming, or trading – then they start work. Children are the only source of prosperity and security for the majority. "We obviously didn't expect Sade back straight away," her mother continued, "but in the afternoon we began to get worried. By seven in the evening there was still no sign of her, and we started looking everywhere. We couldn't find her and went to the police station."

Sade herself explained what had happened to her. "I was selling nylon bags on the streets. A Peugeot 504 pulled up. There were two men in the car. One of them called me over. I thought he wanted to buy a bag, but they knocked me down and forced me into the back of the car. We drove for a long way – right out of Lagos, into the bush. The man got me out of the car and took me into the bush. There was an old man there – a herbalist – and I could see he already had six other children tied up, with their heads shaved."

I wondered whether the purpose of the kidnapping had been to force a ransom payment from the family, but I was told that it is fairly common for herbalists to steal children and then use them as unwilling servants in their magic. It is rare for children to escape successfully when they have been kidnapped for this purpose.

"The two men handed me over to the herbalist," Sade continued, "and he told them to tie my hands and legs so that he could shave my head. The herbalist came at me with a large blade. He lifted the blade up high to bring it down on my hair, when I saw a brilliant white hand holding a shining sword over my head. The sword stopped the old man's blade where it was – he could not touch my hair. He just seemed to change his mind suddenly, and said to the two men who had brought me, 'She can't be used. Take her back to the main road and dump her there.'

"They must have left me by the side of the road. I was dazed – I didn't know where I was or what to do. Then the man saw me and stopped. I explained what had happened and he said he would help me; he even brought me right back to Somolu. It took us over two hours, in three different vehicles, to get home."

That was at nine o'clock at night. The family are rejoicing not only at the supernatural protection which God provided for this child, but also for the generosity and kindness of the man who brought her home. Kidnappings like this only rarely have happy endings.

I had no objective test of whether Sade was telling the truth or not – and I felt uncertain about this testimony. We went over her story three times, but no more details emerged. I suppose I was surprised that she could remember nothing more of what would obviously have been a terrifying experience. (Perhaps that in itself, though, is sufficient explanation for the lack of detail.) I also found myself questioning why the family did not know where Sade had been taken if someone had brought her back – couldn't they have asked the man where he had found her? But they didn't. Furthermore, the whole basis of the story also seemed strange to an outsider: the type of kidnapping from which children are never released sounds like "the land from which no one ever returns alive" – so how do you know it exists?

But Sade didn't seem to be the type of girl who would spin a yarn, and her family obviously believed her, as did other members of Deeper Life I spoke to. There is no doubt that some herbalists get up to wicked things. Was it really the lack of detail and supporting evidence that was raising doubts in my mind, or was it the reliance on what was perceived as a supernatural intervention that I found too simple and unrealistic? Why should it be so strange that God would want to protect his child? Sade saw the shining sword. A European might just have seen a kidnapper inexplicably change his mind.

Christian marriage

The Deeper Life Bible study in Benin City takes place regularly on a Tuesday evening, and the other pastors from the state can attend if they are able. They then take the materials to teach the same study in their own churches the following Monday. The Bible studies are printed out in note form (in English) and distributed to all who attend.

At Sapele I heard Pastor Obe, dressed in a simple beige jacket and trousers, deliver a Bible study in English – number eleven in a series of studies in Ephesians – on "Yieldedness in the family", based on chapter 5 verses 22–4. This was after one brother had led us in singing choruses, and then another brother led us in a time of prayer. A brother standing next to the pastor at the lectern gave a phrase-by-phrase translation into Urhobo. There were a number of other language groups receiving simultaneous translation at the back of the church.

"In general, Christians owe one another mutual sub-mission. We must be of a yielding and of a submissive spirit as we live in the fear of God. In particular, the wife is to be submissive to the husband, under God's authority, as unto the Lord. The wife must submit to the husband in everything lawful and consistent with her faith and knowledge in Christ.

"Where God's authority is made plain, the husband's authority ceases. The husband has no right to require his wife to disobey God (Acts 4.19; 5.29). Whenever the wife is constrained to differ from the husband, it should be with mildness and gentleness. She should state her reasons humbly, obey God faithfully and leave the event to God. After this, she should endeavour to be a better wife and put forth more and more efforts to make her husband and family happy."

Thus we heard a straight exposition of Scripture which was speaking against a context where husbands commonly expect total obedience from their wives (society will condone beating a wife if she refuses); and where a wife may ignore a husband except as a means of providing a home and a chance for her to produce children. Nevertheless I must admit that I did not find much in the study which might help a Christian woman who was suffering in a relationship with an unloving or cruel husband.

The next night in Benin, Pastor Francis presented study twelve to his people: "Love in the family", based on Ephesians 5.25–33.

"God's standard for family life is very high – higher than all Old Testament examples of family life. Husbands are commanded to love their wives, not as Adam, Noah, Abraham, Moses, Boaz, Isaiah, Hosea loved their wives, but as Christ loved the church. What a standard! Before the husband can so love his wife, he must die to self. Then there would be sacrificial, sanctifying, sharing, and sensitive love. Where there is love, there is no animosity, no struggle, no fighting, nothing but a perfectly glorious union. Love must be at the very heart and centre of our homes. The husband must be willing to deny self, bear toil and trial to provide for his wife, care for her, and defend her.

"The great secret conjugal happiness is mutual love, kindness, tenderness and loveliness of character in the home. The wife should respect and obey the husband; the husband should love and care for the wife.

"If you love your wife," continued Pastor Francis, "you will never raise your hand to slap her. Speaking in tongues doesn't matter if you're beating your wife. If your wife doesn't cook the food you like, do you send her home to learn? No! You love her and honour her. Don't insult her. If your wife is an unbeliever, love her and she will be converted, in Jesus' name. Look at Malachi 2.15,16: 'Do not break faith with the wife of your youth. "I hate divorce," says the LORD God of Israel.' Don't think you can run out of a marriage conducted in the court or your home because it wasn't conducted in a church – the Lord was a witness. God hates sending a wife away. If your wife is a witch – love your wife! It's a mystery, but love your wife."

I frequently heard both Ephesians 5 and Genesis 2.18 used in teaching about marriage in the Deeper Life Bible Church. The purpose of marriage was normally described as first, partnership; and very much second was fruitfulness. Marriage is desirable – it is not good to be alone. This is an important emphasis to make in Nigeria, because the popular perception of the purpose of marriage is in order for a man to get children, and for a woman to bear children.

The wife's submission in the marriage relationship, reflected in obedience and service to the husband, fits with traditional expectations. In emphasising partnership before childbearing, though, Deeper Life are making something of a stand against common expectations. But in their ministry to childless couples who desire children, and women with pregnancy problems, they are in practice making childbirth the equal first priority.

The important stand against the low opinion which men often have of women is in the teaching about the husband's love for his wife working out in complete dedication, affection, sympathy, concern for his wife, and no eyes for any other woman, whatever the problem.

So in practical advice, authoritative Bible study, and effective confrontation with the spiritual, Deeper Life are involved with trying to build strong Christian families. In the same way as they are open about the problem of childlessness, so they are also addressing the questions single people have about whom they should marry, and the more complex and painful issues of polygamy and divorce.

10

Marriage, polygamy, and divorce

Singles

In Kano one week for the regular Tuesday Bible study, I heard Pastor Ransom Bello leading the people on marriage, focusing particular attention on those young people who were thinking about marriage, or looking for a life partner.

"Marriage was the first institution by God. God is the only one who can match a man and a woman together. I hope you single people won't think this study is going to be funny or outmoded."

Pastor Bello warned singles not to marry an unbeliever, and parents not to let their child marry an unbeliever:

"Do you think you can change them? Who is wiser – you or God? Are you the Holy Spirit? Some Christians do not learn much about marriage before going into it. Surprisingly, some who are experienced and knowledgeable in other aspects of the Christian life seem to be ignorant of this important area. John Wesley was a great man of God who evangelised effectively, preached santification clearly and convincingly, built up the early Methodists impressively, counselled and built up (through letter writing) many lives, preached and wrote many life-changing sermons. Yet his marriage (contracted after he became a preacher) was an unprofitable union. What a great mistake he made in the choice of a wife!

"Marriage in the dark, marriage without learning, instruction, counsel and guidance, can be a tremendous gamble. And sudden marriage can be a step towards sudden death! For many people, the unprofitable union (2 Corinthians 6.14–18) will be a sure guarantee for an unprofitable, unfruitful life."

At the end of the study, Pastor Bello asked us all to stand and pray, which we did, for three or four minutes. Then those of us who were married (it seemed a minority) were asked to sit, while the pastor prayed for the unmarried. He asked them, "Are you prepared to do the will of God?"

And they prayed, placing themselves and their lives before God.

Polygamy

It is normal all over Nigeria to find polygamous marriages, although not all cultures find polygamy acceptable. Deeper Life teach monogamy; but how does a woman cope who finds herself in a polygamous marriage?

I met Franca Wuyah from the Nasarawa Zone in Kano – she had a tired but smiling round face. She was from Cross River State, and had married a flight engineer from Kaduna State in 1978. They worked and lived happily together, although they were not Christians, and failed to have any children.

Four years into their marriage, in 1982, they moved to Kano from Lagos, and her husband's family started pressing him to take another wife in order to get children. But he was faithful to Franca and they went all over trying to find a solution to their problem. Eventually however, there was no success, so he decided to take a second wife. Franca had become a Christian in April 1985, after someone had invited her to a Deeper Life service. She was a new Christian and very confused still, so she came to see the Deeper Life pastor, and he advised her to pray – there was nothing more that could be done.

They were travelling to the husband's home town for Christmas, and he had arranged his second marriage for December 27th, 1985. Franca drove down with the six children who lived in their house, while he drove with his new wife-to-be. On the way, Franca had a road accident – the car was crushed and cut in half. Her leg was badly damaged, no help arrived for two hours, but nobody was killed.

"But I realised I was a child of God," she told me. "The children in my car thought I was going to die, but I told them not to cry, and I prayed that the Lord would let me live and give testimony to my husband. After I prayed, I felt myself go up into the sky, and I saw three mighty gates made of gold, each with very big padlocks. I waited for one to open so that I could go in. Then someone came from my left. He was dressed all in white. I couldn't see his face, but he talked to me. He just asked me to turn and go back to where I had come from. I looked up and saw a rainbow, and written underneath were the words, 'Go and sin no more.' Not long after that, I woke up and I felt as if something had happened to me. It calmed me down. I was satisfied. I had had an encounter with the Lord. Now every day I thank God and I know there is a reason why I should be alive.

"Not long after that, a couple came and helped me. They took me to a hospital, left me there, and carried the children and our luggage to my husband. Immediately my husband rushed to the hospital to see me." Franca's parents wanted her to leave her husband, but she believed God had instructed her otherwise, and she pleaded with them to let her stay with him.

"I just accept the second wife, and I keep praying that I will have children still. Yet God has given me more than children: he has given me grace and peace. I don't see problems any more – I am happy. I keep asking God to show my husband and his other wife to see the light, and I believe God will do that in Jesus soon. I believe that through me my husband is going to be saved."

As the first wife, she is senior to the second wife, and Deeper Life teach that the first wife is the only true wife before God. Nevertheless, it is clearly far from easy for Franca to be in the marriage relationship in which she now finds herself. But God has shown his love to her by giving her that vision and purpose. She might have come to view herself as irrelevant and useless – but now she knows that she is God's person in that situation.

I asked Kumuyi what his attitude was to polygamy.

"We have always maintained that in the New Testament it's one man, one wife. In the Old Testament, polygamy was practised, but God did not command it. In the original institution of marriage, God made it one man, one wife."

"How do you actually deal with the practical problem of a man who is born again, but who has more than one wife?" I asked.

"Our stand has always been to take the line of the early missionaries in Nigeria," Kumuyi replied. "When the early missionaries came, they taught that every man should stay with his first wife, and release the other wives. That has always been our stand up till the present moment."

"As you have applied that, has it created any pastoral problems with the other wives?"

"Yes, sometimes. And even the men, some of them, have identified with other churches. They were born again here, but they do not accept our teaching. They would rather worship in another church that does not teach what we teach. We have not felt that we should change and follow the path of expediency because of the reaction of those people. We still feel that we should look into the Scriptures. If the Scriptures prove us wrong, then we will change, rather than do so because of the reaction of the people."

"Say a man has two wives, and he has to send the second wife away, what actually happens to her, and do you not feel some responsibility towards her?"

"If she is a member of the church, that means if she is born again, we will take care of her, if she needs our care. Like giving her an amount of money that she needs; or the man himself can do that."

"But she would have to live in a different place?"

"Yes. The man can settle on her any business she wants to do – petty trading, or whatever she has been doing. He still has the responsibility of educating the children, because this is a paternal type of society, and even the Bible is paternal."

"So the husband still has a responsibility for that other wife and children?"

"No – only for the children – helping them and educating them. The woman will cater for herself, but we teach that because she was not properly married, she can still be married if she wants to. It was like she was living in sin, now she has come out of it, and now she can marry somebody."

"Have you had cases of that?"

"A lot of cases were settled like that, and a lot of those women have been able to get married."

Divorce

I went on, then, to ask Pastor Kumuyi what Deeper Life taught about divorce:

"We do not encourage divorce. We believe that we should forgive one another, love one another; and once you are a Christian family, you should keep married 'until death do us part'. We teach a lot on marriage: forgiveness, how to live together, communication, and so on. We have published a number of books on marriage.

"There is a Marriage Committee here in the Gbagada church to help the single people. This is because of the size of the church. We have a lot of unmarried people. Three brothers may go to one lady, and then we will have problems in the church! That is why things are channelled through the Marriage Committee. It helps us to know all that is going on. It also helps us to avoid a situation where someone might nurse hatred or animosity. We want to avoid a situation where someone could say, 'I wanted to marry that lady, and you snatched her from me!' So the Marriage Committee offers a kind of marital guidance. The teaching is there, and also the people to counsel, guide and help them. They make their own choices, the committee is just there to know what is going on."

The teaching on divorce is often tied up with the concept of restitution in marriage. This can be applied, as I understand it, to the fact that the first wife is the true wife, and if a separation has occurred the proper Christian act is to restore that original relationship, even if there has been a subsequent marriage.

I met Martha Obiebi in Ilorin – a large and distinguished, but quietly spoken, woman. She told me her story in pidgin English.

She was married when she was very young, according to traditional custom in her area. Their marriage was normal, and Martha bore her husband seven children. Later, however, her husband married another woman. There were problems in the home, and he drove Martha away. She went back to live with her family – for seventeen years, taking her seven children with her. Due to the outreach of the Ilorin Deeper Life Bible Church the husband started coming to Deeper Life, and in response to the teaching there, he came to faith. He soon came to understand that he was in a wrong relationship and that he had to set things right. He sent his second wife away, and she has since married another man. He brought Martha back in June 1987, and she started attending Deeper Life with him. She is a member of Deeper Life now, and active in her House Caring Fellowship.

"I still need your prayer," Martha said. "Pray for our protection, that peace will continue in our home, and that the Lord will strengthen us in our old age. Pray that we will both be more deep in the Lord."

I asked Martha how she felt after all these years about her

relationship with her husband. "I was unhappy before. Now I am happy," she replied.

I later asked Pastor Kumuyi what he meant by "restitution":

"Imagine we were friends and I had stolen something belonging to you. If I am converted and I witness to you, you would remember that I had stolen what belongs to you. You'll be wondering what type of testimony I have. But if I came to you and said, 'My friend, I'm sorry, I'm apologising for what I did, I know I hurt you some time ago but now I've become a Christian. Please forgive me.' That's what we mean by restitution."

"You'd apply that more widely as well?" I asked.

"Yes, if you were holding malice against somebody, we expect that you would go back to the person, apologise, and discontinue the malice. If you have an unresolved matter with close relations – wife, husband, children – you cancel the whole thing and just forgive them because Jesus has forgiven you. And you will make them know you have forgiven them. It is not enough to say, 'I forgive them in my heart,' while they feel you are still unforgiving. You must be humble enough to tell them that you have forgiven them. If you are offended, you must be able to tell those who offended you that you felt hurt but that everything is settled. That is Christian living."

At the National Ministers' Conference which the Deeper Christian Life Ministry run from time to time for ministers of other churches, I met the Reverend Samuel O. Shittu of the Salvation of God Church. He attributes his understanding on marriage and restitution to Deeper Life teaching. I think it only fair to point out that this is how Samuel understood the teaching, and that Deeper Life leaders that I spoke to afterwards were cautious about his application of the doctrine. Samuel, of course, is not a member of Deeper Life, so is not bound by their understandings anyway.

"Mine is a living testimony," he said. "I heard about Deeper Life, but I felt their teaching and doctrine was too tight. But in 1978 I attended a Deeper Life retreat

and the teaching on restitution in marriage was good. I
was disturbed when I returned home to my wife. I now
understood that we were wrongly married, because she had
been married before. I had to allow my wife to return to her
former husband, or to her own family, or to be settled on her
own. It was wrong that we should be married. I met other
ministers of the Gospel and asked them how they understood
that doctrine. They said the Deeper Life doctrine was
wrong, so I didn't send my wife away – but I had no
peace. We had been married for sixteen years. She had a
son by her former husband, but we had had no children in
our marriage. In 1986, I travelled for a programme. Before I
came back, my wife's son by her former husband came to our
house asking for money. This forced me to make a decision.
We had to make that restitution, and I sent my wife away
with her son. After the restitution God gave me another
wife, my own wife, in 1987. In 1988 God gave me a baby
boy. The Lord helped me to understand that I had been
living in adultery because I listened to the other ministers
and not the Bible. So I want to associate with Deeper Life
because I believe they have the balanced doctrine."

The danger in teaching too strongly against adultery and
divorce and relating that to the concept of restitution and
marriage is that you could end up with a kind of divorce
by the back door. Perhaps Samuel should not have been
married to his first wife – in the sense that she should not
have divorced her first husband and married Samuel. But
Samuel was now in the position of having been married
before, and yet he felt it was all right for him to marry
again! Human relationships are so complex that it is not
easy to have hard and fast rules.

Some churches in Nigeria allow only one man, one wife,
and you stay with your first partner. Other churches allow
polygamy, but not divorce. Yet other churches allow both
polygamy and divorce. In seeking a clear teaching, perhaps
the Nigerian churches in general are displaying a weakness
of wanting an authoritative answer without struggling
through to hear God himself on a particular situation.

The short cut is to describe the ideal, and impose it on us less-than-perfect mortals. That route can lead to unresolved pain.

We strive for perfection, as the Lord himself, by his Spirit, enables and empowers us:

> . . . a man will leave his father and mother and be united to his wife, and they will become one flesh. (Genesis 2.24)

> "Why then," [the Pharisees] asked, "did Moses command that a man give his wife a certificate of divorce and send her away?"
>
> Jesus replied, "Moses permitted you to divorce your wives because your hearts were hard. But it was not this way from the beginning. I tell you that anyone who divorces his wife, except for marital unfaithfulness, and marries another woman commits adultery." (Matthew 19.7–9)

> It is good for a man not to marry. But since there is so much immorality, each man should have his own wife, and each woman her own husband . . . But those who marry will face many troubles in this life, and I want to spare you this. (1 Corinthians 7.1,2,28)

11

"This is God's work"

God is reaching all sorts of people through Deeper Life: a couple who have everything but a child to love, an old Muslim man, a middle-aged man suffering from the after-effects of drug addiction, a young agnostic woman, a marriage tormented by demons. Dupe, Louis, Christian, Ekanem, and Susanna, whose stories are told here, have been persuaded by both God's word and his deeds. And Deeper Life is reaching people all over Nigeria.

Why has Deeper Life grown?

The only reason Deeper Life has grown is because God himself has given the growth. Kumuyi and Deeper Life members would want to claim a dedication to serving the Lord, but in that dedication there is little pride. Men and women cannot change the hearts of their fellows; only God can bring someone to himself. So when we look at the way Deeper Life do things, those things may have contributed to its growth – or they may have hindered even greater growth! Furthermore, if we in other churches look at the way another church – which is growing – operates, that does not necessarily mean that if we do the same things or work in the same way, then our own church will also grow.

The "orthodox" churches, such as the Anglican, have a tremendous strength in their history, tradition, and international relationships. Then within such a "global church" there can be a tolerance of a breadth of Christian understanding while still developing appropriate local expression of the faith. More recent overseas-mission-related churches such as ECWA (related to SIM) have also developed their own distinctive style of life, witness, and worship while benefiting from a firm theological and structural base. The newer, more indigenous, independent churches offer freshness and a distinctively African style of worship. Deeper Life, so far, have not been able to offer their adherents these different qualities.

That said, there were particular characteristics of Deeper Life Bible churches which I felt were important.

Personal invitation to the fellowship

The main reason people go to Deeper Life in the first place is because somebody who is already a member invites them along. There are all sorts of different reasons and all kinds of methods, but that personal commitment and enthusiasm in the membership was common to all the Deeper Life Bible Churches I visited. A lot of the evangelistic work at the personal level was done through House Caring Fellowship members inviting neighbours to their meetings, drawing people into the life of a church through participation in a small, almost intimate group. That said, I got the impression that more people now were coming to Deeper Life through being invited to church services than were coming through the small groups. The only other significant reason why people came to a service or a crusade was if they were spoken to in a dream. We in the West need to encourage and enable Christians to invite friends and neighbours to our services and meetings. And we need to pray that God himself will speak directly to individuals in our neighbourhood.

Mrs Dupe Akinfemiwa married in 1978. Her husband is a marketing manager, and they live in Sogunle, Lagos. Soon after they got married, they started trying for children, and Dupe began to have a series of miscarriages. They went to Britain, Germany, and the USA to see specialists for help. In Germany, for instance, the specialist tried all he could. He diagnosed cervical incompetence and an allergy to beef that gave an infection.

Dupe went to Lagos University Teaching Hospital, and was under a very good doctor. He gave her an operation – "*shirodkar*", where the neck of the womb is tied to keep the baby in. Dupe was on permanent bed rest in the hospital after the operation, but she still suffered a miscarriage. She then had the same operation five more times, with the same result.

Then they tried the Maryland Medical Centre in Lagos, where an excellent doctor did everything he could. She had three more *shirodkars* there, but they all failed.

In 1986, Dupe started her tenth pregnancy. She had a *shirodkar* at the Maryland again, and carried the pregnancy to four months for the first time.

"That gave me hope," said Dupe, "but I lost the child."

Her eleventh pregnancy saw her in the Maryland again for another *shirodkar*. She stayed in hospital for five months before and after the operation. She came home – but started premature labour. She delivered a baby boy at six months, and he was put in an incubator. When she left the boy in hospital, she explained:

"I couldn't go home. I don't know why, but I went to the Deeper Life Bible Church. I had never been there before. I was very sick. It was a Wednesday, and I asked if I could see the pastor, but he wasn't in. I met someone there who prayed with me for that baby – that baby was all my life. One of the Deeper Life members came home with me – and then the house was full of Deeper Life members taking care of me. I decided maybe I would fellowship with them when

I was better. But the next day I went to the hospital and found my baby dead. One of the Deeper Life people came with me, but I just couldn't bear it any more. I wanted to end it all. The Deeper Life sister insisted that Pastor Kumuyi would be able to see me and that it would be all right. She gave me message cassettes from Deeper Life to listen to, but I wasn't interested.

"Because the Deeper Life members kept on coming, three or four weeks later my husband and I went to the church. The pastor mentioned my problem in the prayer time. I had a serious stomach pain after the birth, and immediately after he prayed, the pain vanished. I was just shouting, 'It's me! It's me!' I joined a House Caring Fellowship, and claimed my promise. Later my husband and I saw the pastor and he prayed with us. One Deeper Life brother kept coming and praying, and one day he said we should pray in faith and agree we were going to have a baby. We accepted, and he prayed with us on the basis of Matthew 18.19, where Jesus said: 'I tell you that if two of you on earth agree about anything you ask for, it will be done for you by my Father in heaven.'

"We prayed, and he said we should go and buy the baby things to get ready for the delivery. I wasn't interested in doubting. I went out and bought some baby clothes and kept them in my wardrobe. Three months later I got pregnant. I became frightened – I couldn't decide whether to go to hospital or stay at home.

"I went to the hospital, and they did a test. My Deeper Life brother told me I didn't need to worry about hospital, but I wasn't sure. I was confused. At the third month I went back to the hospital – I wanted a doctor to remove my doubt. When I got there, I was really surprised: he said, 'Don't let's do an operation this time. Let's try it naturally – and may God help us!'

"I had no bleeding, no bed rest. My doctor had said. 'Take your time, but do things naturally.' My Deeper Life brother said, 'This is God's work – do whatever you want to do.' I didn't need to try at all. I had no sickness, no headaches. If

I got a headache, I would just say, 'God, I don't want it, in Jesus' name,' and it would go away.

"I had no problems until the seventh month. My doctor called me in for a Caesarean section. He didn't want the labour to harm the baby. I told him God had seen me through so far, and he wanted the glory for himself so I didn't want an operation. I went to see the pastor, and he prayed along with me. I believed God and told him what I wanted. The hospital had given me November 19th, 1987, as my due date. I wanted the baby before that, and I wanted only two hours labour. On November 18th, after I had been to the clinic, I was shopping and visiting, and I went to hospital to deliver the baby girl in less than two hours. I needed no special treatment at all. The operations had cost N8,000 or N10,000 each time. In all my earlier pregnancies I had used various drugs, sometimes up to ten different drugs, and they would cost a lot – maybe twenty tablets for N100. I used to go to the herbalists too. But for this baby I used nothing except the church.

"I called the doctor who had wanted to give me a Caesarean. At the hospital they called my child a 'wonderful work of God'. After ten years, so many people wanted to give our daughter names. She's called Patience Oluwatosin ('God is worthy to be worshipped') Ndidiamaka ('Patience is supreme') Mary."

A church to participate in

Individuals felt confident about inviting others to the church, because there was a solid sense in which the church was worth going to. The way the services were structured enabled spontaneous participation as individuals and in small groups (the opportunity to join in the simultaneous audible prayer, and the discussion in "Search the Scriptures" groups for example). But people could also gain a sense of participation at the whole church level by giving their testimony to the congregation, asking a question of the pastor, or by submitting a written prayer request which would be read out to all the people, and all the people would pray.

As a Westerner, the length of the services, and the number of services, were sometimes a problem for me. But part of the success of the Deeper Christian Life Ministry is the way it fills the lives of the people – particularly the "workers", of whom there are many – with meetings and outreach activities. I wondered if such a high level of activity might have a detrimental effect upon family and social life, especially when not all the members of a family are involved. I don't suppose, though, that most Deeper Life members spend more time in meetings than we in UK spend slumped in front of our TV (and video). And I suspect the Deeper Life meetings are more beneficial!

Time and availability are the ways in which people express themselves within their own culture. In the UK we go by the clock, comparing how many hours in a day we work, or how many days holiday a year we get. We budget our time, and we can feel embarrassed if we are ten minutes early or twenty minutes late. Punctuality is a Christian virtue – but it is also a virtue to be available. In the UK we may think, "I can give this person/activity fifteen minutes." A Nigerian is more likely to make a looser, more open-ended commitment: "I will talk until the conversation finishes"; "I will work at this until the task is completed." A more flexible attitude is taken to time, and this can cause conflict and frustration in a modern society which is modelling itself on the West.

Deeper Life are right to preach punctuality as a proper expression of Christian witness – it is keeping a promise, being truthful. But Deeper Life remain more flexibly people-centred than tightly clock-centred. One of our problems in the clock-centred West has been that our Christian faith gets allocated out of most of our life. It is the Nigerian's more flexible attitude to time that enables Deeper Life to feed the people – an open-ended commitment with an almost ceaseless round of activity, which once you are entered into it, gradually increases your commitment. In giving their time, Deeper Life members are expressing their commitment, and in providing a lot of opportunities to fill their time, Deeper Life are enabling people to increase their commitment.

Preaching

Kumuyi is an outstanding preacher. People travel a long way gladly to hear him, purchase his tapes, and buy his books. This is a church which, above all, has been preached into existence. But it is not only Kumuyi. He trains his people in the discipline of Bible study, and those who go out to pastor in other cities, towns, and villages, and other countries, are usually also accomplished preachers by the time they are sent.

Apart from exposition, it is worth noting that Deeper Life speak authoritatively from the Bible into African situations, particularly in the areas of the search for God, poverty, the family, and the supernatural.

Like every capital city, Lagos has its transport problems and traffic jams (or "go slows" as the Nigerians accurately describe them). The government in Lagos and throughout the country is pursuing a vigorous mass transit programme and widespread road building projects. One such project is a new dual carriageway and bridge linking the Gbagada/Bariga area of Lagos with the city centre on the island. Driving along a part-completed slip road, finding our own route through the different streams of traffic and contractors' vehicles, we bumped up a hill to a high point in Bariga which the new road will pass over. We parked alongside some houses – the hill was high behind us, but the road was at roof level of the Muslim compound we were due to visit. From our vantage point we could see over the roofs to the distant palm trees, beach and sea. This gave the area an unusually fresh atmosphere, with the sea breeze blowing warmly in the evening air.

The compound was formed in an L-shape of single-storey buildings – the walls painted in pastel colours, cheerful against the red-brown earth and brown rusting iron roofs.

At the top of the L, nearest the road, the end building was a small mosque where, as we walked down to the building at the other end of the L, some boys were receiving their Koranic instruction after getting home from day school.

A young man welcomed us into an oblong sitting room – maybe as long as four metres, but probably less than two metres wide. There were three armchairs, three more red and blue plastic upright chairs, two small coffee tables and a desk with evidence of interrupted school homework on it. As I waited in the sitting room I could hear the Muslim children singing in the mosque across the compound.

After a few moments Louis Obumse came to great us: a large man in a gorgeous pink-and-black patterned long shirt. He is a retired First Class Warrant Officer of the Nigerian Army (and he looks like it!), in which he served for thirty-three years. He sat down opposite me, a delighted smile on his face, proud to tell me his story.

His experience of God had started quite late in life. He remembered that it was a Tuesday in March 1983 when he boarded a bus for Obalande Praying Ground – the central mosque – for all his life he had been a Muslim. In that bus Louis heard somebody preaching salvation and healing. He became interested in what the young man was saying: "God can heal you today. If you have an evil spirit; if you're a leper; if you're blind, deaf, or dumb; if you're barren – today, God can heal you."

"Can this happen in Nigeria?" Louis asked himself, and he said to the young man, "I am an *Alhaji* – although an Ibo – but I have had a lot of sickness. No doctor has been able to help me with all those pills and medicines. Here is my address. If you want to save me, come to visit me."

Louis told me that he was still in the army at this time, and to his surprise the young man turned up at his army flat the next day – Wednesday. He asked Louis whether he was ready to accept Christ as his personal Lord and Saviour. Louis told me, "I had been terribly sick – I had been to Western doctors and native doctors. I was looking for anything that would heal me. In the bus that Deeper

Life member promised healing for incurable disease. I said I would accept Christ if I could be healed."

As well as being a Muslim, Louis had been active in various secret societies and sects including the Lodge, the Rosicrucians, the Reformed Ogboni Fraternity, the Aborigin, and the Freemasons. He had so many regalia in a box that it took two of his children to lift it whenever he had to move. But he said, "I mean to have salvation."

The young man told him to come to the next day's Miracle Revival Hour at Gbagada – and somebody even came to collect him that Thursday to take him there. Louis listened carefully to the message and then it came to the time of prayer at the end. There were some general prayers for various types of needs, then Pastor Kumuyi said, "There's a man here with a protracted eye problem, diabetes, bad breath and hereditary high blood pressure. If you put up your hand, I will pray for you and you will be healed of all these problems, in Jesus' name."

Louis told me, "I was angry – I thought, 'Who has told this man all my personal problems?' But I had to raise my hand. Then I realised that pastor couldn't see me, so I had to wave my hand before he knew where I was. When he saw me he started to pray for me. I was wearing my glasses, and nobody else was near me or touched me, but when he finished praying and all the people said, 'Amen,' my glasses fell off and broke on the ground. At the same time I felt a very cold touch from my head to my toes – it was so cold I felt I was going to die. I felt my eyes start to shine and I realised I could see clearly without my glasses. I started shouting with joy! I used to feel a pain due to the diabetes – but that pain left me. I used to feel heat in my body, and that stopped too. I knew God must have touched me, and dealt with everything that was wrong with me. That was over five years ago, and even yesterday I went to my doctor for a check-up and he confirmed there's still nothing wrong with me. Anyone as fat as me should have high blood pressure! The high blood pressure was hereditary – it was what killed my father, and I had had it for twenty years. I had suffered the bad breath and diabetes for fifteen years. I had been short-sighted for twelve years – I couldn't read at all without glasses. Now I'm a member of Deeper Life as long as I live. I'm a permanent member – nothing could make me leave the church. Even today I preached in the bus. There was a 'No Preaching' sign, but nobody stopped me! Doctor Jesus is great – he has all the spare parts! And when I'm dead, Deeper Life will bury me!"

I asked Louis how his Muslim family had reacted.

"My family are very happy. That bad breath made friends run away from me. My wife and children wouldn't come near me, but now they're so happy. Christ is the answer. All my family are Deeper Life members now, and even if I'm dead I'll still serve God. Heaven is my home."

Obumse is a large and loved character – obviously the current patriarch of his family – so when he decided to accept Christ, the others clearly had to follow. At the same time he is gracious and humble – satisfied to be a House Caring Fellowship member, not seeking leadership or authority in the church. And it is gracious of God to deal in this way with a family. A new convert can feel isolated and alien – but there is joy and security when a household turns to the Lord.

All the time we had been talking the evening light had dwindled, and it was dusk by the time we said goodbye.

Meeting needs through miracles

In dealing with the supernatural, Deeper Life have gained a reputation which attracts those who are in need. A reputation for success raises the level of expectation, and so the work develops. Deeper Life are not "just" a healing ministry – they have always sought to be a ministry which develops a whole ("deeper") Christian life. The miracles ministry is remarkable, but a lot more goes on in Bible study, Sunday worship, the House Caring Fellowships, and in daily Christian living.

Miracles in Deeper Life are not there to create a reputation, they are miracles which are immediately relevant
to African situations, particularly needs for deliverance,
healing and material provision. The miracles are not icing
on the cake. They are the bread, the *eba*.

And so it is that, rather than having a reputation for
performing miracles, what is most effective in terms of
witness and attracting new members is when an individual
is released from oppression, or healed, or provided for in
their poverty. The neighbours – even the whole village – will
notice, and that will make a difference.

I remember meeting a forty-seven-year-old trader in Kano
called Christian Ejeke, originally from Anambra State.
When he was ten years old, his father had abandoned
"heathenism", joined the Anglican Church and had had
Christian baptised. Later, when he was twenty-four and
working in Imo State, he started smoking Indian hemp,
and about the same time developed internal heat. He went
to a number of hospitals and doctors, but no clear diagnosis
could be made, and no successful treatment found. Between
1967 and 1970, Ejeke was in the bush, fighting in the civil
war.

In 1974 he developed hypertension and spent a lot
of money at different hospitals, but with no success. In
January 1985 he moved to Hausawa, Kano, and joined the
Anglican Church there, but in June 1987 someone took him
to Deeper Life. Soon after, he had a dream telling him to join
Deeper Life, so he continued going there. By May 1988 the
hypertension and internal heat were so bad he thought he
was dying:

"I went to hospital. I stayed there for ten days – it cost
me N2,000 – I was unconscious a lot of the time, but
the symptoms persisted. Some brothers brought me to
Deeper Life. I was prayed for and from that day, there
has been no sign at all of the hypertension or internal
heat."

Meeting needs through caring

In developing the House Caring Fellowship system, there is a very high level of personal concern shown towards all the members of Deeper Life. It is a good feeling to be a member – people look after you and you help look after others. It is a general feature of African life that people know they need each other. The House Caring Fellowships help people to express and develop that understanding.

The structure of House Caring Fellowships, and in the larger churches of Areas, Zones, and Districts, means that there is always someone available who is able to help you pastorally. It helps to have available to members people who are pastorally gifted, and who can themselves if necessary, refer you to someone who is more pastorally skilled.

Lifestyle

Deeper Life members are recognisable by the firm stand they take on matters of personal morality and, for example, dress. The demands placed upon members to conform to what are seen as biblical standards encourage them that they are indeed following Christ (although there is a risk here of legalism and "salvation by works"). But that sense of identity is powerful and rewarding for the members themselves, while also contributing to Deeper Life's general reputation as being serious about commitment. A distinctive lifestyle is a most effective witness.

Brothers and sisters

Throughout Deeper Life I found real joy in people feeling free to call one another "brother" or "sister". They loved it! The women also appreciated being given responsible roles in the life of the church and, by and large, their ministry was received by the men.

The Bible

Deeper Life people love their Bibles. They carry them
everywhere, and study them with all their energy. They
wish to take a fundamental, literal approach to Scripture,
but they are usually careful about the context and historical
background of a particular text. Particularly in the cities and
towns, I found that the approach to the Bible was far from
simplistic. In the villages, the level of education of the leaders
and members made a thorough approach to Scripture more
difficult. But they take Scripture as their authority, and are
prepared to change their stand if they can be persuaded from
the Bible.

We drove over to Ebute Metta in Lagos one evening to
meet Ekanem Ekpo, a young woman office worker in her
twenties. By the time we got there it was dark night and
there was a power cut, so once we had parked the car we were
dependent on the candles and hurricane lamps of others.

We crossed the storm drain that separates the road from
the houses in this densely populated part of the city, to a large
four-storey building. I mumbled some greeting to the men
sitting talking on the outside steps and we went through the
front door into a dark corridor. After a moment I could make
out a staircase, which we climbed to the top floor. At the top of
the stairs we turned left towards the front of the house, where
moonlight was coming into the corridor from the balcony at
the end. Finally we were brought into the front room on the
left of the house, which was fairly large and full of furniture –
a dining table and chairs, soft armchairs and a settee. A wall
unit between the two windows opening on to the street held
a variety of ornaments and family photographs as well as a
television. We shared two hurricane lamps – two girls doing
their homework at the dining table had one, while Ekanem
and I talked by the light of the other.

At the end of 1986, Ekanem had a fever, so she went
to a clinic and was given an anti-malarial injection. She

was discharged after a week, but had a hard lump on her bottom where she had been injected. As the days passed, the lump grew bigger and became very painful, giving Ekanem sleepless nights. The hospital gave her some drugs, but the pain kept on troubling her. She went back to the hospital – the lump was by now very big – and they told her to press ice-packs on it.

Some time later, when she was washing one day, she realised she had no feeling there. She asked her sister to pinch her, which she did, and she even stuck a pin in her – but Ekanem couldn't feel anything at all. She went back to the hospital and they admitted her for treatment. She couldn't rest at all, it was so painful. She asked the doctors if they could incise and drain the lump, but they said it was too hard. They had looked at the problem with X-rays, and had tried physiotherapy, but things didn't seem to be getting any better. As they found they couldn't do anything, the hospital discharged her, but by then the dead feeling extended down her right thigh.

"My whole right leg was getting weaker – and this continued into 1987," Ekanem told me. "I was limping badly, but I continued with my extra-mural studies while also working full time as an office clerk. In September 1987 my company sent me to a special clinic in Port Harcourt. They really tried their best for me and gave me excellent treatment. But one day when I woke up I found I couldn't walk. I had lost all my feeling in both legs. They put me in traction, and gave me drugs – there followed a whole series of treatments. After a week or two the doctor told me I would have to start getting used to using a wheelchair. I just couldn't believe I'd have to use one. I knew I couldn't move my legs or feel any pain but I didn't want to agree with him. I wasn't going to give in! It took a lot of convincing before I finally tried the wheelchair. Life was difficult for me in the clinic: I was bed bathed and bed fed. To urinate was painful, and I was incontinent, and had stopped menstruating.

"This went on for a while. All the staff did their best, and things did seem to be getting better, but in the end they

felt I needed to be seen by a specialist, so I was referred
to the National Orthopaedic Hospital in Igbobi in October
1987. By then I had got used to the wheelchair, and was
shown so much support and love by my family and work
colleagues that I was able to cope most of the time. I saw
the gynaecologist about my menstrual problem – he proved
I wasn't pregnant, but I still didn't start having periods. I
used to cry a lot, and feel that God was very wicked. If God
really was there, he wouldn't have let this happen to me.
Many of the nurses would even pray with me. One ward
sister challenged me: 'You keep on crying, "Why me?" Who
do you want it to be then?' and I realised I wouldn't want
anyone else to be like this either. So I stopped complaining,
but I still wept a lot, and cried myself to sleep at nights.

"Much later I even had to see two psychiatrists each
month. They gave me drugs to help me sleep well. But I
got so angry with the doctors. I would shout at them, 'It's
all right for you – you can stand there and talk to me – but
all I can do is lie here.' I started looking anywhere for help.
I sent candles to 'white garment' churches for them to pray
for me. I took holy water. And the hospital continued their
tests, including a special one for my nerves. And I was still
going for physiotherapy."

Then, early in 1988, a woman who worked at University
College Hospital, Ibadan, was admitted to Ekanem's ward.
She had been in a serious road accident on her way to a
Deeper Life retreat, and testified to the other people on the
ward that God had preserved her from worse injury. She was
on the far side of the ward to Ekanem, who noticed how many
people were coming to visit this woman from Ibadan. From
their look she could tell they were Christians, but anything
that had to do with serious Christianity wasn't Ekanem's
style – she never went to church.

This woman would put on tapes of Christian messages
and Gospel songs. When any of her visitors came, Ekanem
would just move out of the ward. Then one Friday (February
26th, 1988) they came as a group to visit in the early
evening – about six o'clock. It was her International

Friendship League fellowship group from the Deeper Life
Bible Church in Ibadan. By this time she had been moved
to the bed right next to Ekanem, and she befriended her.
Their companionship had developed, so that Ekanem was
even turning her cassettes over for her when they ended!
Ekanem told me she had also started keeping a Bible
under her pillow, though she could not really explain
why, except that it seemed to give her some comfort.

"My younger brother and a close friend from work were
with me that evening," Ekanem continued. "I wanted to go
out when all the woman's visitors came, but something made
me stay. I even sang a chorus along with them. My brother
and my friend were going to go, but I told them to wait
outside. The group leader said we should turn to a passage
from James. My brother wanted me to go out with him, but
I took my Bible and I read aloud the passage for them:

> Is any one of you sick? He should call the elders of the
> church to pray over him and anoint him with oil in the
> name of the Lord. And the prayer offered in faith will
> make the sick person well; the Lord will raise him up. If
> he has sinned, he will be forgiven. (James 5.14–15)

"The leader preached a little sermon, then they all started
praying aloud. It seemed strange to me, but I started
praying with them for her. I had recently developed a
liking for her, and at that moment I even forgot my own
need. Then the leader started praying, 'That woman over
there: you're healed, in the name of Jesus.' My eyes were
shut – I didn't know who he was referring to. I listened
and he continued with another prayer. I was waiting to
hear somebody scream because she had been healed, but I
heard nothing. So I thought, 'This man doesn't know where
he is.' When we finished praying we all opened our eyes, and
he asked if they could pray for any others of us on the ward.
The woman said, 'Please pray for Ekanem,' and other people
put their hands up for prayer too. My brother was getting
upset with me, so I told him he should leave now. And there

was another friend in a wheelchair waiting outside the ward to see me, but I told him to wait.

"The man preached a sermon about how sin came through Satan. When he finished he said he wanted us to have faith that God could do anything. I said to myself, 'This man can't be serious.' He said, if we believe, God can do it. If we confess our sins, God will forgive us. I felt God had pinched me, so I thought, 'Let me give God a try.' I prayed like I'd never prayed before: 'I know I'm a terrible sinner. I'm guilty. I want pardon.'

"Then the IFL leader prayed for us. We all closed our eyes, and it felt like someone was whispering in my ear, but I knew there was no one near me. I don't know what language it was, but it said, 'Get up.' I thought it might be the Devil's distraction, but I kept hearing the voice, so I decided to try. At least everyone had their eyes closed, so no one would see me. Earlier I had sprained my wrist, so I knew I couldn't lift myself. I was sitting on a chair, and I tried to get up, but couldn't. The voice continued. Somehow I managed to lift both hands and push myself up. The sprain had healed immediately, and I was able to hold on to the bar by my bed. My waist and knees didn't wobble, and my feet were firm. I started screaming, I was so scared. I lifted my hands from the bar, and leant my head on it. Then I moved my head. I screamed again. I could stand.

"As I calmed down, I heard the voice – and this time I was ready to obey! It said, 'Move.' My first thought was to get in the wheelchair, but I just couldn't move at all. My eyes were still tight shut. 'Take one step,' the voice persisted, and I realised I had to lift my leg. Suddenly there was a snap around my legs like something was removed – and I was able to walk! My eyes were still shut – but I walked right down the centre of the ward. The nurse on duty saw me, screamed, and ran to hold on to me. I just kept on toddling round the ward, and screamed and screamed and screamed!

"The nurse knew I was a paraplegic patient, so she was watching me carefully – but I just shrieked at her to take the wheelchair away! It built up the other people's faith, and the

Deeper Life members started praying for the other patients on the ward. At least three other people started to be able to move limbs they couldn't move before. And later, as that IFL group kept visiting, things kept happening. Two days after I started walking, I started to get the feeling back in my legs – and now my menstrual cycle has returned. Even after all this it took my eldest brother two weeks to come and visit me in the hospital, because he just didn't believe that I was walking again.

"I don't know how to explain it. The doctors don't know how to explain it – but now everything is completely back to normal. I have given my life to Christ, and I want to show my gratitude to God. I always thought these Deeper Life people took things to extremes – but they just told me to read the Bible. Yesterday I went witnessing to some people over the street there. I was arguing with them how we just want to read and obey the Bible. Jesus said:

> If you love those who love you, what credit is that to you? Even 'sinners' love those who love them . . . But love your enemies, do good to them, and lend to them without expecting to get anything back. (Luke 6.32,35)

"I need to tell others about the love of God. I was confused before. I never knew the truth, but in Deeper Life we study the Bible, and exercise our own faith. I now know those things in the Bible are not lies."

Ekanem and I went on talking for quite a while. Some things have not been easy for her since she got back to work, but she willingly testifies to a powerful encounter with God which she is determined will change the direction of her life.

Prayer

Deeper Life believe in the power of prayer. They pray as individuals, in groups, and as a church. In prayer, they will be open to the work of the Spirit in their lives, and so they

are led on into Christian maturity through experiences of
sanctification and the baptism of the Holy Spirit. They will
pray anywhere, at any time. And they see results, as they
pray in Jesus' name.

In Kano we went to the home of Susanna Ilotchonwu,
originally from Anambra State. Two young women were on
the verandah, one plaiting the other's hair. They greeted us
and led us to the room where Susanna lived. Susanna told us
how she fell sick early in 1983. She went to medical doctors
and herbalists – they tried all they could, but there was no
solution. The doctors could not even diagnose the problem.
There was some sort of growth in her womb, and sometimes
she couldn't walk upright for the pain, but had to stoop. Her
husband spent all he had on drugs.

Then one day she prayed, "God, I've heard of many
churches – but I don't know which church to go to." Just
then two Deeper Life brothers came and knocked at the door.
She already knew one of them, and they preached the Gospel
to her. She asked them, "Are you the people who believe Jesus
will come again?"

"Yes, we are."

They invited Susanna to the Deeper Life Bible Church
and persuaded her to join. When she went forward as a
newcomer, they prayed for her there and then, but the
problem did not go away. It got to the point where her family
were so frustrated that they were beating her because of all
the money her medical treatment was costing. Deeper Life
arranged for special prayer for her deliverance. She arrived
for her appointment at ten in the morning. They finished
praying at nine o'clock that night.

During those hours many demons had "manifested",
and subsequently the problem lessened, but still did not
completely go away. Susanna suffered three miscarriages.
She wanted to stop praying, but the Deeper Life members
encouraged her to continue. At the end of 1985, Pastor Bello
announced a covenant year with the Lord in 1986. He gave
all the people forms on which they could write their problems.
Susanna wrote about her sickness – that she had now lost her

job because of it, her husband's business had collapsed, and they couldn't afford to feed their children.

"I decided that as God has done for others, he would do for me. I asked my husband for one week when I would do no work but could be alone with the Lord. He agreed and I prayed all week, and then stopped – I just believed God. Then one day – it was Wednesday, December 4th, 1985 – when I went to the bathroom I heard a great noise buzzing out of me. I was frightened. I said, 'In the name of Jesus, what are you?' It was like a swarm fell from over my head on to the floor. I shouted, 'In the name of Jesus, what are you?' The swarm joined together and became one thing, but it was still moving around. I commanded it to stop in one place – and then I saw it was something like a two-inch nail, but many-coloured. I picked it up and showed it to my husband, but he refused to touch it. My mother-in-law wanted to have it to take to our home town to show the people who had put this curse on me – but the Deeper Life brethren refused. They took the nail and disposed of it. Since then, I have not been troubled with sickness again."

Sometimes a deliverance from demonic oppression can have a physical manifestation, and this was a typical testimony. In January 1986 sister Susanna conceived, and in due course delivered a baby girl. They named her Chikoso ("It pleased God").

Self-supporting, self-governing, self-propagating

Deeper Life are a self-supporting movement, run on a shoe-string – or less. Kumuyi explained to me, "We don't allow anyone to be a full time paid pastor unless his congregation is more than 100, and then the congregation has to agree to support that pastor. We still have some churches of 200 or even 400 where the pastors are not full-time. Each church has to be self-supporting." And in all the time that I was in Nigeria, I did not receive any requests for Western aid of any kind from any Deeper Life member.

They are also self-propagating. I heard the Oyo State Overseer exhorting his pastors to find people to send to the villages in their state to plant new churches:

"We in Oyo State are finding people to go to Kenya – can't we do the same for our own state? Think of the best people in your church, and get them ready to go. Don't underestimate someone. Think of our sister in Kenya – she couldn't lead choruses in her own church – now she is casting out devils!"

There is a vision for growth. Kumuyi told the same group of pastors:

"Our emphasis should be on the practical side of going out. If the Lord comes, let him meet us working for him. Now, every time I preach I try to mention evangelism. I have told all the Lagos District Co-ordinators and Zonal Leaders to spend half their time on evangelism and only half their time on their members. There will always be problems in the church: don't let them take up all your time."

And, of course, Deeper Life are self-governing. Kumuyi is the founder and General Superintendent, and he carries a tremendous weight in pastoring the Gbagada church alone, quite apart from the thousand or so other congregations across Nigeria and the rest of the world. He is a remarkable leader, one of God's people for this generation. Because Deeper Life is a new church, there is no well-established history or structure for passing on authority; but right from the early days Pastor Kumuyi has been training his leaders. Amongst the State Overseers and the leadership in Lagos I met a large group of gifted and godly men and women. Kumuyi has received a great deal from God, but he is adept at passing on what he receives. How Deeper Life will develop in the next twenty years – or until Jesus comes again, whichever is the sooner – we can only wait and see. But already my feeling is that what God has given his people through Kumuyi will be kept and developed long after Kumuyi has gone. This has been God's work, and to him be the glory.

Schiphol – return

The first British "quality" newspaper I had seen in seven weeks was given to me on the plane on the way home. It was full of rape, murder, child abuse, and drug abuse. There seemed to be evil in Britain, too.

Then I found myself back in the place of worship at Schiphol where I had started. Now it was early morning. As I sat there, I knew that my wife and children would be getting ready to come to Manchester to meet me. I was excited at the prospect of seeing them again.

I looked at the picture of the boat on the wall. We're all in the same boat. We're working together there, doing our bit of fishing for the Lord. We're travelling, often not quite sure how we're going to get to our destination. The journey's a bit bumpy sometimes.

We need to know what our own role is in relation to others, and we need to be pliable and responsive. We may be close to one person, and far away from another. Two or three may work together for a time while others rest, or do something else. It is almost certainly true that no one person – or even combination of people – gets the whole picture. The primary role of each person is submission to the direction and co-ordination of the skipper.

The mast of the boat is functional, but is also in the form

of a cross. We're gathered around the cross.

Thank you, Lord Jesus, for all the answered prayers; and for everything else you give us, which is much more.

APPENDIX

1 LORD, who may dwell in your sanctuary?
    Who may live on your holy hill?
2 He whose walk is blameless
    and who does what is righteous,
  who speaks the truth from his heart
3   and has no slander in his tongue,
  who does his neighbour no wrong
    and casts no slur on his fellow-man,
4 who despises a vile man
    but honours those who fear the LORD,
  who keeps his oath
    even when it hurts,
5 who lends his money without usury
    and does not accept a bribe against the innocent.
  He who does these things
    will never be shaken.

(Psalm 15)

Kumuyi made some preliminary comments concerning David and his question in verse 1. He made the point that, "David, the King of Israel, was asking a question not from man, but *he was asking from the Lord*. He considered the question so important, he wouldn't even ask from a prophet here on earth. He must have known what it took for a stranger coming from any other nation to become an Israelite and share fellowship with the people of Israel. And so he must have begun to think, if it took so much and demanded so much, before you can become a part of Israel, what will it take to live in heaven above?"

Then Pastor Kumuyi went on to ask, "*Why should a king even begin to think about heaven* – especially when he had all he could ever get in this world?"

Kumuyi answered that "what David discovered, what Solomon discovered, what everyone is discovering today" about why we should think about heaven can be summarised under three headings:

(a) *Earthly possessions are not satisfactory*. Because of the unsatisfactory nature of the things of this world, David wanted to know what it would take to get to that place where there would be unlimited, unhindered, unspeakable joy and satisfaction.

Comparing Ecclesiastes 2.1–11, Kumuyi said, "This is the testimony of his son Solomon, and you can see that the things of this world will never satisfy your heart. Here was a man who had tasted anything that anybody could taste in this world, and yet there was that emptiness, that void, that unsatisfactory feeling in the heart saying, 'What else will I get that will make me happy, make me joyful, make me fulfilled?' And he couldn't find anything."

"Think about yourselves," said Kumuyi, as he drove the message home. "Think of all the things you've got in this world. They made you happy one day. The following day you forgot about all that had made you happy the previous day. You had joy one moment. The following moment there was no joy any more. You thought, 'This now will satisfy me permanently,' and after you had finished that thing, you became empty. The whole experience was disappointing. And so you begin to wonder, 'Is this how life will continue?' A man like that, a woman like that should be asking, 'Lord, what will it take so that I can live eternally with you?'"

(b) *"Another thing we have learnt is that we do not have any continuing city over here."* Reading from Hebrews 13.14 and then Hebrews 11.10, 14–16 Kumuyi talked about the "enduring city" and the "better country", the "heavenly" country.

"Let me ask you," he said. "You live in this country. We love the country, we pray for the country every time, but let's be sincere, let's be real. With all the robbery, with all the injustice, with all the powers of darkness, with all the atrocious things that are taking place – in all sincerity, would you want to live in a country like this for one thousand years? For two thousand years? Three thousand years? For things to continue just like they are? All the promises in the papers, over the radio, over the television: we don't see the fulfilment. Today it is one trouble, and when we think that trouble is over, another trouble comes upon us as a nation. Think about it. Would you like to live in a country like this for the rest of eternity? Of course not. We seek a better country."

(c) *"Not only that – we see the signs of the end of the world all around us."* In Matthew 24.3 the disciples asked Jesus Christ when the world would end. In response to Jesus' reply (specifically verses 4–11), Kumuyi asked us:

"Have you not seen these things? Human beings with all their frailties and all their sins will declare they are Christ, and they will deceive some people. We've seen that in this nation. Have you not seen wars? And rumours of wars? We see it, we hear about it. Would you not say all those signs are around? Someone who knows the world is coming to an end will want to know, where do we go after here? And if I ever have any desire of wanting to live in heaven, what does it take, what are the qualifications, what are the things I need to have, what do I need to be, as a person, so that I will be able to make heaven my goal?

"The moment you are born again there's a change in your life, and the desire of going to that place which Christ has gone to prepare will be in your heart. Look at Philippians 3.20–21. As a child of God your heart has a desire, a longing:

'I want to go that place. When Jesus comes I want to go with him.'"

In his preamble, therefore, Pastor Kumuyi drew us into his subject by challenging us effectively on why we needed to be thinking about heaven. What are the qualifications for heavenly citizenship? Pastor Kumuyi identified five essential qualifications.

(1) Real Conversion Kumuyi's first point demanded the adult decision to live for Christ. Deeper Life expect an individual to make a change in their lives and to be able to say at what date (and what time) he or she was born again. (I think this is fine if that has been your experience, but there are those who call themselves Christians – and who call God their Father, and Jesus Christ their personal Lord and Saviour – who have grown into faith over a period of time, maybe many years, maybe even since childhood. I have no doubt there can be a need for commitment and radical change – but I also believe there can be a type of re-commitment, a re-alignment, which is the adult acknowledging the lordship of Christ, without denying the work of Christ in his or her life so far. Jesus told Nicodemus that he needed to be born again. Jesus also warned his disciples that they needed to become like little children in order to enter the kingdom. Interestingly, Pastor Kumuyi referred to both these passages (John 3 and Matthew 18) as he talked about conversion, while not particularly referring to the faith of a child.)

"In John 3.3,5,7 we see that there needs to be a real conversion. The Bible says that all have sinned and have come short of the glory of God. The Bible says that no man can be justified or saved or redeemed by the works of the law. You must take Jesus as your saviour.

"And look at Matthew 18.1–3. The disciples wanted to know who will be the greatest. But Jesus Christ was not going to talk about the greatest in the kingdom, he knew you must talk about entering before you can talk about being great when you enter. It takes real conversion, brothers and sisters. It takes a change of life, a change of heart, a change of direction. You are washed in the blood of the Lamb. You are cleansed in the blood of the Son of God. And now, after that change has come, now you can say, 'I know him as my Lord. He has come into my heart.' And that is the very first step on your way to heaven.

"In Acts 3.19–20 you can see that after you have turned your back on your sin and you have received Jesus as your personal saviour, he lives inside you; and the time is coming when Christ himself will come back and he will receive you unto himself.

"Look at Psalm 24.3–4. If you are still a sinner, your hands are not clean. If you have never given yourself to the Lord Jesus Christ, your hands are not clean."

(2) *Right conduct* Battling against the acoustic problems of this large, open, building with cement walls and floors, and with the hubbub of simultaneous translation echoing around, Kumuyi had no problem in keeping the rapt attention of his congregation as he went on to make the point that it is not only our response to God, but also God in us through our faith in him and his grace towards us, that lead us into righteous conduct. Deeper Life preach "sanctification" in the sense that it is an identifiable work of God in the believer which enables him or her to sin less and to lead a more righteous life. Other strands of Christianity place even more emphasis on God in the believer, and teach virtually no level of personal responsibility in right conduct. Some of these churches might emphasise, for example, that although we are sinful, when God looks at us, he looks through Christ, and therefore does not see our sin. Others emphasise the work of the Spirit in the child of God to the extent that the believer ceases to be sinful at all. In the other direction, there are churches which do seem to be saying that it is by our own efforts – as God works in us and helps us – that we live righteously. This was how Pastor Kumuyi described the need for right conduct that morning:

"Look at Psalm 15 again, verses 2, 3, 5. There are people who will tell us they are born again, but they are still as sinful as ever. Some people will say, 'Well once I'm born again, that's all. I don't have to live right, I don't have to do anything in line with obedience to the word of God, and I know that by and by, when Jesus comes I'll be getting to heaven . . .' Somebody deceived you. Do you think you could make heaven without conversion that has the evidence of the right conduct? Somebody deceived you.

"And look at Deuteronomy 10.12–13. It's for your own good.

"Look also at Matthew 5.20. Jesus was saying there's a type of righteousness that will try to manifest without grace and faith, which is all by your self-effort. That's self-made righteousness, just like the scribes and the Pharisees. But, Jesus said, if you do not have anything beyond that superficial righteousness, if you do not have an in-depth righteousness that is wrought by grace and faith in the Lord, 'right-standing' with the Lord, you'll never be able to make it. It takes more than your self-effort. It takes more than just trying and struggling to obey the laws of the Bible. You need to go to the cross and be born again, *then Christ himself puts the righteousness there within.*

"Now in Matthew 23.27–8 you can see that it takes more than what you can do on your own. It takes the word of the Lord making that change within you. And in 2 Corinthians 5.17: 'Therefore, if anyone is in Christ, he is a new creation; the old has gone, the new has come!'

"Let no one deceive you. Let no religion blindfold you. Your conduct will change when you are really born again. And that is the evidence that you know the Lord. That's what it says, before we can live with God for ever."

(3) Right conversation But when it comes to "right conversation" as an aspect of a righteous life, the responsibility is firmly on the believer:

"Notice in Psalm 15.2–3 that if you want to know whether someone really belongs to the Lord or not, listen to them talk. You will find that some of the people who say they are born again are not genuine. With abusive language and curses in their mouth, you'll know that they are not genuine. It says if you are really a child of God, you must speak the truth in your heart. You know what caused Moses a real, terrible problem? When he spoke rashly with his mouth and he struck the rock twice, and he couldn't enter into the physical land of Canaan. He was denied that benefit of enjoying the physical promise that had been given to them. We know he went to heaven, but in his own case he was not able to enter into the land of Canaan.

"And you know the problem of Rehoboam the son of Solomon in 1 Kings 12? He let the younger people speak roughly, and he lost the kingdom.

"Look at Matthew 12.33–4. You call Jesus your Lord, but what if he should look at you and say, 'All those professions of faith I do not accept, you are part of the brood of vipers'? What a terrible thing! And you know, that is what happens when you are misusing your tongue every time.

"Look at 2 Peter 3.10–11. People do not understand that one day, everything will be folded up, and the only thing that will matter is whether you have been with the Lord in reality or not.

"Look at 1 Peter 3.9–10. You know what sometimes shocks you: the rough attitude to life and rough conversation of the people who call themselves people of God. The abusive language, the cursing, that will come out of people who profess to be born again. You want to make heaven? It takes more than what you have got.

"And I'd rather get into trouble speaking the truth, I'd rather be misunderstood speaking the truth, rather than covering it up and lying and using what the worldly people call 'diplomacy', and lose my soul. There is no ministry of tale-bearing given to the children of God. There is no ministry of gossip given to the children of God.

"Now come back to Psalm 15.1–3. Let me just say something here. All that God said here in his answer is in the present continuous tense. There are people who will tell us, 'I got saved many years ago.' They think that's enough. But it says he 'whose walk *continues to be* blameless'. Not that

I walked blamelessly ten years ago, but I'm not walking blamelessly now. You continue to walk blamelessly. You keep on doing righteousness. You can't say, 'When I was righteous before, or when I was consecrated, when I was devoted and yielded and decided for the Lord it was a nice time, it was a wonderful time. But now I know that I'm having problems, I'm backsliding, but God is a wonderful God, and I'll make it to heaven at last.' I'm not sure of that."

(4) Right company One of the charges levelled against Deeper Life over the years has been that they appear to be exclusive. I have taken up some of these doctrinal arguments in the main text of this book, but this is what I heard as I began to enter into Deeper Life:

"If you want to make it to heaven at last, you must have the right company. Look at Psalm 15.4. A real child of God is not in the gang of robbers, is not in the gang of the night people, the people who will kill, the people who will smuggle, the people who will rob houses in the night. A child of God is not part of them. Do you tell me that somebody is born again and still belongs to secret cults? Never. And still has all the people in those secret societies as friends? As intimate, close friends and advisers? It cannot be. Can you tell me that somebody who has been born again will still have the herbalist and the witch doctor as their adviser? If you are a child of God, you will not have the people who are in touch with familiar spirits and evil spirits and the powers of darkness as close, intimate friends to you. It will shock you to look at the people who say they are Christians. On Sundays like this they cannot come to the house of God. You know why? They have to be at the meeting of the palm wine drinkers. They have to be in the meeting of their tribal people, and they say, 'Well, I go to those meetings because when I die I want my people to bury me.' And when they don't come to bury you . . .? You want the evildoers to bury you! You want the people who are still worshipping idols to bury you! What – do you want to give your soul to the Lord and then give your body to the idol worshippers? Why don't you come out totally from among them and live a real Christian life? You will not be in partnership with people who are doing evil when you are a real child of God.

"Look at Psalm 50.16–22. There are people who will build their houses, give their houses to prostitutes, and will still come in to church. 'Oh,' they say, 'thank God. When I was in the world . . .' Where are you now? 'When I wasn't born again . . .' You are born again now that your whole house is rented out to prostitutes? And you are sharing an apartment with those prostitutes? The Lord is righteous, the Lord is holy, and he wants his own children to separate themselves from the people who are doing evil.

"Now look at 2 Corinthians 6.14–18. Can you tell me that a person is really born again and goes to marry an unbeliever? They tell me that somebody is born again and goes into business partnership with the people who are not following the Lord? That's not biblical. 'Oh,' you say, 'that's Deeper Life doctrine.' Look at it. That's the word of the Lord. That's the standard of the Bible, that you should not have anything to do in the way of committing evil with the people of the world.

"And in 1 Corinthians 5.11 the word of the Lord commands us to not be in partnership with the people who are doing evil. But we will be with the people who are doing right.

"Romans 16.17–18. You know there are people, you wonder whether Christ is really in their hearts, whether the Holy Spirit is really living inside them. There are people who will go white garment wearing and candle burning and incense burning. Then they will come to your house and say, 'Well, I am going to be living with you but you know I go to this other place. I burn candles, I burn incense, but I just love you and we are together.' You won't accept such a thing, you won't accept such a person to be your close friend, if you are a real child of God. What did Jesus say about false prophets? He said, beware of them. And he said, by their fruits you shall know them (Matthew 7.15–16). He didn't say, 'We should accept those false prophets, be nice to them, fellowship with them, be united with them, and not care about what they believe, how they live or what they do. Whether they are using magical books or not, don't worry or fret about it, just love them and fellowship with them.' That's not the word of the Lord."

(5)   Real consecration As Kumuyi reached his final point, he was emphasising how much is expected of the disciple. That the Christian life does not stop once one has been born again. God is at work in the believer, but there is also responsibility on the part of the believer to live in holiness. Pastor Kumuyi built his summary around the words of Psalm 15.4 to describe the committed, "consecrated" believer: "who keeps his oath even when it hurts."

"Now let's look at Psalm 15.4. That's consecration, real consecration. You know what consecration is? It's commitment to the Lord, to the word of the Lord; and here today I can see faces of people who years ago put everything on the altar, saying, 'Lord, I will stand for your word.' But today you are not standing on that word any more. You have changed. You and I knew each other before you were married. You went by, 'Thus says the Lord' before you were married, but at the time of your courtship, you know how you changed. At the time you were going up and down planning that marriage, you know how you changed. And after your marriage you found you could not go by the teaching of the word of God any more! Do you know what it takes to get to heaven?

"And you know how you committed your life to the great commission? Years ago. We know one another. We went through this country preaching the Gospel, and serving the Lord: 'They must be saved'; 'Give your life to the Lord Jesus Christ.' We knocked on every door, we went through every street, and we said, 'Lord, until the last living soul has heard the Gospel of the Lord Jesus Christ, we shall not rest. But we shall go on preaching the Gospel.' We had opposition then, we had persecution then, we had difficulties then.

"Are we doing it today? 'No, you know, we are tired now. And we cannot keep knocking on doors like we used to do, going through the streets like we used to do, preaching in the buses like we used to do. We are getting older now.' Older than the word of God? Older than our past consecration? Older than the commitment to the Lord? Older than the great commission which Jesus gave to the church? 'We are getting more mature now.' More mature than the authoritative word of God upon our lives? You know what it takes to get to heaven?

"Are we not backsliding? Are we not going away from the Lord? Are we not going away from the word of the Lord? You believed the word of God before. You are the people who taught those people 'one man, one wife'. But now that the rich people are coming to the church, our mouths are closed. Were we not humble in the past? Were we not the people who will humbly serve our fellow men? Wash their feet and help them up? What are we now – so proud! Too proud to go and talk to them! We are changed! But the Bible has Psalm 15.4. 'Well,' you say, 'the commitment I made before, it's become inconvenient.'

"Where do you stand today?" Pastor Kumuyi concluded. "You can tell the Lord, if you've backslidden, if you've gone back from the Lord, you can say, 'Lord, I'm coming back home. Lord, I'm coming back home.' Rise up and talk to the Lord in prayer."

So 12,000 people stood and started doing just that. Confessing, arguing, pleading, and talking. From time to time Kumuyi would encourage them to continue in prayer, helping them to focus on what he had been saying:

"The end is approaching. The Lord is about to come. Call upon the Lord. Let him meet you prepared. Let him meet you consecrated. Let him meet you yielded to the Lord. Stand on the totality of the word of God. In the last days there will be a lot of compromise. Stand on the word."

And then, "Are you born again? You have real conversion – a change of heart, a change of life, a change of direction. Talk to the Lord about it. If you have not been born again, this morning you can give your life to the Lord. Any sin in your life, confess to the Lord, repent of all the evil things, and take the Lord as your personal Saviour."

And as people continued to pray: "Are you obedient to the word of the Lord? Or do you fear your neighbours more than you fear God? *It takes a little bit more than what you have got now to make it to heaven*! Believe the Lord. The blood of Jesus Christ his Son cleanses from all unrighteousness."

And finally – one hour after the sermon started: "In Jesus' name we pray. Amen."